The Hindu Tantric World

The Hindu Tantric World

An Overview

André Padoux

The University of Chicago Press
Chicago and London

The University of Chicago Press, Chicago 60637
The University of Chicago Press, Ltd., London

Printed in the United States of America

26 25 24 23 22 21 20 19 18 17   1 2 3 4 5

ISBN-13: 978-0-226-42393-7 (cloth)
ISBN-13: 978-0-226-42409-5 (paper)
ISBN-13: 978-0-226-42412-5 (e-book)
DOI: 10.7208/chicago/9780226424125.001.0001

Originally published as André Padoux, *Comprendre le tantrisme: Les sources hindoues* (Paris: Albin Michel, 2010).

Library of Congress Cataloging-in-Publication Data

Names: Padoux, André, author.
Title: The Hindu Tantric world : an overview / André Padoux.
Other titles: Comprendre le tantrisme. English
Description: Chicago ; London : The University of Chicago Press, 2017. | "Originally published as André Padoux, Comprendre le tantrisme: Les sources hindoues (Paris: Albin Michel, 2010)." | Includes bibliographical references and index.
Identifiers: LCCN 2016025208 | ISBN 9780226423937 (cloth : alk. paper) | ISBN 9780226424095 (pbk. : alk. paper) | ISBN 9780226424125 (e-book)
Subjects: LCSH: Tantrism. | Tantrism—History.
Classification: LCC BL1283.84 .P3413 2017 | DDC 294.5/514—dc23 LC record available at https://lccn.loc.gov/2016025208

♾ This paper meets the requirements of ANSI/NISO Z39.48–1992 (Permanence of Paper).

To the memory of A-C, irreplaceable life companion

The road of excess leads to the palace of wisdom.

WILLIAM BLAKE, *The Marriage of Heaven and Hell*

Contents

Note on the Pronunciation and Transcription of Sanskrit

The Sanskrit alphabet has forty-nine letters, which are transcribed here, when necessary, using diacritical signs according to a common international system.

The vowels are pronounced very much like Spanish or French vowels.

The short *a*, however, is pronounced like the *u* in "but" and the long *ā* like the *a* in "balm."

As for the consonants, *g* is pronounced like in "guest," *c* as *ch* in "church," and *j* as in "jungle." The aspirated consonants (*tha, dha, pha, bha*) are pronounced marking the aspiration, like in "top hat," for instance. *R̥* is a vowel pronounced more or less like "ri."

Acknowledgments

This is not a translation of the French book *Comprendre le tantrisme: Les sources hindoues* published in Paris in 2010 by Albin Michel, but a different book along the same lines. The French book was meant for a French readership and included passages useful for such a readership, which could (and have been) translated into Italian, Spanish, and Romanian but are unsuitable for English readers. Wishing to modify several such passages, I eventually redrafted the first part (chapters 1 through 4), enlarging it and giving it a somewhat different emphasis. It was also necessary to take into account recent discoveries in the field of Tantric studies, a field that has considerably changed in recent years due in particular to the rediscovery of Tantras until then unavailable or unknown. This consideration also affected chapters 5 to 10 (part 2), which were therefore updated, corrected, and often enlarged. The two chapters of part 3—11 and 12—are also largely revised. The bibliographical references throughout the book and the bibliography have naturally been updated and adapted for an English readership. On the whole, this book is longer, more detailed, and somewhat more "technical" than the French one, which was written for a large and supposedly uninformed public at the publisher's behest. This is not, I believe, the case for the readers I am writing for now in English, and I hope that these readers will find this book readable and perhaps useful. I would like to thank here all those who helped me with their advice and who offered suggestions for improving my English.

Special thanks are due to Dominic Goodall of the École française d'Extrême-Orient, who, in spite of his many professional duties as a scholar, spent hours not only carefully reading the whole book, correcting it whenever necessary but also redrafting whole passages—this especially in the first part, which as it stands now is in some details more his work than mine.

He also made a number of suggestions and emendations in the second and third parts. To him, I feel deeply indebted.

My thanks are also due to my friends France Bhattacharya, Véronique Bouiller, and Gilles Tarabout for their help on Tantra in different areas of India, to Jim Mallinson for his advice on Nātha texts and notions and, last but not least, to Denis Matringe, without whose timely help I would not have been able to send a decent manuscript of this book to the publisher, whom I was able to contact thanks to the kind intervention of David G. White.

Paris, October 2015

Preface

Why write a book on Hindu Tantra for readers interested in India? The reason is that one cannot give a complete account not only of Hinduism but of Indian thought—of what was (and still is) the vision of the world and of what transcends it for many Indians—without taking Tantrism into account. For some fifteen hundred years, Tantra has been an essential element giving expression with particular clarity to some of India's fundamental tendencies, ways of thinking, or of existing. Admittedly, some Tantric beliefs and practices are bizarre. There is, too, an important esoteric initiatory side. But even such peculiar traits are not to be disregarded, for they express some tendencies one may well consider as essentially Indian. Without Tantra, Hinduism—as well as Buddhism as it was in India and as it has spread over Asia—would not have been what it was and still is.

To deal with Tantra is not merely to deal with a strange minority aspect of the Indian religiospiritual world; it is to deal with some of its fundamental traits.

One may also ask why we should be interested in India. Why is India, why is the Indian civilization, one of the few that particularly captures the interest? Fascinates, even? Is it because the past—a fascinating one—is still, in some respects, present there today? Or is it because some of the fundamental spiritual or existential problems of mankind have been perceived and dealt with so subtly, sometimes so beautifully, there? I cannot deal with this last question here. But for what it is worth, if there were no such questions and not such an attraction, this book would not have been written.

The Tantric domain includes also Buddhism. An important part of Mahāyāna Buddhism—spreading from India across Asia to Japan—is Tantric. However, I will sometimes refer to it here without considering it. This is not because it is not interesting. Tantric Buddhism developed side-by-side with Tantric Hinduism, Mahāyāna Buddhism being strongly influenced by Śaivism. The two religions interacted; they shared some deities with common iconographic traits as well as some notions. They also elaborated concepts in opposition to each other. Examining both Hinduism and Buddhism would have been entirely justified. But doing this would necessitate a much longer work than this one and, since the traits and problems of Tantric Buddhism are different from those of Tantric Hinduism, their inclusion would necessitate a different, more global, approach.

Even limited to its Hindu side, giving an overview of the Tantric domain, both ancient and modern, is not an easy task. This is not only because one is to examine and describe a large ensemble of socioreligious facts and notions but also because of the very nature of the Tantric phenomenon and of the manner in which it has been seen in India, where it still exists, and in the West, which became aware of it and has partly "fabricated" it, since the nineteenth century.

This being so, I will first show how this phenomenon was perceived and defined from outside in the Western tradition and from inside in the Indian tradition. I will then try to show how it appeared in India, spread to the whole subcontinent and, with Buddhism, extended over most of Asia, an expansion during which it underwent many transformations due to the local contexts where it developed. There is also a textual aspect of Tantrism: it has an enormous textual, essentially Sanskrit, basis, a great part of which was only recently discovered and studied, opening new vistas on the nature and scope of the Tantric domain as well as on its historical development. Then, looking at the main traits of the theologicometaphysical notions—the beliefs—of the main Tantric traditions and systems, I will try to give the reader an inkling of the power, originality, and diversity of the Tantric vision of the cosmos and of the human being as part of the world.

Fewer problems are met with in the second and third parts of this book because, being more descriptive, they deal with the concrete, perceptible reality of the Tantric domain—what constitutes it from the point of view of both the notions, which are essential, and the practices, which are numberless, the former being closely bound with the latter, since there is no practice without a theory that gives it a meaning and explains it. I will thus first consider the Tantric body, which is a fundamental element because, except for the abstract thinker, there is no Tantrism (or any creed) without its being experienced, lived, in the body—or, more exactly, in an indivisible body-mind totality. From this bodily basis I will then take up the Tantric notions and practices concerning speech, sex, asceticism, and spirituality. After this, I will come to what we may call the spatial side of the Tantric world—temples with their rites and iconography and sacred sites and pilgrimages. These chapters are based on ancient texts that describe ancient notions and practices. But Tantra went on existing and evolving down to our time, preserving many elements while modifying others or creating new ones—a "change in continuity" that is characteristically Indian. This also appears in the third part where, looking at the contemporary Indian scene, we will briefly see what Tantric presence still survives there, a presence that is at the same time pervasive and largely ignored even by its actors. We shall meet there again the problem of what is and what is not Tantric. Finally, I will look at a few aspects of what the West has done with Tantra, reinventing it so as to answer to its needs or desires. Though mostly questionable, unreliable, and/or frivolous, this Western approach is not wholly uninteresting, at least in some respects.

I must add that I do realize the arbitrariness of all descriptions, especially when dealing with uncertain historical elements, subtle notions, and socio-religious factors both complex and difficult to define. What I boldly offer here is my own view of the Tantric domain. I believe it is not unfair, but one could, of course, see and describe the whole thing differently.

PART I

The Hindu Tantric Domain

1

The Hindu Tantric Field: Terminology and Attempts at Defining a Tantric Domain

Et si j'affirme, je m'interroge encore.
JACQUES RIGAUD

The very nature, extent, and continuity in time of the Tantric phenomenon raise a problem. How can one explain the appearance and the gradual overall diffusion of practices and notions that, albeit diverse, have enough common traits to permit their being considered as forming a specific, recognizable, perhaps definable socioreligious phenomenon in the Indian religions (Hinduism, Buddhism, even Jainism) in India and in a large portion of Asia? How can it happen that, facing a particular notion and practice, we can say "This is Tantric"? When reading certain texts (but what kind of texts?), when observing certain ritual practices together with the notions that accompany them, how can we perceive enough characteristic elements for us to feel that what lie before us are aspects of a common phenomenon? Or are we mistaken? Do we perceive a global phenomenon where there are, in fact, merely similar elements—having, as one says, a family likeness—that cannot properly be considered as being aspects of a common phenomenon? A phenomenon born in India that has (notably with Mantrayāna Buddhism) overstepped the limits of the subcontinent and spread across almost the whole of Asia: central Asia (Tibet, Mongolia), Southeast Asia (Indochina, Indonesia—Bali down to our days), and even the Far East.

Considering there is here a common general phenomenon is perhaps a Western, "etic," way of thinking. In effect, European scholars were the first to discover or to believe they had found in what they knew of Indian religions—Hinduism and Buddhism—traits that they called "Tantric" and that they first believed to be limited to a particular area. Then they discovered their wider presence, and finally, today, saw their pervasiveness, and even sometimes denied their specificity. Though questionable, this "etic" approach is not entirely unfounded, for in spite of the fact that the notion of Tantrism as an entity is Western and unknown in traditional India, Indian works called "Tantra" were being written for centuries, and the character of these texts, rites, or observances was recognized as "Tantric," some texts being even recognized as a form of divine Revelation.

There is undoubtedly a "Tantric problem" that we must first tackle, namely that of the term *Tantrism*, or *Tantra*. How is the socioreligious domain that we shall see here to be named and defined? Now, to define is to determine, delineate, and to understand—to name in the religious field is fundamental, foundational even. Being French, I am tempted to quote here the French poet and thinker Paul Valéry, who said (half-jokingly), "Great gods were born from a word-play that is a kind of adultery." One could also say about "Tantrism" what an American Indologist once said of karma: that it is more a problem than a notion—a notion and a fact. As we shall see, it is surely an important fact. But let us first look at what can be said on the subject.

The extension in time and space and the diversity of the Tantric presence make it difficult to define and delimit. Its textual basis, essentially but not entirely in Sanskrit, often arcane, is huge in extent. Moreover, these texts have, for the most part, been recently discovered (since the 1950s, mostly) and are still being explored and taken account of. Therefore, new elements may very well be found that will alter our view of the subject on some points. In addition, the Tantric side of Hinduism appeared some fifteen centuries ago and still survives, while having evidently evolved in the course of time. Can we really grasp it in the diversity of its historical dimension? And if so, how can we describe it properly? Also, Tantra was (and still is) approached from different angles and interpreted in different ways. It is a field where, in many cases, no final point of view can honestly be offered. All I can do, therefore, and what is attempted here, is to give a general overview as I perceive it now—to strive toward the truth, hoping to find it while not being sure of being able to do so.

What's in a Word?

First, how are we to name the domain we explore here? *Tantra*? *Tantrism*? *Tantricism*? *Tantrisme* is currently used in French, *Tantrismo* in Italian and Spanish, and *Tantrismus* in German. *Tantrism* or *Tantricism* is less frequent in English, where one usually uses *Tantra*. The term as such, however, is not important. The importance is in what it means or designates for those who use it. In the original French version of this book, the term *tantrisme* was discussed at length, for its current use was the main reason for the idea that there existed not a Tantric aspect of Hinduism but a particular Indian socioreligious entity—a "Tantric" section of Hinduism, distinct from mainstream Hinduism—or, at least, the idea that one could study the Tantric field as different from other current forms of Hinduism. Of course, such a misconception needed to be disproved.[1] I will not do this here because *Tantra* is the usual English term for the Tantric domain. However, the fact remains that for centuries in India, there have been, and there still are, elements that are Tantric and others that are not—a duality some Indians were evidently not unaware of, which we will consider here.[2]

We may note first, concerning other terms that reflect a Western approach to Asian cultures, that applying the label "Hinduism" to the infinite diversity of beliefs, cults, and practices of the socioreligious world that developed in India over the course of centuries on a Vedic basis is also foreign to India. Like *Tantricism*, the word *Hinduism* denotes an Indian reality as seen from outside—by the Muslim conquerors and the Arab travelers (Ibn Batuta, notably), rather than by those who succeeded them in India. As there is no global Sanskrit term for the Tantric phenomenon, there was also no Sanskrit term meaning *Hindu* before the presence of Islam, and this term emerged perhaps in the fifteenth or sixteenth century.[3] The word *Hinduism* only appears in the nineteenth century with the British. Having noted the "etic" character of the terms *Hindu* and (still more) *Hinduism*, we must also note that Indians were not unaware of the common traits of the brahmanical/Hindu traditions. If the upholders of the different Hindu systems abundantly condemned their opponents' doctrines, they were nevertheless conscious of their common fund or traits and of their being different from "others." There are, dating from the sixth to the sixteenth century, a few hierarchically classified Indian Sanskrit descriptions of these systems, distinguishing them as those of believers (*astikas*) and different from those of unbelievers (*nāstikas*), such as Buddhists or Jains.[4]

In contrast with these European or Indian globalizing approaches, some Western Indologists have recently tried to deconstruct the global vision of Hinduism, considering it as an ensemble of related religions rather than one religion with different aspects. Some also stress the fact that these religions are to be studied and understood by applying their own categories rather than our own.[5] Western conceptions also explain that Hindu nationalists recently coined the word *hindutva* as a name for what they consider as the original nature of an Indian Hindu motherland.

But we must now first see, briefly, when and how the Tantric aspects of Hinduism were discovered and interpreted by Europeans, then how they were seen in ancient India.

A list of Tantras was published for the first time in volume five of the *Asi-*

atick Researches, the "Transactions of the Asiatic Society of Bengal," founded in 1784 by Sir William Jones. The first texts that were studied were probably those read by H. H. Wilson, who wrote a *Sketch of the Religious Sects of the Hindoos* in volume seventeen of the *Asiatick Researches*, published in 1832. However, he does not call the practices he describes *Tantric*. He calls them the practices of "vàmis or vàmàcharis . . . the left-hand worshippers of the Goddess," whom, he said, "are very numerous among the Shaivas," such rites being "derived from an independent series of works known by the collective name of tantras." Wilson also notes that "the worshipper of Shakti, the power or energy of the divine nature in action, are exceedingly numerous amongst all classes of Hindoos." These statements show a good and unprejudiced grasp of the facts, with a realization of the widespread nature of Śākta (therefore Tantric) practices. A few years later, the French scholar Eugène Burnouf, in his *Introduction à l'étude du bouddhisme indien* (1844), devoted a whole section to Tantras (Buddhist Tantras, of course), noting their relationship with Śaivism—what he called "the ridiculous and obscene practices of the Shaivas." These first scholars to note the presence of the Tantric phenomenon mentioned only the practices and not the notions that accompanied them (or sometimes were at their origin). They were not, in their time, in a position to realize its nature and extent—still less its pervasiveness.

Half a century later, the first to do this was the pioneer of Tantric studies, the British judge Sir John Woodroffe (1868–1936), alias Arthur Avalon, who wrote in the preface to *Principles of Tantra* (1913): "Mediaeval Hinduism (to use a convenient if somewhat vague term) was, as its successor, modern Indian orthodoxy is, largely Tantric. The Tantra was then, as it is now, the great Mantra and Sadhana Shāstra (Scripture), and the main, where not the sole, source of some of the most fundamental concepts still prevalent as regards worship, images, initiation, yoga, the supremacy of the guru and so forth."

The style of this passage is that of another time. But to have realized the problematic nature of the notion of Hinduism and the pervasiveness of the Tantric phenomenon a century ago is remarkable. Sir John Woodroffe's role in the development of Tantric studies must not be undervalued. He was the first to proclaim the importance of the Tantric world and to publish studies on some of its aspects as well as a number of texts, using either his name or the pseudonym Arthur Avalon. The *Tantrik Texts* series of books he edited was the first of its kind. It is still in print (as are his other works), some of its volumes remaining useful. Tantric studies have enormously progressed since his time—in the last twenty years especially, as we shall see—and although Avalon / Woodroffe appears as an icon of another epoch, one must not fail to remember the importance of his role.[6]

On the nature of what is Tantric, an overall and global statement is all the more difficult to give because—as will be shown in this book—if the Tantric phenomenon was limited and therefore definable to begin with, over the course of centuries it took on (quite early perhaps) a twofold aspect. On the one hand, there were (and there are to this day) initiatory traditions or transmissions whose (sometimes transgressive) practices and doctrines were properly Tantric, assumed and lived as such. On the other hand, there existed—to a different extent and intensity and in different forms throughout the Hindu world—a number of Tantric practices and notions in addition to the former traditions (this is what Sir John Woodroffe wished to say).

I need to expand on these two aspects, but I must not oversimplify. The two aspects I have just mentioned do not exist side by side—they often interpenetrate. There are more, and less, "Tantric" traditions and systems. Further, if we come across Tantric practices and notions nearly everywhere in Hinduism, they are not always the same ones and they are not always present in the same way; their context may differ, and practices exist only in particular (social or ideological) contexts. There are also more or less "Tantric" texts. Finally, the Tantric metaphysical systems, pantheons, and ritual practices often include elements common to Hinduism in general, some of which go back to Vedic times. As I have said, the social and ritual rules of the brahmanical *dharma* are generally admitted in the Tantric sphere as valid on the level of social life. More important perhaps, the basic forms of reasoning and of intellectual approach to reality in the brahmanical culture as found in the *darśanas* are used in Tantric exegesis and philosophy. In this respect, we must not forget that the majority of Tantric texts are in Sanskrit, composed by Brahmins brought up in their communities and steeped in intellectual brahmanical culture, the culture of India.

Some Attempts at a Definition

THE INDIAN VIEW

The Sanskrit word *tantra* is from the verbal root *TAN*, which means "to extend," "to spread," hence "to spin out," "weave," "display," "put forth," and "compose." By extension, it comes to mean "system," "doctrine," or "work." A Tantra is thus a work, a text—any text. It is, says the fifth-century Indian author Pakṣilasvāmin, "a collection of facts." Many Sanskrit works that are not Tantric are called Tantras; for instance, the main Indian collection of fables is called the *Pañcatantra*, "The Five Books." Conversely, a large number of Tantric works are not called Tantra—this is especially the case in Tantric

Buddhism but also in the Hindu domain where basic Tantric scriptures are called *āgama*, *saṃhitā*, *sūtra*, and so on. The current Sanskrit expression *asmin tantre* may mean "in this Tantra," but most often it means simply "in this work." This being so, the fact is that from around the sixth century, a number of works named Tantra appeared in India that propounded new practices and notions while presenting themselves as revealed by non-Vedic deities. Such texts and their teachings were first described as Mantramārga ("the way of mantras"). Then came the adjective *tāntrika* ("Tantric") and later the term *tantraśāstra* ("the teaching of the Tantras").

The adjective *tāntrika* thus came to be used as opposed to *vaidika* (Vedic) to contrast two forms of the revealed religious tradition, the *śruti*: one originally embodied in the Veda and continuing as the "orthodox," "mainstream" form of Hinduism, the other based on Tantras or such texts and revealed by various deities. The best-known expression of this dichotomy, and the most often quoted, is by Kullūka Bhaṭṭa in the fifteenth century (therefore after the times of the main Tantric developments in the eighth through the fourteenth centuries) in his commentary on the Laws of Manu (*Manusmṛti* 2.1.), where he said that Revelation is twofold—Vedic and Tantric (*śrutiś ca dvividhā vaidikī tāntrikī ca*). The formula is all the more important because it uses the term *śruti* (revelation) for the Tantric as well as the Vedic Revelation, both being recognized as having a divine origin, be it the eternal self-revealed Word of the Veda or the Tantric teachings of a god or a goddess.

A characteristic trait of Tantric traditions is, in effect, that they appear as revealed by a divine being who, by doing so, brings what he or she proclaims from the transcendent plane—where it exists eternally still unexpressed—down to the level of this world. This is called the "descent of the Tantra" (*tantrāvatāra*), a metaphysical process that is often described at the beginning of the texts (Tantras, āgamas, etc.) that propound their doctrines. These revealed teachings are considered superior to the Veda (and as its continuation), for they are more effective in leading humans toward liberation, leading them more rapidly and up to a higher spiritual plane than the Veda-based teachings. They also claim to be better adapted to the needs of beings living in the present dark cosmic age (*kaliyuga*), where desire or passion (*kāma*) prevails.

Tantric traditions, however, do not usually entirely reject the brahmanical Veda-based teachings and rules. Those who follow Tantra consider them valid on the lower plane of social life as general, basic rules to be followed on the social plane, which can lead to salvation but not to liberation, as only the higher and more sophisticated Tantric teachings can bring the adept to liberation.

In effect, as is the case nowadays when one contrasts orthodoxy and heterodoxy, the *vaidika/tāntrika* opposition is not absolute. The two categories it contrasts are not clearly definable, and Hindu orthodoxy is defined more by social behavior than by beliefs. As has often been said, Hinduism is more a religious world of "orthopraxy" than of orthodoxy—what a Hindu does and how he behaves is more important than what he believes. One may very well behave as a good, observant Hindu—fully respecting the Hindu traditional rules of caste and purity and yet be devoted to a fearsome Tantric god or goddess—or simply attend cults or rites in temples (or having rites being performed there for his benefit) by priests who, if they are Śaivas, are Tantric initiates[7] and Brahmins.

As we shall see, Tantric traditions may be more or less "heterodox," or transgressive. Transgression itself can coexist with the outward respect of brahmanical norms. Among these are notably the rites of passage (*saṃskāras*),[8] which mark the stages in the life of the twice-born and are practiced by caste Hindus even if they are Tāntrikas. Such rites are Vedic and are still being performed today. They differ from the ancient, solemn Vedic cults that largely do not exist in India anymore except in exceptional cases of survival, or as a voluntary "quasi-archeological" return to a bygone past—a return sometimes subsidized by Western Hinduizing groups or promoted by an Indian reactionary political ideology. (It happens in such Vedic reconstructions that elements of Tantric origin are anachronistically included, for they are so current in Hinduism that one is not aware of their nonorthodox nature.) Apart from such cases, *vaidika* and *tāntrika* elements run alongside one another or combine variously to different degrees more or less everywhere.

Because Tantric rites, practices, and notions are so widespread, over the course of time their validity came to be more or less fully admitted—if not socially then at least ritually—as valid alongside the "Vedic," "orthodox" Hindu tradition, this even by strictly observant Brahmins. Thus around 900 AD, the philosopher Jayanta Bhaṭṭa (whom we will see again later on) said that the validity of the revelation of the Tantras and their teachings could be admitted insofar as they fulfilled some criteria of authenticity and were not contrary to the Vedic tradition and to respectable standards of behavior. A few years later, one of the masters of Vaiṣṇavism, Yāmunācārya (918–1038), who was indirectly the master of the great Vedānta theologian Rāmānuja (therefore of perfect orthodoxy), wrote the *Āgamaprāmāṇya* ("The Authoritativeness of the Āgamas"[9]), upholding the Vedic validity of the scriptures of the Pāñcarātra (or Pāñcarātra), the dominant form of Tantric Vaiṣṇavism. Of course, one may remark that what Yāmunācārya defended was the validity of a particular non-Vedic revelation, not "Tantric" notions and practices as opposed to the generally admitted "orthodox" ones.

As I have already noted, what India recognized is not the existence of a particular "Tantric" socioreligious "recognizable totality" but merely the fact that there are different approaches and experiences of religion, and these "non-Vedic" practices and notions were revealed by deities that are but aspects of the one supreme *brahman*, worshipped by all. I may add that the deities who revealed the āgamas, or Tantras—Viṣṇu, Śiva, the Goddess—had been worshipped for centuries. To recognize the validity of their revelation was therefore not recognizing much. Let me add that though perfectly Tantric, the Pāñcarātra practices and doctrine whose Vedic validity was upheld by Yāmunācārya were not at all transgressive, some masters of the Pāñcarātra going even so far as to describe their tradition as a Vedic school (*śākhā*). Tantric traditions raise a problem only insofar as they are transgressive, but even this problem, as we shall see, can be solved by carving out a place for transgression.

In this respect, we must look at what Abhinavagupta, the great philosopher and mystic of Kashmir (tenth through eleventh century)—one of the most remarkable Indian thinkers and a master of a very transgressive Tantric system—had to say. In his vast treatise *Tantrāloka* ("The light on the Tantras"; TĀ 35, 26 ff.), which hierarchically classified (as was usual in India[10]) the various revelations (the Vedic one being on the lowest level of the scale), he said that they were all valid in their own way and on their own plane because they answer all to particular needs and circumstances, but also and essentially because they are all originally issued from the same supreme godhead—who, for him, was of course Śiva. "There is," he said, "in truth only one unique tradition (āgama). On this tradition everything is founded, from popular doctrines up to the teachings of the Vaiṣṇavas, Buddhists or Śaivas." It is true that, for him, his own Kaula-Bhairava nondualistic Śaivism of the Trika was the only completely valid one; nevertheless, all other traditions were to be recognized, respected in their own field and within their limits.[11]

Abhinavagupta's position was not without scriptural support. An important Tantra devoted to the cult of Kālī, the *Jayadrathayāmala* (seventh through eighth centuries), for instance, prescribes that the adept respect the social rules of caste so that their gurus should not be disrespected. Another Tantra, quoted in the *Tantrāloka*, says that Śaiva initiates are to follow Vedic rules—they must act according to the traditional rules of their caste "to preserve the social order" (*sthityartham*)[12] for their own sake and for the benefit of their caste. This is possible, explains Jayaratha when commenting on this passage, because Vedic rules do not partake of the highest truth (*paramārtha*). Following them is therefore of little consequence. I could quote other Tantras to the same effect.

Not all philosophers, however, were as open-minded. Kumarīla Bhaṭṭa, "Mīmāṃsā-Kumārila"[13] (of the seventh or eighth century), for instance, condemned Tāntrikas outright, saying that one should have no contact with them, even in words. Another author, Aparārka (eleventh century), stated that according to the scriptures, there is no such social group as the Śaivas; therefore, there were simply no persons who could follow this teaching. One may study the Tantras, he said, so as to know what they say, but one must not follow their doctrine, only that of the Purāṇas (Antiquities), which is "Vedic." This in spite of the fact that in Aparārka's time, many Purāṇas—which form a section of the Veda-based tradition, the *smṛti*[14]—included a number of Tantric notions, practices, or mantras, sometimes even whole sections of Tantric treatises. A passage attributed to the *Skandapurāṇa* describes two methods (Tantric and Vedic) for the worship of the Goddess.[15] The most obvious and characteristic case of the interpenetration or juxtaposition of Tantric and Vedic texts is perhaps the admittedly later (eighteenth century) canonical collection of the 108 Upaniṣads, several of which were composed or rewritten at that time on the basis of earlier Tantric, Nātha, elements.[16]

In fact, much earlier than the eighteenth century, perhaps very early, followers of the main Tantric traditions came to consider their teachings not as replacing the Vedic tradition but as forming an esoteric initiatory superstructure—a special teaching completing, crowning, the exoteric "Vedic" base—which was considered unable to lead to liberation though it was valid on its own plane of social life. This hierarchization of doctrines and the claim of superiority of particular Tantric traditions was formalized in the theory of the progressive ascending position of doctrines (*uttarottaravaiśiṣṭya*). A new doctrine does not abolish a previous one; rather, it transcends it by giving details—precisions (*vaiśiṣṭya*) that allow the adept to reach a higher spiritual level by following higher and higher (*uttarottara*) teachings and practices. The more specific a rule, the higher the spiritual level. Thus, for instance, Abhinavagupta states that the "left-hand" (*vāma*) Tantric tradition is higher than the "right-hand" (*dakṣiṇa*) one, Kula being higher than *vāma* and his own Trika the highest and most specific of all, transcending even the Kula. It is interesting to note here that in such hierarchical presentations of Tantric traditions, the term *Tantra* usually refers not to the most but to the least "Tantric" systems. We shall return to this subject in chapter 4.

As we shall see in chapter 2, the presence and impact of Tantric notions and practices was not limited to the religious field. It played an important role in the social and political domain (this, of course, together with the "Vedic" notions ruling the Hindu socioreligious world). The Hindu conception of the king, for instance, is not Vedic but Tantric, and it has survived down to modern times—Nepal was until recently a Hindu monarchy ruled according to Tantric principles.[17]

Regarding the present, we may note that in India today, in spite of the pervasive presence of Tantric notions and practices, such practices tend to be perceived in current popular opinion as dangerous, immoral, perverse magic when overtly practiced and affirmed. Even in India, the approach to Tantra is complex and problematic. We will see this in chapter 11.

WESTERN ATTEMPTS AT A DEFINITION—OR THE FABRICATION OF TANTRA

Having looked at the discovery of Tantra by European Orientalists and at their first attempts at understanding it, I will now briefly review some more recent attempts at a definition of the subject by Western scholars. I will then outline what I believe to be the main distinctive traits of Tantra—that is, the view that guided me when writing this book. I naturally believe this view to be as objective, as "scientific," as possible. But I do not forget that there is always a measure of arbitrariness in an overview that, being necessarily guided by a preconception of the subject, will itself be a partial fabrication.

The following quotations of Western definitions or characterizations of Tantra represent only a few instances, not a complete survey of such statements.

As far as I know, the first description by a European scholar of Tantra understood as an important aspect of Indian religions is by Mircea Eliade in *Techniques du Yoga*, first published in 1948 in French.[18] He wrote, "It is not a new religion . . . but rather an important stage in the evolution of the main Indian religions." "Tantrism," he added, "becomes after the 5th century A.D. a pan-Indian 'fashion.'" One may not agree with some of Eliade's ideas, but to notice the pervasiveness of Tantra—to underline the importance of *śakti* in the Tantric vision of man and the cosmos, the Tantric construction of a vast pantheon, the fundamental role of mantras, of meditative and ritual techniques, as well as of the body—to say also that "Tantrism embodies in a certain sense the widest conception of the concept of the status of the liberated in this life (*jīvanmukta*)" showed an exceptionally discerning perception of the real place and significance of Tantra in a time when this was unusual in the West.

This was shortly after the last world war, a time when scholars still believed the Tantric aspects of Hinduism to be of little importance, and when only a comparatively small number of Tantric texts were known to exist and still less had been edited—a time when not many manuscripts were accessible (or deemed to deserve the effort of deciphering them). However, some felt that the field was worth investigating. Thus, in the two-volume handbook of Indology, *L'Inde Classique*,[19] in the section devoted to "Rites et pratiques," seven closely printed pages described "le tantrisme" not as a recognizable totality but, implicitly, as particular aspects of mainstream Hinduism. (These pages were written by Lilian Silburn, who was to become a pioneer of Tantric studies.) Later, Louis Renou (a master of Indological studies), pointed out in volume six of his *Etudes védiques et pāninéennes* (1960) the omnipresence of Tantric elements: "All literary statements in texts later [than the tenth century]," he wrote, "which appear as free from Tantric elements, are in all likelihood simply reflecting a quasi-archeological will to revive ancient Hinduism."[20]

Madeleine Biardeau, in *L'hindouisme, anthropologie d'une religion* (1981),[21] wrote about Tantrism: "It does not bring anything new. It only takes up upside-down well-known values, reading the Tradition in an esoteric way." On the Tantric notions about the Word, she said, "It merely amplifies to the point of madness an authentically brahmanical form of thought." This was, in both cases, acknowledging that there existed no particular limited Tantric domain but an ensemble of notions—admittedly specific, but part of Hinduism. Referring to the brahmanical theory of the four aims, or purposes of human life—Eros or passion, the enjoyment of the pleasures of this life (*kāma*), all that has to do with material life (*artha*), all that concerns the sociocosmic order (*dharma*), and liberation (*mokṣa*)—Madeleine Biardeau described the Tantric position as an attempt to place *kāma* as a means to progress toward liberation, which was an apposite way of explaining the ideologically central, though limited in practice, place of Tantric sexual or more generally transgressive practices. A view that can be taken as supporting the idea sometimes put forward is that for an adept, the Tantric domain could be perceived as his private, inner domain as opposed to his outer, public person.[22] This view is confirmed in India by the often-quoted Kaula description of the Tantric householder as being "inside *kaula*, outside *śaiva*, and *vaidika* in public life." However, this is only valid on the individual, personal plane for private, domestic rites—a very small part of the Tantric field, which includes nearly all aspects, private or public, of religious or social life.

But rites are very important in Tantra. Tāntrikas are hyperritualists, as we shall see. This explains the definition of Tantra by Jean Filliozat (1906–82), a scholar whose contribution was essential to the development of Tantric studies. Professor of Indology at the Collège de France, Jean Filliozat was the founder (in 1955) then the head of the Institut Français de Pondichéry. He determined that one of the main activities of the Indology section would be the collection, classification, and editing of Śaiva āgamas. In a review published in 1968 in the *Journal Asiatique*, Jean Filliozat described Tantrism as "merely the technical, ritual aspect of religion, whether Śaiva, Vaiṣṇava, Buddhist or Jain." He added, "A treatise of religious architecture is necessarily Tantric." One might explain this judgment by the overwhelmingly ritual character of most of the āgamas collected by the Institut Français de Pondichéry. The judgment is, however, not totally unfounded. It has a hermeneutic (as one says) usefulness if one takes into account the totality of the Tantric field—Hindu and Buddhist, Indian and Asian. The pattern of the rites of worship in the whole area is practically always based on the pattern of the Tantric *pūjā*.[23] However, its usefulness is limited because, aiming at finding a defining element common to everything Tantric in Asia, it is inevitably minimalist and therefore inadequate.

In spite of this restriction, I would like to underline the importance of ritual as a general Indian trait. For the Vedic "orthodox" tradition, neither prayer nor devotion but ritual is necessary to maintain the cosmic order. Ritual precision, not devotion, ensures the efficacy of a rite. Ritual mistakes are not sins with moral consequences but technical faults with religious or cosmic effects. The spread of devotion has progressively destroyed the essential importance of ritual precision, though it has not entirely obliterated it even today, for ritual is not mere action without meaning, as is sometimes said. For a devotee, it is meaningful and a source of intellectual or spiritual developments.

In contrast, as all-embracing a definition of Tantra as possible was put forward in *Hindu Tantrism* by Teun Goudriaan in a short (sixty-seven pages) but precise and perceptive overview of the subject, described as "one of the main currents in the Indian religious tradition of the last fifteen hundred years . . . the extremely varied and complicated nature of which . . . renders . . . a single definition almost impossible." Goudriaan then summed up some of the constituents of Tantrism (in its wider sense) as he understood it, enumerating eighteen traits of ritual practice, behavior, or doctrine—an interesting and valid, though not undisputable, list. The section of the book by Goudriaan included two more chapters, one on "Tantrism in History" and another on "Tantrism in Hindu Religious Speculation," both giving a good overview of what was known then, which is far from the present (still in progress) state of knowledge[24] on the subject.

This knowledge of, as well as the attitude toward, Tantra has changed markedly in recent years. It is now a recognized subject in university departments of oriental studies, religion, or social sciences in Europe and the Americas.[25] This is the case notably in the United States, where the Society for Tantric Studies is active, contributing to a better view and understanding of the Tantric phenomenon.[26] Important contributions to this better view of our subject have also appeared in Europe and Japan. There are now excellent and gifted scholars on Tantra in Austria, France, Germany, Hungary, and Italy, to name only a few. In England, retired professor Alexis Sanderson is at present the best and most learned specialist of the Tantric field. One cannot write on the subject without referring to his work. All this, however, takes place in the academic field. It is to be found in books or journals not easily available except in university libraries, and is meant for those who know Sanskrit, which is not likely to be the case for most readers.

Among those who have recently contributed to the better understanding and definition of the Tantric field, I would like to quote Professor David G. White who, in *The Alchemical Body*, underscored the links between Tantra and alchemy, a very interesting and useful point. In the more recent *Kiss of the Yoginī*,[27] he identified Tantra with the Śaiva traditions of the Kula, where he considers the sexual element (rites and notions) as central. White is right in distinguishing between a "hard-core," transgressive aspect formed by some texts (Kula mostly) with their practices and notions and a "soft" Tantrism found nearly everywhere as the usual practices and notions of Hinduism. He believes the first aspect is the most important one. But I believe the importance of the Tantric phenomenon lies precisely in its pervasive interpenetration with brahmanical elements. White also edited a collection of studies called *Tantra in Practice*, to which he contributed an excellent introduction where, taking a larger perspective, he describes Tantra as "that Asian body of beliefs and practices which, working from the principle that the universe we experience is nothing other than the concrete manifestation of the divine energy of the godhead that creates and maintains that universe, seeks to ritually appropriate and channel that energy, within the human microcosm, in creative and emancipatory ways," a definition perhaps too general but unobjectionable.

To this I would finally like to add a more recent one from a 2011 article, *Tantric Traditions*, by Dominic Goodall and Harunaga Isaacson, both particularly knowledgeable on Tantric matters. The article begins as follows: "Starting from about the sixth century of the common era, initiatory religions claiming authority for scriptures called Tantra, and promising liberation as well as various worldly and supernatural goals through the power of mantras, came to the fore in South Asia. That these Tantric traditions were not marginal can be seen not just from the huge quantity of textual material that their followers produced, but also for instance from the importance which Tantric gurus played in the life of kings and the court."

The next sentences of the paragraph would very much deserve quoting—as would the whole article, to which we will come back in the next chapters.

Having thus quoted some definitions of the Tantric phenomenon, and before reviewing in the following chapters its different aspects, I would like to enumerate what I believe to be its main traits. It being understood that this is a modern synthesis of a long series of historical developments (fifth to early eighteenth centuries) during which notions and practices changed, appeared and disappeared—Tantra never was at any precise time as we synthetize it now. Nevertheless, here are the points I would like to make.

Tantra is inseparably made up of notions, of ideology, *and* of actions and practices, all being linked—a vision of the world, then, the means to give substance to this view on the existential plane of body-mind and in the world one lives in.

On the ideological plane, the Tantric vision is that of a world issued from, upheld and completely permeated by, divine energy (*śakti*), which is also present in the human being who can harness and use it (her, rather) for worldly as well as ritual aims and for liberation. In all Tantric systems, nondualist as well as dualist, the deity is ever present (when not immanent), pervading the universe, which is not illusory but the result of a "transformation" (*pariṇāma*) of the supreme *brahman*. The deity, too, when acting, is nearly always conceived as polarized in masculine and feminine, the female pole being that of power (*śakti*), a power that may be auspicious and favorable but also fierce and fearsome—this especially if in the form of a goddess. The hugeness of Hindu pantheons, their "maṇḍalic" pattern, is Tantric. Tantric traditions are initiatory—a Tāntrika adept is an initiate, which implies an initiating master, a guru, then a transmission from master to master. This explains (at least in part) why Tantric teachings are secret in principle, a point that is constantly underlined.[28] Secrecy is linked to another basic Tantric element: transgression—be it the mere disparagement or the complete rejection of brahmanical rules, especially those concerning ritual purity. By participation or immersion in the forbidden, the Tāntrika transcends his limits, gains all powers as well as salvation—a salvation in this world.

Concerning practices, the ritual Hindu worship of deities (*pūjā*), in its usual pattern, is originally Tantric. Therefore, it is always Tantric in its pattern but not always in its spirit, for a *pūjā* can be done for any deity, Tantric or not Tantric. The pervasive presence of mantras, the fact that mantras are the highest form of deities, that one can approach the godhead and progress toward liberation only using mantras, is Tantric. The fundamental place, beside mantras, given to the Word (*vāc*) and everything that concerns it is also typically Tantric (though Vedic in origin). Typically Tantric, too (and also originally Vedic), is the complexity and superabundance of rites. The link between Tantra and yoga should also be mentioned. (The important magical side of Tantra is not typically Tantric. It is generally, essentially, Indian.)

Those are only a few landmarks given to the reader before entering into a more detailed description that, I hope, will show the interesting specificity of Tantra as a pervasive aspect of the Hindu socioreligious world.

2

Origins, History, Expansion

As we have seen, giving a definition of Tantra is not easy. Equally difficult is the task of outlining its historical development, as there is little data available. Therefore, in this chapter, I will put forward deductions—hypotheses more often than certainties. However, even with the very few well-established facts to be found, I can show the importance of a socioreligious phenomenon that has permanently marked not only the religions but also the history, the very life, of South Asian and Southeast Asian societies.

India, it is often said, has no sense of history. Without being wrong, this statement is not entirely true. The fact is, however, that for the most ancient period, very few really informative documents are available—and there are not many for the following age. Therefore, what can we say about the beginnings of the Tantric phenomenon? Two points can be made: First, contrary to what is sometimes said, there is nothing Tantric in the Veda. Second, contrary to what some Indian authors have said, Tantra was, in all likelihood, born quite early in the Indian subcontinent.

As for the Veda, one does find in Vedic times—that is, from the R̥gveda to the oldest Upaniṣads (those called "Vedic," dating from the seventh to the third century BC)—elements that are of consequence in the Tantric world. Such are the notions concerning the cosmic role and the presence in the body of the Word[1] (*vāc*) together with the role of mantras (even though the meaning of the term *mantra* is not the same in the Veda as in Tantra—but Vedic mantras are sometimes made use of in Tantric rites.[2])

Such is the case, too, of micromacrocosmic correspondences (together with the "mystical physiology," to speak like Eliade), or of sexual symbolism, or of the conception of kingship. Other instances could be cited. These notions, however, existed there in embryo without the developments that appeared later, especially in the world of Tantra. This world followed the Vedic one. They were different but, developing as they did on the same soil, they shared some elements. More precisely, Tantra did not abolish the socio-religious Vedic tradition; it merely wished to transcend it. We may also note that the Tantric view of this world—considered as a reality worth being taken into account—as well as the intense ritualism of Tantra are nearer to the Vedic attitude than to the spirit of renunciation and the antiritualism of the Upaniṣads and of ancient Buddhism. However, this does not prevent many Tantric texts from recommending the transcendence of ritual and from extolling renunciation. Change and continuity is a characteristic of Indian philosophy and religion.

Where and how did the Tantric phenomenon begin? On one hand, the frequent worship of female deities and the importance given to the notion of energy (*śakti*), which is feminine, are sometimes seen as supporting the idea that several Tantric notions or practices can be traced back to the Indus civilization. However, there is no proof of this, and the very existence of goddess cults in Mohenjo-Daro or Harappa is not proven. There were also Vedic goddesses. On the other hand—and this is certain—the worship of feminine forms of the deity is a characteristic trait of modern popular Hinduism. But because Tantric scriptures are in Sanskrit, the Tantric notions and practices are not popular but learned. In addition, they are initiatory, secret. Ascribing them a popular origin is therefore questionable. There are, however, exoteric, festive Tantric rites that are "popular" because they are attended by many, even by crowds.[3] There are also common elements between some popular cults and some Tantric practices, so much so that one may be tempted to consider them as related.

This being so, we can be tempted to believe (if we do not limit our view to the early period but consider the historical evolution of Tantra) that it arose from two aspects of the same Indian source—one popular, diffuse (more linked to the soil), the other learned, lettered, socially more limited (more "Indo-European"?). The contact or interaction between these two resulted in the appearance and development of the practices and notions that were to constitute the Tantric phenomenon within the Veda-based brahmanical orthodoxy.

The basis or starting point of these practices and notions appears, however, to be ancient and brahmanical. Asceticism—renunciation as a means to gain not only liberation but also, or mainly, divine or magical powers—is as old as India. Magical rites are described in the ancient *Gṛhyasūtras* and in the *Arthaśāstra*, the traditional brahmanical treatises on practical life. The value given to this world, too, is Vedic. These elements, appearing and developing in contact with popular cults and beliefs, could have been influenced by them and, due to this contact, the particular traits that were later called Tantric appeared and developed. (As we shall see, there is a continuity between the learned and the popular in many domains.) Admittedly, this is a hypothesis, which some will not accept because resorting to the substrate as an explanation is often criticized.[4] Nevertheless, the hypothesis seems not impossible to me. Several facts that will be mentioned later could tend, I believe, to support it.

Not to be underestimated are the ancient ascetic (*śrāmaṇic*) movements of wandering renouncers from which emerged Buddhism and Jainism and which were not "popular." Also important are the ancient ascetic (Vedic, even) practices (*tapas*)[5] as well as observances (*vrata*) from groups such as the Pāśupatas, from which (as we will see) issued a proto-Tantric Atimārga. Therefore, the role of the substrate must not be overvalued.[6]

However, I would add that even if conjectural, this view is more plausible than the idea sometimes put forward of a shamanistic, central Asian origin of Tantra. In my view, Tantric practices and doctrine are not in the least shamanistic, and there is no reason to believe that they come from anywhere but India—except, of course, if one considers them detestable and prefers therefore to place their origin in some other part of the world. (The idea has also been put forward recently by some scholars that Dravidian, South India, may have played a role in the beginnings of the Tantric phenomenon.)

A Few Historical Elements

Of course, no trace remains of the small initiatory ascetic groups in which I believe Tantra germinated. It is also not certain that it appeared within such groups rather than resulting from a creative evolution taking place more generally within post-Vedic Hinduism. Elements usually considered characteristically Tantric, such as the quest for supernatural powers (*siddhis*), magical powers or even sorcery (*abhicāra*), and rites for prosperity, are found in the *Gṛhyasūtras*, Vedic texts on domestic rites. Sexual symbolism is omnipresent in the *Mīmāṃsā*, the ritual exegesis of the Veda. Tantra does not always innovate. Epigraphical evidence from the first centuries AD show that while kings accepted their role as guardians of the brahmanical socioreligious order (*varṇāśramadharma*), imposing its observance in their kingdoms or in the regions they conquered, they were personally devoted to Śiva, Viṣṇu, Sūrya, or the Goddess—that is, to the deities whose cults were to be extolled in the Tantras.

Quite early within Tantra, as Sanderson has noted, there was "a determination to be fully embedded in the brahmanical tradition" shown not only by the rule that Tantric initiates should keep their social brahmanical obligations but also by innovations in their "ritual repertoire to bring it into greater congruence with the brahmanical."[7] This helped the expansion of Tantric beliefs and ritual practices from limited ascetic groups to the larger social stratum of married householders (*gr̥hastha*), who were henceforth to form its social basis. Their condition was summed up by the formula quoted earlier: "*Kaula* inside, outwardly *Śaiva*, and socially *vaidika*."

One of the best-known relevant inscriptions, and the most often referred to before the recent discovery and study of more ancient evidence, is the Gangdhar inscription, dated 423–24 AD. The inscription records that a minister of a king from Malwa ordered a temple to be built to the Mothers (*mātr̥*), female deities described as uttering loud and terrible shouts of joy and stirring up the oceans by the powerful wind "born from the Tantras" (*tantrodbhūta*). This temple was reportedly peopled by *Ḍākinīs*, goddesses who, like the Mothers, appear often in Tantric pantheons. Less picturesque but more interesting are manuscripts (recently studied) of Tantras that appear to date, in part, from the fifth century. Such is the case of the *Niśvāsatattvasaṃhitā*, a Śaiva Tantra that contains very early, quasi-pre-Tantric elements.[8] The *Vīṇāśikhatantra*, on the cult of the god Tumburu, probably also dates from the fifth century. All other more or less datable ancient Indian elements showing the existence of Tantric pantheons we know of are from the sixth or seventh century or later. Some Yoginī temples of Orissa date perhaps from the eighth century. As for literary evidence, the vast (sixth century) astrological treatise, the *Br̥hatsaṃhitā*, mentions the worship of troops of Mothers (*mātr̥gaṇa*); Guṇāḍhya's *Br̥hatkathā* (sixth century?) and Bāṇa's seventh-century *Harṣacarita* describe possession rites performed in a burning ground; a play by Bhavabhūti (eighth century) describes Tantric rites, as does another play of the same period, Bhaṭṭa Jayanta's *Āgamaḍambara* ("Much Ado about Religion"[9]). Other documents of that period, which we will see, concern the social, political, or economic domains.

A precise reference that has often been mentioned is the Sdok-Kak-Thom stele, dated 1052 AD. It reports that a certain Brahmin "expert in supernatural powers" (*siddhis*) brought the cult of Tumburu to Cambodia together with four important Tantras, the *Sammohana*, *Nayottara*, *Siraśccheda*, and *Vīṇāśikha*, during the reign of Jayavarman II at the beginning of the ninth century. It appears now that at least one of these texts, the *Vīṇāśikhatantra*, dates from much earlier. However, this inscription remains important because it documents the expansion of Tantra outside India. Much older are Chinese documents concerning the ancient kingdom of Fou-Nan, and Sanskrit inscriptions from Champa proving the existence of apparently Tantric Śaiva cults in that part of the Indo-Chinese peninsula. From India, no written (manuscript) document earlier than the ninth century has been found. Fragments from Gilgit, however, date from the seventh century. But cults and doctrines may well have existed centuries before being mentioned in an inscription. Therefore, there is no reason not to believe, in the present state of knowledge, that the Tantric phenomenon was already present in India in the fifth century. In fact, if one refers to evidence outside India, an earlier date appears possible, since Indian Buddhist texts were translated in Chinese from the fifth century.[10]

If one knows very little about the beginnings of Tantra, its expansion to most of the Indian subcontinent from the eighth or ninth century is certain. Kashmir was an especially important and intellectually brilliant center for Buddhism and Hinduism, two closely linked domains. Some of the main religious and philosophical (as well as literary and historical) Indian texts are from Kashmir—an efflorescence that went on until the thirteenth century, after this region was reached by Islam. Even then, it did not entirely disappear: cults survived and—as is well known—Śaiva pandits went on teaching there down to very recent times. Bengal, the center, and the south of India were also regions of Tantric activity and culture, as proved by written works as well as, more visibly, temple architecture and the arts, this going on for centuries. Generally speaking, one may say that the main Tantric period in India was from the eighth to the fourteenth century when, no longer limited to small ascetic esoteric and transgressive groups but spreading and expanding, both attenuated and enriched, fully embedded in the brahmanical world, it "Tantricized" Hinduism, changing it in many ways while continuing to be in a way its secret core.

Geography and Expansion

From the geographical as well as from the historical point of view, there are practically no certain data on the beginnings of Tantra. It seems to have been present relatively early in the whole subcontinent. Is this because it appeared at the same time in several places and in similar initiatory groups? Or is it because it spread rapidly everywhere? If so, how did it spread? We cannot say. Some believe that Tantra was disseminated by wandering ascetics such as the ones still found in India today. As we shall see, the link between Tantra and kingship may also have played a role.

It is generally believed that the region where the Tantric phenomenon first appeared is the northern and Himalayan part of India, a reason (rather than a proof) for this belief being that three of the four centers (*pīṭha*) of the great Kaula ensemble of Śaiva Tantric traditions are located there, the main one being one being Oḍḍiyāna, which is the Swat Valley of the Himalayas, now in Pakistan. A valley mythically believed, by Buddhists as well as Hindus, to be the birthplace of some of their spiritual traditions. At the other end of the Himalayas, Bengal and Assam were equally Tantric regions, notably with the Buddhist and the Hindu Sahajiyās (very active from the eighth to the twelfth century), Tantra being still very much present there today. In Nepal, Buddhism and Hinduism were very early "Tantricized" and have remained so today. The oldest Tantric manuscripts are found in Nepal (due to the fact that the climate is more favorable to their preservation than that of most of India[11]).

However, Jayaratha (twelfth century), commenting on Abhinavagupta's *Tantrāloka*, said that *madhyadeśa*, which we can take as meaning central India, was the place of origin of all the sacred scriptures, the *śāstra*—that is, the Tantric scriptures. Gangdhar, whose important inscription of 423–24 AD was mentioned above, is in that region (in the state of Madhya Pradesh today). Not far from Gangdhar are the Khajuraho temples, built in the tenth and eleventh centuries by the Chandella kings, whose structure and ornamentation are generally considered as typically Tantric. In Khajuraho as well as in the neighboring state of Orissa, temples were built and dedicated to the Yoginīs, fearsome Tantric goddesses whose importance we will see later.[12] Only a few such temples survive, the most noteworthy being at Bheraghat, a remarkable circular structure with eighty-one statues of Yoginīs. There were surely many in ancient times, which shows the hold these deities had on ancient society. In Ujjain (also in Madhya Pradesh), according to the Chinese pilgrim Yi-Tsing (683–727), Bhairava-Mahākalā surrounded by *Ḍākinīs* was worshipped, a worship that is still alive today. In the same period, Bāṇa, in his novel *Kādambarī*, places a queen wearing amulets, performing magical rites, and invoking the Mothers in that same town. In his *Harṣacarita*, he also describes a South Indian *ācārya* in a manner that evokes a very Tantric atmosphere. The Śaiva Tantric tradition of the Siddhas (*cittar* in Tamil; a category we shall see again further on) has long existed in Tamil Nadu in the south. Karnataka, where there are today many goddess temples, was also a very "Tantricized" region in ancient times. (I will note here that from the twelfth century onward, the originally Kashmirian Śaiva Tantric tradition of the Śrīvidyā existed in South India, of which several authors were important. It is still active at the time of this writing.[13])

I have mentioned above a few Tantric monuments. But what is to be underlined in this respect is that from a certain time (eighth century?) onward, Hindu religious architecture was (and remains) essentially Tantric. As we shall see (in chapter 10), the rules concerning the construction of temples and their iconography—be it the making, placing, or consecration of images—were practically always given in Tantric scriptures or manuals.

The vast number of ancient temples or sanctuaries still seen in India today is proof of the deeply rooted presence of Tantra not only in the Indian landscape but in the life of Indians. When attending temple rituals, Indians see and pay homage to images of deities that are Tantric in their aspect and conception. Very often, this is also the case for the images used at home for private, domestic, daily worship. Living as we all do in a world peopled with images, concrete or mental, the fact that these images are generally Tantric must have some effect on those Hindus who constantly see them. However, this does not mean that they become unconsciously Tāntrikas.

Be that as it may, we must underline the fact that even though some historical, textual, and iconographical data are available, we know next to nothing about the social context of ancient Tantric texts, which alone would permit us to understand the nature of their presence and impact. What did they mean in their time for those who lived with them? In what social milieu, in what castes, among what kinds of ascetics did the Tantric cults and practices first appear? How did they develop and how were they performed? How did the Tantric notions and practices spread from their first initiatory limited presence to larger social groups (with the inflections this necessarily brought about)? There are many important questions to which one cannot give a precise answer, even though, as we shall see, one can perceive the importance of the link between religion and social and political developments.

Outside India

Although we do not know much about the early period of Tantra's development, the fact that it soon overstepped the limits of the Indian subcontinent is well known. Possibly as early as the fourth century, it spread in different ways together with the religious and political Indian presence throughout a great part of Asia. Monks, teachers, ascetics from India—and notably from Kashmir—were mostly responsible for this expansion. We do not know exactly how this went on, but the early and overall presence of Tantricism in Asia is very visible—a very important cultural fact. Following the silk road,

Tantric Buddhism spread to Mongolia, central Asia, and China, as shown by frescos and manuscripts from Khotan, Turfan, and Dun-Huang, and it was introduced in Tibet in the eighth century.[14] Ultimately, it reached Japan, where there are still important Tantric Buddhist sects or institutions. As we have seen, Chinese documents as well as surviving inscriptions and iconography are proofs of Tantric—Buddhist and Hindu—presence in the Indochinese Peninsula, where the Indianization of the local kingdoms of the Chams and the Khmers produced such masterpieces as Angkor. This Hindu Tantric presence survived until the fourteenth century. In what is now Indonesia, Buddhism was evidently present in the eighth century in Java, where monuments such as the extraordinary structure at Borobudur—a Buddhist mantrayāna "maṇḍalic" structure built, some say, on a Hindu basis—still survive. Tantric Śaivism coexisted with it, and is still alive today in Bali. There were therefore several centuries of the "Tantricization" of Asia.

A Tantric World?

We have seen until now mainly textual, epigraphic, or iconographic evidence showing the Tantric pervasion of Indian religious and philosophical thought. Without Tantrism, their course would have been very different. But the presence and effects of Tantra went much further. It left its mark on the whole Hindu or "Hinduized" world beyond the religious field—in the social and economic field and on the polity. This very important aspect has too often been left out by scholars who, working mainly on texts, are tempted to forget that these texts appeared, were received, and put into effect not in the abstract but in a particular social and political context. This context first marked them and then marked what they acted on, thus contributing to the modification of this context that, as it were, gave them a practical impact in return. "To be interested by gods is to speak about men," a French anthropologist[15] once wrote. It is humans who have created gods—partly in their own image. Such interactions are still seen today.

Historically, a main point is the social extension of Tantra, to which we have already alluded. If they appeared, as we tend to believe, among small initiatory groups of renouncers—visionary transgressive cults, magic performed by ascetic, esoteric "virtuosi"—the first Tantric cults and their related scriptures spread progressively. They penetrated larger milieus not of renouncers but of people living in the world—householders (*gṛhastha*) accepting (at least secretly) some Tantric beliefs and practices only insofar as they were compatible with the society of castes. Unfortunately, we cannot follow the evolution of this important social development throughout the course of history. We do not know how and in what circumstances this transition from a transgressive minority to a larger, less intense, "routinized" presence in the social establishment took place. We do not know the nature of the relationship or the interplay of these two aspects of Tantra—the "hard core" and the "soft" middle ground.

The Hindu form of religion that spread over the Indian subcontinent and beyond from about the fifth century was in fact essentially Śaivism, even if brahmanical rules and practices were also socially upheld (and imposed on conquered countries). Vaiṣṇavism, Buddhism, and sometimes Jainism were also present, but Śaivism was predominant, including naturally the worship of goddesses (Śāktism, as this aspect of Tantra is usually called), since such cults were present in the earliest forms of Tantric, or pre-Tantric, religion.[16]

I do not need to expand here on the fact that the Tantric pervasion of Hinduism does not transform the average Hindu devotee into a Tāntrika, even if he worships divine forms that are originally Tantric and follows a procedure of worship (*pūjā*) that evolved in a Tantric milieu. Tantras, too, are after all not uniformly transgressive: some—those of the Pāñcarātra—do not typically involve the transgression of socioreligious norms at all. In general, the Tantric domain gradually ceased to be the realm of secrecy and of transgression (there were and are exceptions). This became only its esoteric part, its "hard core"—a very limited and not very visible part that remains essential because it is the original, basic element whose spirit has marked many aspects of the beliefs and of the personal life of the average Hindu for centuries (if unnoticed). In the course of this book, we will meet these two aspects of the existential experience of Tantra from time to time.

Tantra had also a very important political and economic aspect. In the Hindu kingdoms that settled in India after the Gupta era from the seventh century onward and that lasted, at least formally, until 1947, the king was considered divine—a condition that grounded his authority. The term *deva* (god) was applied to him as to a deity. His consecration (*rājyābhiṣeka*), performed according to the traditional rules, was followed by a Tantric (generally a Śaiva) initiation performed by a specialist in mantra rituals, which transformed him into a kind of Tantric initiate. Ritually transformed into an embodiment of a deity, usually Śiva, the monarch was symbolically married to a goddess, usually Durgā. His power was thus supported by the power (*śakti*) of a goddess, of Yoginīs, or of Mothers (*mātṛ*), powerful and often fearsome Tantric deities.[17] The monarch, who lived in a palace built according to the rules given in Tantric manuals, had Tantric rites performed and Tantric mantras used for the benefit of the realm, to promote the success of his patrons, to remove the obstacles to his power and to frustrate or defeat his enemies.[18] In this he was helped by the royal preceptor (*rājaguru*), who also helped him on the way to liberation because he was, as a consecrated king, also an initiated adept (*sādhaka*). He was surrounded by spiritual masters (*ācāryas*), holders of magical powers (*siddhis*), who put the teachings of the Tantras to use for his benefit. He also had a royal chaplain (*rājapurohita*), a Tantric initiated Brahmin, of less importance. The Hindu monarch thus appeared as the sacrificer par excellence.

The Tantric presence in the Hindu realm was also felt through the temples, which proliferated there, often endowed with large gifts of land.[19] The monarchs who ordered such temples to be built wished to give the legitimacy and solidity of their power a material form. Seats of divine forces, the temples were also symbols and seats of temporal power. Essential to the divine and territorial power of the Hindu monarch was the concept of *maṇḍala*—the realm conceived as a diagram, theoretically circular in shape, whose center was the king—a formula that had official value in Nepal until recently.[20] In this perspective, the Tantric goddesses were not present merely near the king. Being clan goddesses (*kuladevīs*) or deities of local territories (*kṣetradevīs*), they peopled the *maṇḍala*, where their cults confirmed their power—one thus sees the social and political rootedness of Tantric deities.[21]

The rules concerning the layout of the royal palace were also prescribed in the Tantras. So too were those on the layout of the town built around the palace, with rules on what we would call "town planning": the layout of markets, of the dwellings of different castes or activities, and so forth. All such rules were evidently also applied to other urban settlements and other types of buildings. For instance, in the domain of irrigation, in the creation of wells or reservoirs, the ancient rules given in *vaidika* texts were extended and completed by Tantric manuals. Tantra (mostly in its Śaiva form) also played an active role in the assimilation of the communities in conquered regions where brahmanical society came to be extended, thus integrating new populations who benefited from the less rigorous (on the religious and ritual plane) Tantric conception of caste.

Finally, we should not forget that the linguistic means of this cultural expansion was Sanskrit. Tantra spread outside India through texts written in Sanskrit. The Tantras and their exegesis, as well as votive or dedicatory inscriptions (the sole signs still visible now in many countries of that ancient Tantric presence[22]) are in Sanskrit, the language of ritual in all Hindu temples in Asia—as well as of the Buddhist *sūtras* or Tantras—transposed into Tibetan or Chinese.

With this political-religious organization where the power is divine, where the human space is subsumed by the divine, where the people participate in festive rituals, there came to exist a Tantric world—or at least a world where the link to the transcendent is marked in many respects by Tantric conceptions and practices. This world was brought, together with the cult of the divine monarch, from the various parts of the Indian subcontinent to Cambodia, Champa, and Indonesia. In Tibet, China, and Japan, Tantric rites and Buddhism were made use of in support of political power.[23] We may therefore speak of a Tantric civilization—a veritable Tantric world—that existed for centuries in India and in all the "Indianized" parts of Asia, a world whose imprint is sometimes still visible today.[24]

3

The Textual Material

The textual material of Tantra consists mainly of texts called *tantra* in Sanskrit, hence the name of the Tantric phenomenon whose basic fabric ("fabric" being one of the meanings of the word *tantra*) they constitute. As we have already said, not all Tantric texts are called Tantra. They are also called *āgama* ("tradition"), *saṃhitā* ("collection"), or *sūtra* ("aphorism"). All these texts form the Tantric scriptures, we may say[1]—the Tantric Revelation, as all these works are deemed to be divinely revealed. There are also other revealed Tantric texts. The Purāṇas ("antiquities") are vast, sacred texts of Hinduism, some of which are Tantric or include Tantric elements or portions. There are also the Tantric Upaniṣads. All these texts are in Sanskrit, the "perfect," "refined," or "hallowed" (*saṃskṛta*) language, the language of the gods. The Word (*vāc*), "mistress of the gods," speaks in Sanskrit.

A very important body of literature must be added to these revealed works—namely, commentaries, digests, compilations, monographs, collections of hymns or of names of deities, and mantras and works on mantras (forming what one usually names the "teaching or science of mantra"[2] [*mantraśāstra*]). There are also technical or iconographical treatises, mystical works, and philosophical, speculative, or literary works of all sorts. All this forms a huge ensemble that began being produced in the first centuries of our era and went on appearing practically until today. Most of these texts are not dated. Very often, we do not know when or where they first appeared. It should be noted that they are predominantly philosophical and normative—they propound theories and express rules. They say what is to be believed or conceived and what is to be done but they do not describe what was actually done by whom or when they were produced. They remain, however, our only and irreplaceable source of information.

Works of all types written in the vernacular languages that have been used in India since the middle ages should also be added to this basic body of texts. Generally more recent than those in Sanskrit, closer to everyday life, showing often interesting forms of popular devotion—not infrequently of literary value—they are also to be taken into account if one wishes to grasp the full extent and diversity of the Tantric phenomenon. There were also such Tantric works in Southeast Asia and notably in the Southeast Asian Peninsula. One cannot give here more than a rough overview of this huge textual ensemble of Sanskrit and vernacular texts. While doing so, I will not enter into their doctrinal import or into the practices they describe—this will be (briefly) done in the next chapter.[3]

Sanskrit Texts

The Sanskrit Tantric texts are predominantly Śaiva. Those of other Hindu persuasions are of less consequence in both number and variety of doctrines and practices. There are also Jain Tantric texts, but they are not important or original enough to be described here.

ŚAIVA WORKS

Because they constitute the majority of Tantric literature, the Śaiva works form a huge body of texts, of which only a very cursory description can be given here. Furthermore, it happens that the range and quantity of the texts available has considerably and rapidly increased in recent years. Tantras or exegetical works hitherto known only by name have recently been discovered or become easily available in photographs or even online. The whole study of the Tantric field has thus entered a new phase; a phase of work in progress where what is propounded one day may be proved (at least provisionally) false or uncertain the next. Of course, I will not expand on such problems here. However, I feel it is fair to tell the reader that they exist.

Revelation/Scriptures

There are several Indian traditional classifications of Śaiva scriptures of different origins. They are complex, largely theoretical, partial and incomplete, and need not therefore be quoted here.

There is, however, an ancient classification of Śaiva scriptures into two great categories or "streams" (*srotas*), which is useful and valid. It divides them into the Outer Path (Atimārga), accessible only to ascetics—seekers only of liberation (*mokṣa*/*mukti*)—and the Path of Mantras (Mantramārga), open to both ascetics and married householders (*gṛhastha*), and entered to attain liberation, supernatural powers (*siddhis*), and the enjoyment of pleasures or rewards (*bhoga*/*bhukti*) in this world or in other worlds.

The Atimārga is composed of two main divisions of ascetics, the Pāśupata and the Lākula, which can be described as "proto-Tantric." Many of their constituent beliefs and practices survived in the Tantric Śaiva systems that followed them. The Pāśupatas, worshippers of Rudra as Paśupata, Master of the Bound (of humans, that is), were renouncers—initiated, living separated from society (*lokātīta*), and behaving strangely. They followed particular, often antisocial, observances (*vrata*), ending their lives in cremation grounds (*smaśāna*). Their scriptures, as well as some notions and observances, survived for centuries. The Lākulas, a school of the Pāśupatas, used to wander half-naked, their bodies smeared with ashes from a funeral pyre. They carried a skull-topped staff (*khaṭvāṅga*) and an alms bowl made from a human skull, worshipping Rudra in a vessel filled with alcoholic liquor. Their observance being generally called "that of the skull" (*kapālavrata*), they were therefore called *kāpālika*, a term (along with related observances) we shall meet again further on.

The other stream, the Mantramārga, the Path of Mantras, which grew out of the Atimārga, is properly Tantric and includes all the scriptures of Tantric Śaivism from its origin to the present day (being Śaiva, this classification does not include the Pāñcarātra, the Vaiṣṇava Tantric tradition). The texts of the Mantramārga are divided into five groups, which include *bhūtatantras*, on the cults of spirits or demons (*bhūtas*), and Tantras of Garuḍa, most of which have disappeared. The other Tantras (which still exist) are divided into Tantras "of the right" (*dakṣiṇa*), "of the left" (*vāma*), and of the Śaivasiddhānta. All these are the texts we will review here. There are also other traditional classifications that need not be mentioned here because none of them include all Tantras deemed to have existed or to be still existing, some of which being, in fact, later than these attempts at distributing them into different groups.

The Śaivasiddhānta

These texts, generally called āgamas by Sanskritists, are often called Tantras, sometimes saṃhitās. They should be noted because they embody the common Śaiva fund of doctrines and practices: they are its common doctrine (*sāmānyaśāstra*), to quote Abhinavagupta. The main Śaiva private or public rites, in the past as well as today, are usually performed according to their prescriptions, completed by a number of commentaries and exegetical works. The basic Śaiva doctrine, instructions on religious architecture or iconography, as well as a large number of rules governing the social and private behavior of Śaivas, are to be found in these āgamas. We must therefore consider them first.

Traditionally, there are said to be 28 such āgamas. Ten of these are called *śaiva* because they are generally deemed to have issued from Śiva's mouth. The 18 others are called *raudra*, as having been revealed by the 18 Rudras.[4] Scriptures forming a "secondary division" (*upabheda*) and formally considered as being 207 in number—some lists including only 198 or even 120—are connected to these āgamas. But these classifications are artificial and their numbering debatable; they do not reflect the actual importance or the real position of these texts, whose modes of composition, mutual relationships, as well as dates (ranging arguably from the fifth to the thirteenth century) remain largely uncertain.

I should add that some of the officially existing texts have not reached us, others only partly—only some have been edited, very few have been studied, and still less have been translated.[5] In addition, manuscripts of still-unknown texts may be discovered whose content may modify the views we have now.[6] But however partial our knowledge of these works may be, it remains essential for our understanding of Tantric Śaivism, be it from the doctrinal, the social, or the ritual point of view.

Their role as prescribing the general rules for the life of the observing Śaiva is conveyed in the theory that all āgamas are made up of four topics, each of which may be treated in a separate text section (*pāda*): doctrine (*vidyā*), yoga, ritual (*kriyā*), and behavior (*caryā*).[7] Not much space is usually given to doctrine. The Tantric ritual superabundance results in the ritual section usually being the longest one. The bounty and precision of ritual prescriptions in the āgamas is also due to the fact that, for what was to become "classical"[8] Siddhānta, only ritual practice leads the adept on the way to salvation. This teaching is, in fact, not meant so much for the Śaiva householder (*gṛhastha*)—the average Śaiva adept living in this world—but for the initiated adept wishing to reach liberation.

The prescriptions of the āgamas are also those followed in Śaiva temples, especially in South India. This explains why most āgamic prescriptions are moderate, faithful in most cases to those of "orthodox" Brahmanism. With very few exceptions, there are no terrifying deities or ecstatic cults or animal sacrifices in the Siddhānta āgamas. On the social plane, the āgamas usually respect caste rules and, in some cases, even say that their teaching is meant only for "twice-born," therefore excluding *śūdras* (and *a fortiori* outcastes).

Of these texts, I may quote some of the main or best known ones, which are edited (sometimes translated) and to which I shall refer in this book. These are, for instance, the probably South-Indian *Ajitāgama*, which includes many iconographic precisions and was recently translated into English; as well as the doctrinally rich *Parākhyatantra*;[9] the *Mṛgendra*, mentioned above; the *Raurava*;[10] the *Kiraṇatantra*; the *Dīptāgama* (critically edited in Pondicherry); and the *Mataṅgapārameśvara* (some observances [*vratas*] of which are the same as those of Bhairavāgamas). Others could be mentioned.

The Tantras of Bhairava and of the Goddess

The traits I consider as most characteristically Tantric are found in this group of canonical Śaiva texts, which are also those I refer to most often. It includes a large number of Tantras of different sorts and different dates, probably dating from the fifth century down to modern times. They are variously classified. The main classification to which I will refer here is in two *pīṭhas* ("seats"; ensembles, that is): the Seat of Mantras (*mantrapīṭha*), grouping the Tantras dedicated to Bhairava, and the Seat of Vidyās (*vidyāpīṭha*), these being either Union Tantras (*yāmalatantras*) or Power Tantras (*śaktitantras*), within which one may distinguish between different categories of texts.

The basic cult of the *mantrapīṭha* is that of Svacchandabhairava, a fearsome aspect of Śiva, also known euphemistically as Aghora (the "Not-Fearsome"), worshipped with a female consort. The Tantras of this *pīṭha* traditionally number sixty-four in eight groups of eight.[11] These traditions are Kāpālika, their basic ascetic observance being that of the skull (*kapālavrata*). Ascetics bear a skull staff (*khaṭvāṅga*) and worship several terrifying deities in a cremation ground in addition to Bhairava and also Śiva conjoined with Śakti.

In the other *pīṭha*, the *vidyāpīṭha* (a *vidyā* is a feminine mantra),[12] the dominating divine form is feminine, and the goddess being worshipped is either associated with a male consort or, sometimes, alone as the Solitary Heroine (*ekavīrā*). There are two categories of Tantras of this group. The first is the Union Tantras (Yāmalatantras), where Bhairava, Lord of the Skull, is worshipped in union with the furious Kāpālinī, Goddess of the Skull, surrounded by secondary deities. One of its main texts is the twelve-thousand-stanza *Picumata-Brahmayāmalatantra*. There are also Power Tantras (Śaktitantras), which are considered higher than the preceding ones. Among such Tantras are those of the Trika, such as the *Siddhayogeśvarīmata* (edited and partly translated), the *Tantrasadbhāva* (in manuscript), and the *Mālinīvijayottaratantra* (edited, partly translated), with the cult of the triad (*trika*) of the goddesses Parā, Parāparā, and Aparā. There are also the Tantras of Kālī, notably the twenty-four-thousand-stanza *Jayadrathayāmala* of the Kālīkrama or Kālīkula, also known as the Venerable King of Tantras, *Tantrarājabhaṭṭāraka*. Because of the dominating place and role of goddesses and of the power (*śakti*), the Tantras of the Vidyāpīṭha are often said to be Śākta or *śāktaśaiva*. Their deities are nearly always paired as sexual couples. Their practices are often described as being "of the left" (*vāma*), as opposed to those of the Siddhānta, said to be "of the right" (*dakṣiṇa*).

As we shall see in the next chapter, due to their different origins and the initiatory lineages that developed historically with the cult of Yoginīs, the nondualist Śaiva traditions came to form different schools, or systems, grouped in the Kula (or Kaula) ensemble with its four "transmissions" (*āmnāyas*), their Tantras being always (though more or less) *kāpālika*. Although they are devoted to different deities, they share many common beliefs and practices. The Tantras quoted above are referred to in different *āmnāyas*. There are also other texts, such as the *Devīpañcaśataka* of the Krama system, the *Mahākālasaṃhitā* (edited) on the cult of Guhyākālī, the *Kubjikāmatatantra* (edited), the *Kubjikā Upaniṣad* (edited, translated) of the Kubjikā cult, the *Ciñcinīmatasārasamuccaya*, the *Vāmakesvarīmata* and the *Yoginīhṛdaya* of the Śrīvidyā (both edited and translated), the *Tantrarājatantra* on the cult of the thirteen Nityās, Lalitā, and so forth.

The Tantras we know of are often described as résumés of an original text of enormous dimension. This is mere imagination. But as already said, Tantras are often very long (a recently published part of the *Manthānabhairavatantra* on the cult of Kubjikā is twenty-four thousand stanzas long).

Of the Śaiva Tantras, I want to mention particularly—because of their place in Kashmirian Śaivism—the *Svacchandatantra* (a dualist work) on the cult of Svacchandabhairava and the *Netratantra* on the *netramantra*, the mantra of Śiva's (third) Eye. These are two texts of moderate size, dating probably from the eighth century. They are in print[13] with interesting (nondualist) commentaries by the Kashmirian author Kṣemarāja. A short ancient text is the *Yonitantra* (edited and translated). It describes the ritual worship of *yoni*. The *Rudrayāmala* is often referred to in other texts that say they belong to its tradition, but no reliable version of this Tantra is available today—or any proof that it really existed. Also worth mentioning are the *Kulārṇavatantra* (fourteenth century) and the *Gandharvatantra* (both edited in the Tantric texts) and the *Śaktisaṅgamatantra* (edited).

There are also texts that, though not called Tantras, are considered to have been revealed. An example of this is the *Śivasūtra*, one of the main texts of Kashmirian nondualistic Śaivism, which is deemed to have been revealed to Vasugupta (early ninth century).[14] Very much worth mentioning, too, is the *Vijñānabhairava*, a short but exceptionally interesting work (see chapter 9). For the Krama system, also called the Great Way (Mahānaya) or the Way of the Goddess (Devīnaya), I will mention the *Devīpañcaśataka* and the *Kramasadbhāva*. For the Kubjikāmata, the *Ṣaṭsāhasrasaṃhitā* (edited and translated), the *Kubjikāmatatantra*, or the *Kubjikā Upaniṣad* (all edited); for the cult of Tripurāsundarī, the *Vāmakeśvarīmata/Nityāṣoḍaśikārṇava* and the twelfth- through thirteenth-century *Yoginīhṛdaya*. Some texts called Tantra are, in fact, compilations. These are sometimes interesting, like the *Vidyārṇavatantra*, whose author is known. We shall look briefly at the doctrinal content of these texts in the next chapter.

Indian culture is a culture of commentaries. In a traditional system of thought where truth is deemed to have been revealed at the beginning of time (or even to exist eternally, in the Absolute) and is therefore sacred and untouchable, tradition, which is alive, can only evolve—adapt to a changing context—through commentaries, which propound new interpretations of the original discourse or revelation under the guise of clarification. Tantras or āgamas are also works in verses drafted in stanzas and composed according to very strict prosodic rules that often do not permit a clear expression of meaning, which only a commentary can clarify. This point is worth underlining, for the way a text is drafted is important—it reflects the spirit of the text, it influences the way it "functions" and is made use of. Because of the traditional Indian prejudice in favor of brevity, a notion is very often put forward as a brief statement or aphorism (a *sūtra* or *kārikā*), which is often so dense and compacted as to be unintelligible unless expanded and clarified by a commentary. Because an important teaching can only be given by word of mouth, it is first to be orally explained by a master, then further clarified and interpreted in written commentaries, which will be further commented and explained. This is characteristic of the whole religious or philosophical discourse of India.

This postscriptural exegetical collection of literature is huge. This is where the whole body of Tantric thought, beliefs, and practices can be found. I will constantly refer to it not only in the next chapter but in the whole book, for there one finds all that concerns mantras, ritual, yoga, asceticism, iconography, and so on. Thus, for instance, the best source on Śaiva domestic and public ritual is (with its commentaries) the *Somaśambhupaddhati*, a ritual treatise of the eleventh century.[15] In the field of mantras, the *Prapañcasāra*, attributed to Śaṅkara (but it is later); the *Śāradātilaka* of Lakṣmanadeśika (with its commentary); the *Īśānaśivagurudevapaddhati* of Īśānagurudeva; and the seventeenth-century *Tantrasāra* of Kṛṣṇānanda are essential reference works. Many other works could be mentioned.

But what cannot be passed over here is the Śaiva exegesis of Kashmir, for one finds there some of the most brilliant philosophical works that have an important place not only in Tantrism but in the history of Indian thought.[16] It flourished from the ninth to the thirteenth and fourteenth centuries. Built on the scriptures of the Mantramārga by Kashmirian Brahmins, this commentarial literature deals either with the entirely Śaiva texts of the Siddhānta or with the more diverse scriptures dedicated to Bhairava or to the Goddess (therefore of the Mantrapīṭha or of the Vidyāpīṭha).

The ritual and doctrinal synthesis of the schools of the Krama, the Spanda, the Pratyabhijñā, the Trika, and the Śrīvidyā—all of which are remarkably interesting, some of their authors being among India's foremost philosophers and spiritual masters—were based on the Tantras of Bhairava or of the Goddess. Some of these authors were Somānanda (c. 900–950), author of the *Śivadṛṣṭi* ("The Vision of Śiva"—partly translated[17]); Utpaladeva (c. 950–75), author of the *Īśvarapratyabhijñākārikā* ("Aphorisms on the Recognition of the Lord"), an arcane but very interesting work (edited, often translated); Vasugupta (c. 875–925), author of the (translated) *Spandakārikā* ("The Aphorisms on Vibration"); Kṣemarāja (eleventh century), who wrote the commentaries on the *Netra* and the *Svacchanda* Tantras; and many others. Special mention must be made of the incomparable Abhinavagupta (c. 975–1025)—philosopher, yogi, and mystic—India's foremost aesthetician. His *Tantrāloka* ("Light on the Tantras"[18]), a vast ritual and spiritual treatise referring to a number of Tantras is—together with Jayaratha's (thirteenth century) commentary, the *Viveka*—a basic work, essential for the knowledge of the Tantric domain. More exclusively philosophical are his *Parātrīśikāvivaraṇa* (edited, translated) and his two vast and infinitely subtle commentaries on the *Īśvarapratyabhijñākārikā.* Interesting, too, is his *Paramārthasāra.*

There are Krama works, too. In addition to the texts named *Mahānayaprakāśa* ("Illumination of the Great Way"), there is the (thirteenth-century) *Mahārthamañjarī* of the South Indian Maheśvarānanda, which incorporates elements from the Pratyabhijñā. Also from South India is the *Cidgaganacandrikā*, a commentary on the *Kramastotra.* The Śrīvidyā tradition also claims some interesting Southern authors, notably Bhāskararāya (eighteenth century). We will revisit all these exegetical texts in the next chapter.

Less accessible to the readers of this book (for they are seldom translated) are the exegetical works on the Siddhānta scriptures. However, to be mentioned here are such authors as Bhaṭṭa Rāmakaṇṭha, commenting on several āgamas but also on philosophical works;[19] Nārayaṇakaṇṭha, on the *Mṛgendra*; and Śrīkaṇṭha, author of the *Ratnatraya*; Sadyojyotiḥ, the author of several treatises that arguably shaped all subsequent Śaiva thought; and also Bhojadeva, king of Dhārā, author of the *Tattvaprakāśa*.

Let me add that the few textual references above have been chosen somewhat arbitrarily from a huge ensemble.

VAIṢṆAVA WORKS

The canonical Tantric Vaiṣṇava literature is that of the Pāñcarātra. Its scriptures usually go by the name of *saṃhitā*, a term that means "collection," "compendium." But they are also sometimes called āgama, or Tantra, and their ensemble is often called *pāñcarātrāgama*.

Like the Śaiva scriptures, they are not easy to date. They were long believed to date from the eighth to the fourteenth century, thus being later than the Śaiva āgamas or Tantras by which they were often noticeably influenced. However, some recently discovered documents point toward earlier beginnings. Their geographical origins are difficult to ascertain. Like the Śaiva texts, they include theoretical notions, theological and cosmological elements, but their content concerns chiefly rites and observances. The worship and ritual services of most of the Vaiṣṇava temples of South India are still performed today according to their prescriptions,[20] which hardly differ from those of Śaiva texts when concerning ritual or yoga. From the doctrinal point of view, they are nearer to brahmanical orthodoxy (proudly asserted by some of their affiliates[21]) and their mantras are indeed often Vedic.

The saṃhitās are traditionally believed to number 108—a sacred number—but there are, in fact, more than 200, some of which have not reached us.[22] Many of these texts have been edited. They are not all equally important or interesting. Three saṃhitās are traditionally considered as being especially authoritative (they are called the Pāñcarātra's "Three Jewels" [*Ratnatraya*]): the *Pauṣkara*, *Sātvata*, and *Jayākhya*. Others (the *Ahirbudhnya*, for instance) are also important and worth studying. The *Lakṣmītantra*, an often-quoted text, very much influenced by Śaivism, is also interesting.[23] Geographically, the saṃhitās seem to come from different parts of India, south and north. For instance, the *Ahirbudhnya*[24] may have come from Kashmir, where the Pāñcarātra once played a major role, influencing the local religion. The main cult there was that of Vāsudeva in his form as Vaikuṇṭha. This form had four faces, the mild human face being flanked by those of Viṣṇu's incarnation as the Man-Lion, Narasiṃha, and of the Boar, Varāha, with the face of the wrathful sage Kapila behind.

OTHER TANTRIC TEXTS

In addition to the Śaiva and Vaiṣṇava texts, there were also (as I have said) *saura*-saṃhitās devoted to the Sun god, Sūrya. An ancient text lists eighty-five such Tantras, all of which seem to be lost. One (not on this list), the *Saurasaṃhitā*, has recently been identified in Nepal. However, there are other Tantric texts on Sūrya that are not Tantras but hymns, such as the *Sāmbapañcāśikā*, which is a short but fine and philosophically interesting work, commented on in the spirit of the Trika by Kṣemarāja. At one time, the solar cult was very active in India (linked to kingship) and present in many places, but it progressively disappeared. This cult survives only as an initial part of Śiva's ritual worship.

Of the *Gāṇapatya* Tantras, with Gaṇeśa/Gaṇapati as main deity, none have survived. There is a list of twenty-eight *Gāruḍatantras* and one of twenty *Bhūtatantras*—scriptures related to snake poison (because of the bird god Garuḍa, the chief enemy of snakes) or magic and exorcism (*bhūtas* are spirits or demons), which must have been of considerable importance, considering the foremost place of magic in India from the Veda to this day. They were long deemed to have been lost, but recently several seem to have been identified.

An important and still existing category of texts are the Nāthas, a noteworthy category of Śaiva yogis whose notions and practices can be considered as Tantric. Apparently of ancient origin, they are still present today in India and Nepal (see chapter 11). Their texts, a number of which have survived (some are edited, a few translated) are authoritative. One of them, the *Kaulajñānanirṇaya*, is one of the oldest Tantric texts we know of. It is attributed to the probably mythical Matsyendranātha, traditionally believed to have lived in the tenth century. He is sometimes called (or identified with) Lui-pāda/Lui-pā and honored in Tibet as a master of the Buddhist Siddhācāryas. Also worth mentioning are several works attributed to Gorakṣanātha (twelfth century?), sometimes deemed to have been—together with Matsyendranātha—the founder of the Nātha sect. A few of these texts are the *Gorakṣaśataka* (twelfth century?) and the *Sidddhasiddhānta-paddhati*.[25] Abhinavagupta (eleventh century) quotes Macchanda/Matsyendranātha as one of the founders of the Kula tradition (the Yoginīkaula?), but we do not know if he was referring to the same person. As I said above, elements from the Nātha tradition were used in the eighteenth century to draft some of the canonical 108 Upaniṣads. Some of these are Tantric, sometimes ancient, either redrafted or fabricated for this list of scriptures. They were edited and translated in English in the *Yoga Upanishads* and the *Shākta Upanishads* collections of the Theosophical Society, Adyar.[26]

Tantra is inseparable from yoga. Tantric ritual practices and doctrines always include yogic elements. There are Tantric works on yoga (not always easy to distinguish from the Nātha ones because the Nāthas are the main promoters of haṭhayoga) and yogic portions or yogic elements in most Tantric texts. As we have seen, a section on yoga (*yogapāda*) is theoretically one of the four sections of an āgama.

Therefore, practically all āgamas or Tantras are, in some respects, works on yoga, some including long developments on the subject—eleven chapters of the *Mālinīvijayottaratantra*,[27] for instance. There are also Tantric treatises on yoga, such as the *Ṣaṭcakranirūpaṇa* by Pūrṇānanda—which was edited and translated in 1919 by Sir John Woodroffe (Arthur Avalon) in his *Tantrik Texts* series—the *Āmaraughaśāsana* (fifteenth century?), the (fifteenth-century) *Gherāṇḍasaṃhitā*, and naturally Nātha works like Svātmarāma's (sixteenth-century) *Haṭhapradīpikā* (or *Haṭhayogadīpikā*). There are also the so-called Yoga-Upaniṣads—twenty Upaniṣads of the "canonical" list brought together and published under that title by the Theosophical Society.[28] They are mostly Tantric in their practices and notions, and some are ancient.

Among the main Hindu texts, the Purāṇas should also be noted. These sacred Hindu texts of mythical history—often considered equal to the Veda—the drafting of which apparently went on from the fourth century to the present day, were undoubtedly influenced by the context of the times when they were composed, which overlapped with the appearance and main development of Tantra. Some were very much influenced by it. Such is the case of the *Liṅga-*, *Śiva-*, *Kālikā-*, and *Devībhāgavata*-Purāṇas, to mention only a few. The *Agnipurāṇa*, a vast encyclopedic work, includes purely Tantric sections—including a part borrowed from the best-known Tantric ritual manual of Śaivism, the *Somaśambhupaddhati*. This Purāṇa is also a first-class source of information on Tantric iconography.[29] One may also note, in spite of the fact that it is not exactly Tantric—but it does reflect the Tantric vision of the universe and of power—the *Devīmāhātmya* ("Praise of the Goddess"), which is a portion of the *Mārkaṇḍeyapurāṇa*. It is an ancient (seventh-century) work, still used for ritual and pious recitation in North India for the worship of the Goddess, Durgā or Caṇḍī.

Finally I will allude here to the vast literature concerning mantras, the *mantraśāstra*. In this category are, for instance, the *Prapañcasāra*, attributed to Śaṅkara, and Lakṣmaṇadeśika's *Śāradātilaka*, which I have already mentioned. Together with their commentaries, they are an indispensable source of information. I will cite, too, the *Mantramahodadhi*, and the more recent *Mantramahārṇava* and Kṛṣṇānanda's *Tantrasāra*, reference works often made use of in India today. Many others could be cited. There are also ritual compilations (*nibandhas*) such as the *Kaulāvalīnirṇaya* and the *Śrītattvacintāmaṇi*. There are also Bhāskararāya's works (eighteenth century) on Tripurā's cult, such as the *Paraśurāmakalpasūtra*, the *Nityotsava*, and so on. The sixteenth-century *Tantrasamuccaya* is a ritual treatise still very much in use in Kerala. There are also works on iconography, collections of hymns of praise (*stotra*) to deities—the *Saundaryalaharī*, attributed to Śaṅkara, for instance—and the litanies of "a thousand names" of a deity, such as the *Lalitāsahasranāma*. I must pass over mystical works and works on magic and on alchemy. Finally, there are literary texts that include Tantric elements. One of the richest examples of these is Somadeva's *Kathāsaritsāgara* ("Ocean of Stories"),[30] a vast work of the eleventh century. Also worth mentioning are plays, such as Bhaṭṭa Jayanta's *Āgamaḍambara* ("Much Ado about Religion").[31] Indeed, Sanskrit works that include Tantric elements are innumerable.

Works in Vernacular Indian Tongues

In this review of Tantric textual sources, I cannot ignore those that are not in Sanskrit because they show the extension beyond the learned, elite portion of the Tantric field and the variety of local forms it sometimes assumed. They are also proof of the Tantric presence across the whole Indian subcontinent as well as of its survival down to our days.[32]

Tantric texts, being in Sanskrit, were (and are) accessible only to a literate minority, mostly Brahmins. Their teaching is often arcane, their ritual complicated, and their practices not always easy to follow. They are, however, the textual base of the whole Tantric phenomenon. Due to its extension (and because perhaps it had links with the local popular substrate), this phenomenon reached a larger section of the Indian population, and therefore had to be expressed in the languages spoken by this vast and varied ensemble of worshippers or adepts. In this respect, we must not forget that for more than a thousand years, Sanskrit had ceased (with very minor exceptions) to be the mother tongue of any Indian. It was no longer a current, living language but a learned idiom of restricted use. Therefore, it was quite normal that Hindus of the Tantric milieus should express their beliefs using their own particular, regional tongues. This they did (and go on doing) in hymns, poems and epics, and in didactic or technical works on yoga, temples, pilgrimage, mantra, and so forth. Devotion (*bhakti*) expressed in vernacular tongues had a place quite early (from the sixth century, perhaps), as devotional hymns and songs became an integral part of the religious action along with the Sanskrit formulas of the ritual worship—both private and public—of Śaiva as well as Vaiṣṇava deities.

Appearing, as they mostly did, after the Sanskrit texts, the Tantric vernacular literatures developed in a religious context where pride of place was not given to gnosis nor to ritual precision but to the devotional relationship with the deity, to *bhakti*. In some cases, the singing of devotional hymns (and yogic meditation) became more commonplace than ritual. Hence, in vernacular sources, one finds a more emotional religion closer to the everyday Indian context and new poetical conventions and vocabulary—sometimes reflecting local cultural conditions—very different from the "technical" Sanskrit formulas and the abstract, normative tone of the Tantras.

The larger and also the best known ensemble of vernacular Tantric works comes from Bengal, both because Bengal was an important center of Tantric activities and produced a large corpus of literature in the medieval period[33] and because this literature soon became (and remained) fully available.

Its earlier forms were short Buddhist poems, the *dohas*, and the *caryāgītī*, sung by the Siddhas. They were followed, from the fifteenth century onward, by chants and poems in praise of the Goddess—in particular, the *maṅgalas*, hymns glorifying (this is the meaning here of *maṅgala*) different forms of the Goddess (Kālī, Manasā) sung by bards at festivals or during worship or recited by devotees. One of the best-known contributors of these hymns is Rāmprasad Sen (1720–81), who composed many hymns in praise of Kālī,[34] some of which were quite remarkable. Such poems were very popular and went on being produced down to our days.

The literature of the Nāthas is important and still very much alive in Bengal today. It consists mainly of short poems sung by yogis (and by Muslim Fakirs[35]). It also includes poems and yogic hagiographical tales ascribed to such mythical authors as Mīnanāth, Gorakhnāth, Jālandhari-pā, or to their disciples.

If Bengal was, and still is, one of the centers of Śaiva or Śākta Tantrism, it was also the location of one of Vaiṣṇava Tantra's main developments with the Vaiṣṇava Sahajiyās, who produced a quite fascinating, mystical literature devoted to the intensely experienced worship of Kṛṣṇa and Rādhā from the beginning of the sixteenth century down to the twentieth.[36]

One might mention also here, in addition to these often elaborate literary works, the oral literature of the Baùls and of the Fakirs, whose poems are popular but very Tantric. The mystical poems of one of them, Lalan Fakir, are still often sung today.

There is no equally important Tantric or Tantra-influenced literature in the other Indo-Aryan tongues. But because Tantric practices and notions are still prolific today throughout the subcontinent, it goes without saying that a vast amount of Tantric or Tantra-influenced publications went on appearing in different vernacular languages. I will not take account here of the innumerable translations from Sanskrit texts because they are not original vernacular works, but we must not ignore their existence.

In the works of the "poet-saints," the "saints" of the Indian medieval period, one often finds Nātha terms or practices. Such is the case of poems in Hindi and Rajasthani. In Hindi, the work of Kabīr shows some Nātha influences; he uses the term *sahaj* for the Absolute.[37] In Marathi, Jñāndev (an important poet-saint of the thirteenth century) was a Nātha yogi. Such elements are also found within the Vaiṣṇava sect of the Manbhau. There are Tantric yoga aspects in the texts of the Dādupanthis, in Rajasthan. Tantric yoga conceptions, with the image of the yogic body, are present throughout the Indian subcontinent, spread orally as well as in writing by itinerant yogis—a production of little literary value but too widespread to be ignored. There is also the encounter of the Nāthas with Sufism, which resulted in the writing of yoga manuals in Bengali, Hindi, Urdu, and even in Persian (for the Moghul court).

Also in the south, a region of numerous and vast Śaiva and Vaiṣṇava temples—and notably in Kerala, where a number of very active goddess temples exist even today—there exists a large body of vernacular Tantric literature.

In Tamil (whose literature is ancient and most noteworthy), I can only quote here very few works and names. On the Śaiva side are the Siddhas (*cittar*, in Tamil), ascetic poets, the best known being Manikka Vācakar (ninth century?) and Tirumūlar (eleventh/twelfth century). Their works are sometimes said to form the textual base of the Tamil Śaivasiddhānta. Tirumūlar is notably the author of the three-thousand-stanza *Tirumantiram*, a very remarkable eclectic text. Some would include the mystical poems of Kāraikkālamaiyar (sixth century), a strange devotional figure (but it is not certain that her religion of devotion to Śiva as the frantic dancer of the cremation ground was really Tantric). Civavākkiyar (tenth century) and Paṭṭinattār (fourteenth through fifteenth centuries) are also very interesting—theirs are brief and intense works, close to everyday life, far from the artificiality of Sanskrit texts. Also to be mentioned are the hymns of the Āḻvārs, Vaiṣṇava poet-saints.[38]

Important Tantric or "Tantricized" works in Tamil continued being written throughout the course of centuries. Tantric texts in other Dravidian tongues appear to be of lesser value in spite of the vitality of Tantric cultural and religious activities, notably in Kerala.[39]

Last, I should add that although English is not an Indian tongue, it is one of the languages of India. From the nineteenth century to the present day, works or studies in English were written by Indians that are not negligible and contribute to the continued presence of Tantra in India. I will review some of them in chapter 11 of this book.

4

Tantric Traditions: Fundamental Notions, Beliefs, and Speculations

Having seen the place in history, the geographical extent, and the textual basis of Tantra, we must now look at what it really consists of, beginning with an overview of Tantric beliefs and notions. I will describe ancient traditions—what was thought and believed in the past. This overview is, however, not purely historical. The Tantric notions we shall see are still (in some cases, very much) alive because they are the base of all that is Tantric (or generally Hindu) in India (or elsewhere). One must know them if one wishes to understand not only Tantra but Hinduism as it is today. I will constantly refer to them in the following chapters of this book.

Readers will perhaps find this chapter too long. But as I have just said, to know the main Tantric notions is to know more about the Hindu world, since these notions permeated mainstream Hinduism. It is also useful to discover important aspects of Indian thought, for some Tantric philosophers—Buddhist as well as Hindu—were among the most remarkable and interesting Indian thinkers.

In this chapter, I will review a few notions that are basic elements of Indian thought, then traits that are properly Tantric. I will explain first those given in Tantric scriptures then the exegetical developments based on these scriptures. As we saw in the preceding chapter, these texts and exegeses go roughly from the fifth to the seventeenth centuries, a period during which beliefs and notions evolved and changed considerably, including new elements. Unfortunately, I can only give a static image of this continuously changing reality—a change, however, in continuity, as is always the case in a tradition. India never ceased to create while remaining true to its earliest textual foundations.

Let me add that what will be briefly described here are the main traits of the different Tantric traditions, or schools, leaving aside—however interesting and noteworthy they may be—the sometimes quite remarkable individual contributions of the different thinkers who elaborated or developed these systems.

Beliefs, Pantheons

The religious systems—the deities and pantheons together with the beliefs that go with them—are varied, this diversity being more important on the Śaiva side than on the Vaiṣṇava side, the Tantric domain being mainly Śaiva/Śākta. Therefore, this chapter will deal mainly with Śaiva traditions, giving a general overview of the beliefs and of the cosmic, theological, or metaphysical notions of this Śaiva ensemble, stressing their common elements rather than their differences—however, these differences will be described when noteworthy.

Such an overview is necessary. The basic scriptures, Tantras, or āgamas, though different, share many common elements because they are part of the same "lettered" traditional Sanskrit base; because of the common, shared ritual and doctrinal fund of the Śaivasiddhānta; and also because the main Śaiva texts are those of the vast Kula ensemble—hence, a common vocabulary and many shared basic notions.

I will also add the fact that this Tantric textual base is made up inseparably of the scriptures and of their commentaries, which share a number of elements, either generally Hindu or generally Tantric, though they are from different persuasions. For instance, the Trika tradition brings together elements from the Krama, the Spanda, and the Pratyabhijñā systems. Furthermore, those who wrote the Tantras and their exegeses were Brahmins, all members of a Vedic school (*śakhā*) and steeped in the traditional forms of thought based on Sanskrit grammar and phonetics and using the traditional Sanskrit forms of reasoning as found notably in the so-called six *darśanas.*[1] All shared elements of the Sanskrit culture. The somewhat simplified description I will give here is therefore justifiable, notwithstanding its limits.

Before looking at the content of this textual ensemble, we must first recall some elements common either to all Hindu-brahmanical or specially to Tantric traditions. To recall their presence is also to show that Tantra is but an aspect of the Hindu world.

A Few Common Notions

The reader is surely aware of some general notions. I need not mention them. Of those to be mentioned, I will only make a brief reference to them, noting their presence in Tantra and sometimes the particular aspect they assume there. Other notions, more properly Tantric, will be looked at more closely.

In the first category are notions such as the divine Absolute (*brahman*), the self (*ātman*), the quest for liberation from the fetters of this world (*mokṣa/mukti*), the divine nature of the Word (*vāc*), the notion of *karman*, and so on. Those are common elements I do not need to expatiate on. One common element, however, must be underscored: the system of the *tattvas*, first propounded in the Sāṃkhya, is a hierarchical classification of the constitutive principles (or "realities") of the universe—a classification going downward (as in creation) from the deity at the top to the principle earth at the bottom. This system is made use of in all Tantric traditions when referring to the cosmos or to the human being.

According to the Sāṃkhya, there were twenty-five *tattvas*. They shared out the cosmos, going from the male spiritual principle (*puruṣa*) and the female primary matter, or nature (*prakṛti*). Then, going downward, they followed decreasing levels of subtlety from the levels of consciousness or awareness and the senses to the subtle then to the gross elements (*bhūta*) that make up the material world, the lowest of these being the principle earth. To these twenty-five *tattvas*, Tantric systems added eleven others[2] at the top, which corresponded to eleven transcendent levels through which the supreme godhead, Śiva or Viṣṇu—in conjunction with the god's energy (*śakti*) or the Goddess—passes when creating the world (*sṛṣti*) through successive stages of contraction of their infinite power down to the level of *puruṣa* and *prakṛti*, which are the source of the manifested universe (see table). These additional *tattvas*, which reach up to the highest planes of the deity (that initiates may reach spiritually) are, for Tāntrikas, one of the proofs of the superiority of their traditions over those of the Veda-based brahmanical revelation, which refers only to the twenty-five *tattvas* of the Sāṃkhya.[3]

THE THIRTY-SIX *TATTVAS* OF TANTRIC TRADITIONS

Śiva	
Śakti	
Sadāśiva	the eternal Śiva
Īśvara	the Lord
śuddhavidyā	pure wisdom

māyā	cosmic illusion	
kalā	limitation	
vidyā	(limited) wisdom	the cuirasses (*kañcuka*)
rāga	passionate attachment	
niyati	necessity	
kāla	time	
puruṣa	Spirit, or the Lord	
prakṛti	the source matter, nature	
buddhi	intellect	
ahaṃkāra	"egoity"	
manas	understanding (*sensorium commune*)	
śrotra	hearing	
tvak	touch	
cakṣus	sight	organs of perception (*buddhīndriya*)
rasana	taste	
ghrāṇa	smell	
vāk	speech	
pāṇi	holding	
pāyu	excretion	organs of action (*karmendriya*)
upastha	copulation	
pāda	movement	
śabda	sound	
sparśa	contact	
rūpa	form	subtle elements (*tanmātra*)
rasa	savor	
gandha	smell	
ākāśa	ether, space	
vāyu	air	
tejas	fire	gross elements (*bhūta*)
jala	water	
pṛthivī	earth	

Another element common to all Hindu traditions (as well as to Mahāyāna Buddhism) and that is constantly found in Tantra is yoga—not as a philosophical system but as a somatopsychic practice used in ritual as well as for spiritual ends. I will take up the subject in chapter 5 when describing some of yoga's aspects. Here, I will only point out the fact that Tantric yoga differs from the yoga of Patañjali's *Yogasūtra* in that its practice (and speculations) are based on the imaginary pattern of channels (*nāḍī*) and centers, or nodal points (*cakra*, *granthi*, or *padma*), conceived as present in the human body (sometimes extending above it). This pattern's central element is the *kuṇḍalinī*, a power both divine and human that is present in the body, through which it is to be encouraged to ascend, while also overstepping the body's limits. Tantric yoga also includes elements of haṭhayoga. In addition to these common Hindu elements, there are other elements proper to Tantra—though also found elsewhere—notably in the Purāṇas ("Antiquities"), the sacred mythicohistorical texts of Hinduism. These are mentioned here because their notions, tales or legends, and theology are, for the most part, deeply steeped in the Tantric view of the universe, as I have explained above.

These cosmic and human elements naturally take place within the traditional Indian cyclical conception of time, where worlds (whose duration is divided in *kalpas* and subdivided into *yugas*) cyclically appear and dissolve during divine "days" and "nights." Of such cosmogonies, the Purāṇas give different versions. However, these versions always have the same overall structure. The human aspect of this divine cosmic play is found more in the Tantras rather than in the Purāṇas. The human process toward liberation as described in those texts is not only isomorphic (exactly corresponding in form and process, that is) with the process of cosmic resorption (*saṃhāra*); it proceeds with the same elements. These are internalized by the adept, and—notably during initiation (*dīkṣā*)—ritually placed on his body so as to open a path toward liberation for him.

This correspondence in form and nature—this isomorphism of the human and the divine, taken up in the same cosmic, expanding, irradiating flow of creation, or in the backward movement of cosmic resorption into a godhead constantly pervading the world with its infinite generosity, bestowing joy and grace on humans it had previously bound by fetters[4]—is typically Tantric. This "anthropocosmic" vision underlies all aspects of Tantric thought or action.

A last general observation I will make here is the social fact that the Tantric teaching is, in principle, open to Hindus of all castes, male and female. As already stated, Tantras do not reject the basic socioreligious Hindu traditional rules of behavior. It is not socially transgressive. Women can be initiated, but though their spiritual perfection and power may be acknowledged and even extolled, they cannot perform rites. The status of the Hindu woman is ambiguous. They are "goddess and slave," to quote a French social worker. An American anthropologist puts it differently, reminding us that the divinizations of the Hindu woman and of her *śakti* are "male constructions of femaleness."

But let us turn now to the main traits of the various Tantric traditions, most of which are Śaiva, while some are distinctive contributions of Vaiṣṇavas.

On the Constituent Traits of Tantric Traditions

Here, too, I will merely give an overview of the subject, stressing common points more than differences. Rather than giving details that could be useful only if they were more numerous than is possible in this book, it will be more useful to give a general view, perhaps one that is too simplistic, that underlines the fundamental aspects of Tantric metaphysics and theology (or perhaps psychology) and gives some idea of how a Tantric adept approaches, perceives, or conceives the world he lives in. The reader in need of more details will find them in the books referred to in the notes or the bibliography.

To the best of our knowledge, the basic collection of Tantric religious beliefs and practices appears to go back to the cult of female deities or spirits called Yoginīs—a cult that one generally assumes to have existed very early—thus forming the underlying element of the cults of the Vidyāpīṭha[5] and therefore of the Bhairavatantras, but perhaps not of the early Śaivasiddhānta. Yoginīs were wild, blood-drinking deities radiating out from the heart of a main deity as an all-pervasive network of power (*yoginījāla*). They are often described as hordes (*gaṇa*) organized in families, clans (*kula*), or lineages (*gotra*), usually considered as grouped in eight families presided over by a "Mother" (Mātṛ),[6] who is often a very powerful deity. Yoginīs concentrate in power seats (*pīṭha*) where they are worshipped, while also possessing women and their devotees. They are numerous; a common number is sixty-four (the [twelfth-century?] *Yoginīhṛdaya* says that ten million other Yoginīs emanate from each of them). Their worship, through the course of which they possess their devotees, has survived until today. The main deity presiding over the Yoginīs was Rudra, the original form of Śiva. Tantra, as we have already seen, is mainly—and appears as having been originally—Śaiva, these ancient elements having perhaps also played a role in the apparition of Vaiṣṇava Tantrism.

Such groups of deities, or pantheons, are characteristically Tantric. They usually consist of a main deity with a consort of the opposite sex—for instance, Śiva and Śakti, with the supreme Absolute *brahman* metaphysically above them.[7] Other examples are Kālī or Durgā with Śiva or Bhairava, Tripurasundarī with Bhairava, Kubjikā and Navātman, and so on, the male deity being the dominant one but also often dominated (even if still metaphysically supreme). This occurs notably in the cults of the four *āmnāyas* of the Kula, whose main deities are goddesses. Their main deity can also be solitary, as is typically the case for Sadāśiva, the central deity of the Śaivasiddhānta, as well as for forms of Kālī. They can also be threefold, as are the three supreme goddesses of the Trika: Parā, Parāparā, and Aparā, placed above Śiva. The central deity is nearly always surrounded by a retinue (*āvaraṇa*) of ancillary deities issuing from her, spreading her power in the cosmos. In ritual and in meditation, these are visualized as placed in concentric circles, forming a *maṇḍala*.[8]

This "maṇḍalic" pattern of pantheons is typically Tantric. The multiplication of divine hypostases, Yoginīs or others, seen as active both in the cosmos and in the human body is typical too. Constituent elements of ritual—objects or actions—are sometimes also considered divine entities. The mudrās of the Yoginīhṛdaya, for instance, are at the same time bodily gestures or postures and deities. Mantras are gods or goddesses (called *vidyās* in that case). It is said they number seventy million—so many supernatural entities that all have shapes to be seen or visualized. But mantras are also the highest aspect, the essence made of the speech (*vāc*) of deities. The mantra *is* the deity, hence the name Mantramārga, which means "way of mantras"—the way of the quest for power and liberation in the Śaiva Tantric traditions, in which mantras play an essential role.

Although made of mantras, Tantric deities have sanctuaries usually called *pīṭhas*. Each tradition has its own ensemble and pattern of such sacred places. The Kula, for instance, has four main *pīṭhas*. This geographical placing of the deities makes sacred the Indian space, as we shall see in chapter 10. The divine realm thus pervades the world of humans, and both are hierarchically linked by the structure of the *tattvas*. From the theological point of view, this proximity—this interpenetration of the divine and of the manifested world, this mutual pervasiveness—is strengthened by the fact that Tantric traditions (Śaiva as well as Vaiṣṇava) are "emanationist." This means that the deity does not create a world that it dominates from on high by an initial *fiat*; rather, it eternally manifests the cosmos by projecting it outside (but also inside, since it is omnipresent). This is done through the divine creative power (*śakti*) that continuously pervades, sustains (*sthiti*), and animates the whole cosmic manifestation (*sṛṣṭi*), which will be reabsorbed (*saṃhāra*) in its source at the end of each cosmic cycle.

Philosophically, many Tantric traditions[9] (as well as some *darśanas* and devotional Hindu movements) consider the world as a transformation (*pariṇāma*) of *brahman*—just as clay is transformed into the multiple forms of pots, cups, and so forth. *Brahman* is the material cause of all the visible entities forming this world, which participates somehow in the divine reality and is, therefore, not entirely unreal—it can be made use of to progress toward liberation. The alternative to this model is the *vivartavāda*, the theory that the world is an apparent but an unreal transformation (*vivarta*) of *brahman*. This is the position of the nondualists, the Advaitins, followers of Śaṅkara. Therefore, one must never identify the nondualism of Tantra (and of others,

Advaitins included) with the nondualism of Śaṅkara, which—in spite of its very visible social position in India today—is, and has always been, a minority doctrine.

Such were the ancient cults, ritual practices, and philosophical or theological notions that are the basis of the nondualist or dualist Śaiva Tantric traditions I will review now. In doing so, I would like to emphasize the fact that all these traditions were not only theological and metaphysical constructions but also attempts at explaining how the world appears and goes on existing—visions of the cosmos and human beings' place in it. Though parts and reflections of the cosmos, humans wish to be liberated from it. Therefore, they try to free themselves from its fetters by dominating its constituting powers while using them as aids on the path to liberation—a liberation that frees them from the world while also being a source of joy and power. Such is the Tantric conception of liberation, attained not through mere pleasure but through ascetic practice (*sādhana*), a basic element of every Tantric spiritual quest for freedom.

This spiritual quest is pursued within two metaphysical models: dualism and nondualism—those of the Śaivasiddhānta and of the Bhairavatantras. In dualism, God and the world are separate. Liberation is not identification with Śiva and can be reached only through ritual practice. In nondualist Tantric traditions—those of the Kula, mainly—liberation is reached only through gnosis (*jñāna*), the mental cum bodily understanding and experience of the divine essence of the world and of man. Rites here are merely (but necessarily in most cases) aids on the way—a way along which divine grace (*anugraha* or *śaktipāta*) plays an important, sometimes fundamental, role. Nondualistic systems are where the most extreme, sometimes transgressive, rites—as well as the most subtle philosophical developments—are to be found. In these systems, one can see better than elsewhere how the human being—part of and involved in the cosmic cyclic process, prisoner of this divine play—identifies with the cosmic movement of return to the source when progressing toward liberation. These typically Tantric conceptions and rites are so fascinating that one often tends to believe that they are the sole aspect of Tantra, which is not the case. The world of the Vaiṣṇava Pāñcarātra traditions is different, more sober. The Śaivasiddhānta, which I will now address, is also more staid.

THE ŚAIVASIDDHĀNTA, A TEMPERATE TANTRISM?

Śaivasiddhānta is the way of ritual. It is important for two reasons. First, its doctrine and practices are still alive today and can still be seen, notably in

South Indian temples. Second, and more important for us, its teaching is regarded in the various Śaivite traditions, even nondualistic ones, as their common doctrine. It is the basic ritual teaching to which nondualistic Tantras add esoteric, often complicated, ritual and doctrinal elements.

The teaching of the so-called classical Śaivasiddhānta is a moderate form of Tantrism. While at first it did not seem to differ from the Bhairavatantras and those of the Goddess, it evolved progressively over the course of centuries. However, I cannot give an account of this evolution here because it is still being discovered.[10] In giving a brief summary of its traits, I will inevitably rigidify them, leaving aside an evolution that did not attain its final, so-called classical aspect before the tenth century of our era. In light of this restriction, I will say that in this Śaivasiddhānta, there are no transgressive ritual practices (ritual offerings are "vegetarian" and nonalcoholic). There are no fearsome main deities. Śakti is not an autonomous, often fearsome, power but merely Śiva's energy, the latter being worshipped as the peaceful Sadāśiva. It is also a dualistic system. The human soul and the godhead, matter and consciousness, are entirely separate. The world is distinct from the deity; it is the work of *māyā*, seen as an all-pervasive power animating the cosmos, a prime mover but not a conscious creator of the multitudinous universe in which humans may reach liberation at death but will not be identified with Śiva. Rather, they attain "śivahood" (*śivatā*): they become "released śivas" (*muktaśiva*), identical with but distinct from the deity. If an adept gains supernatural powers (*siddhis*) during his spiritual quest thanks to mantras, he does not become deified. Such traits are not those one usually regards as typically Tantric.

The Śaivasiddhānta is typically characterized by an overabundance of rituals, which are necessarily accompanied by mantras. These rituals are not so much a succession of actions as a play of mentally visualized and experienced images, a situation common to all Tantric traditions, where rites, meditation, and yoga are exercises in creative identifying imagination. If this is a common Tantric trait, in the case of dualistic Śaivism, it is based on a particular notion—namely, that the fundamental impurity (*mala*) with which every human is born, a sort of original sin that binds him to the cycle of rebirth (*saṃsāra*), is a substance (*dravya*) and can therefore only be destroyed by an action. More precisely, the ritual action of Śaiva initiation (*dīkṣā*), which is the initial step toward liberation. Ritual action—together, of course, with the necessary knowledge (*jñāna*)—can open the way to liberation, which will take place at death, not while living. These notions are to be underscored, for they differ from those of the nondualists, which are generally better known in the West. I must also add that the notion that only rites lead to salvation has, over the course of time, tended to be less absolutely asserted. In the last thousand years, the development of devotion (*bhakti*), which has become the usual Hindu religious attitude, even in Tantra, has lessened the importance of ritual. Socially, some āgamas limit their teaching to the twice-born. Temple priests are, in principle, always Brahmins.

But let us now turn to nondualistic Śaivism.

THE NONDUALIST ŚAIVA TRADITIONS

Nondualistic Śaivism is a vast ensemble of initiatory traditions whose doctrines and practices are not always the same, but all go back to the same ancient source and sometimes refer to the same Tantras (in addition to the common ritual base that is furnished by the Śaivasiddhānta, and all that is yogic). They also share many theological and metaphysical notions—they are not closed systems. These traditions are extremely rich from the philosophical, yogic, and mystic points of view. This is where the "theoanthropocosmic" (or "cosmotheandric," to use Raimundo Panikkar's term) vision characteristic of Tantric Hinduism, "the existential attitude on which is based the doctrinal construction"[11]—a vision that sheds light on the speculations and underlies, gives their basis to, the practices—is most clearly to be found. However, I can only give a brief overview of all this, stressing a few particularly typical or (for us) surprising points.[12]

These traditions (as I have mentioned in chapter 3) originated in the ancient transgressive Yoginī cults, their scriptures including Union Tantras (*yāmala*), with the cult of Bhairava, Lord of the Skull; Kapālīśa-Bhairava, its main scripture being the (*Picumata-*)*Brahmayāmalatantra*; and Power Tantras (*śakti*), with the cult of the Triad (Trika) of goddesses and such scriptures as the *Siddhayogeśvarīmata*, the *Tantrasadbhāva*, and the *Mālinīvijayottaratantra*. This cult of the triad of goddesses was regarded (at least by Abhinavagupta) as a "higher" teaching. Beyond the cult of the three goddesses and considered the most extreme was the cult of Kālī as the Destroyer of Time (Kālasaṃkarṣiṇī), propounded in the *Jayadrathayāmalatantra*, also known as the Venerable King of Tantras, *Tantrarājabhaṭṭāraka*. This cult was later to converge with the Trika and give rise to a system of twelve deities, the Kālīs of the Kālīkrama. These different Yoginī cults were practiced by skull-bearing ascetics living outside orthodox society. However, they were (as I have noted above) to evolve, becoming less extreme and penetrating the wider community of married householders. They formed an ensemble of systems with different main deities but with a common esoteric kapālika source and shared basic notions and practices. Developing from the Yoginī cults where these deities were grouped in clans or families (*kula*), they kept the term *Kula* as their designation while also giving different meanings (the "body" and, by extension, the whole "cosmic body") to this term. They also worshipped the eight Mothers, while giving them different roles. One of their characteristics was the propitiation of deities in sexual intercourse with a female partner (*dūtī*). These cults also usually involved possession (*āveśa*) of the adept by the deity. In spite of such ritual practices, the theologies of these Kula (or Kaula) systems usually insisted on the fact that spiritual perfection and liberation, not powers (*siddhi*), were the true goal of their cults. They developed in particular in Kashmir, giving rise to the metaphysics and soteriologies of the various schools of nondualistic Śaivism.

The Kaula ensemble developed into four "transmissions" (*āmnāya*) named according to the four points of the compass, each having its distinctive sets of deities, mantras, *maṇḍalas*, seats (*maṭha*) of origin, and so on. They are as follows:

- The Pūrvāmnāya, the Eastern (or the first[13]) Transmission, which appears, in effect, as the first Kaula system.
- The Uttarāmnāya, the Northern Transmission, with the Kaula Kālī cult, which includes three systems: the Mata, the Krama, and the Mahānaya.
- The Paścimāmnāya, the Western Transmission, whose main deity is the humpbacked or stooped goddess Kubjikā, with the beautiful mantra-god Navātman as consort.
- The Dakṣiṇāmnāya, the Southern Transmission, with the cult of Kāmeśvara and Kāmeśvarī, deities of love or eroticism (*kāma*) and Tripurasundarī.

The cults of these four āmnāyas differ on many points, but they have the same general conception of the deity. There were carved or drawn images of the deity, but it was to be mainly mentally visualized by the adepts. Tantric cults are visionary. The reader will see this in chapter 8 when I describe the Tantric *pūjā*. Such visualizations also play a role in Śaivasiddhānta cults but, for nondualist traditions, the interiorized vision of the deity is particularly important as a means for bringing about possession by the deity. Kaula cults performed ritual sexual union to obtain the sexual secretions to be offered to the deity (together with pieces of flesh and alcohol—sometimes with excreta and other impure substances or objects). Consuming such transgressive oblatory substances (*dravya*) was believed to help the adept transcend his ego and become deified. Kaula traditions regarded such ritual unions with an initiated partner—a "female messenger" (*dūtī*)—as one of their characteristic traits. Such unions were sometimes performed during meetings of several pairs of adepts, named *yoginīmelāpa*, where the *dūtīs* embodied Yoginīs. A sexual practice named the "Great Sacrifice of Kula," believed to have an exceptional ritual and spiritual import, is described in chapter 29 of Abhinavagupta's *Tantrāloka.*[14] In Abhinavagupta's time (c. 1000 AD), however, this union was probably practiced not to produce sexual secretions for oblations but rather, in a different metaphysical (and social) context, to allow the practitioner to step through orgasm beyond the limits of his ordinary human condition and, by such an expansion of consciousness, attain union with the deity, while also showing his disregard for the brahmanical rules of purity.

On the ritual and mental plane, transgression was an essential trait by which the nondualistic Tantric traditions set themselves apart from other traditions—so much so that they used the term "nondualistic practice" (*advaitācāra*) to refer to the Kaula transgressive practices as a rejection of the duality (*dvaita*) of pure and impure in brahmanical society. Let us also note that for the nondualistic Śaiva systems, the Yoginīs were not active merely in the world of spirits; they were also powers present in humans—mistresses of their senses, governing their affects, which acquired an intensity and supernatural dimension through this divinization. This led adepts to an identification of their individual consciousness with the infinite divine Consciousness, thus also helping them transcend the sexual plane.

Though having this common base, the cults of the four āmnāyas differed in many ways in their pantheons, metaphysical notions, and practices.

The basic cult of the Pūrvāmnāya is that of Kuleśvara and Kuleśvarī, god and goddess of the Kula, surrounded by the eight Mothers, Brāhmī, and so on, together with other ancillary deities or supernatural beings. It has particular esoteric practices and code language, but perhaps the most important and interesting thing about this āmnāya is that the Kashmirian Trika tradition developed from it. The tradition was named so because of the role played by various triads (*trika*) and especially the triad of the three goddesses, Parā, Parāparā, and Aparā. Parā is the Supreme—white, peaceful, immutable. Parāparā is the Supreme-Non-Supreme, red and active. Aparā is the Non-Supreme, black and furious. Together they embody the three aspects of the Absolute, which is both transcendent and dynamic. There were no material representations of these goddesses, who seemed to have been only visualized. They are described in the *Tantrāloka* (with reference to the *Devyāyāmalatantra*) in a meditative practice, where the adept is to visualize them seated on lotuses and resting on Bhairavas placed on the apex of the three prongs of Śiva's trident (see chapter 5). Parā could also be worshipped as Mātṛsadbhāva, the Essence of the Mothers, gathering in herself the powers of all the Yoginīs.

The scriptures of the Trika included the *Jayadrathayāmala* and therefore the cult of Kālasaṃkarṣiṇī, Destroyer of Time, and also of Vīryākālī, mistress of the five powers—black, emaciated, with six heads surrounded by flames, astride Kalāgnirudra, the Rudra of the fire of cosmic destruction—a deity whose unlimited power dissolves eventually in the formless Absolute, which is her essence. In spite of such intense visionary cults, rather than being ascetics, the adepts of the Trika were initiated, married householders who could worship these deities in secrecy without being excluded from their social milieu. As I have remarked above, the Trika doctrine was expounded by the great Tantric master, Abhinavagupta. The main scriptures of the Pūrvāmnāya included such Trika texts as the *Tantrasadbhāva*, the *Siddhayogeśvarīmata*, and the *Mālinīvijayottaratantra*, as well as the *Svacchānda* and the *Netratantra*.

The Uttarāmnāya transmission is that of the Kālī cults. It includes three major traditions: the Mata (the Doctrine); the Krama (the Sequence), also called the Mahārtha (the Great Truth); and the Mahānaya (the Great Way) or the Devīnaya (the Way of the Goddess), with the cult of Guhyakālī.

Very little is known of the Mata tradition. Its cult is rooted in the *Jayadrathayāmalatantra*. It is also described in the *Ciñcinīmatasārasamuccaya*. It worshipped the twelve Kālīs, its cult including sexual intercourse. Its deities often had animal faces and were usually fearsome.

The Krama is a better-known and more elaborate system of Kālī worship. Its main characteristic is that it is sequential (as the Sanskrit term *krama* indicates). In it, one worships sets of deities in a fixed sequence (*krama*) as the phases of a universal cyclical pulsion, which gives life to the cosmos, humans, and consciousness or cognition (*saṃvit*). These phases are emission (*sṛṣṭikrama*), maintenance (*sthitikrama*), resorption (*saṃhāra*) of the emitted, and the Nameless (*anākhya*)—also named "phase of the Kālīs" (*kālīkrama*)—to which is added in most texts a fifth phase of pure light (*bhāsakrama*). The Krama also worships a system of sixty-four Yoginīs. Interesting in this Krama version of the generic Hindu vision of the cosmic cycle is the fact that it is animated not by the main deity but by groups of Kālīs. These are active both in the cosmos and in the human body, which they animate, thus giving a cosmic (and divine) dimension to the senses (*indriya*)—an aspect we shall see again when looking at Śaiva exegeses. Its scriptures include the *Devīpañcaśataka* and the *Kramasadbhāva*.

The cult of Guhyakālī or Devīnaya appears as a concretization or popularization of the Krama metaphysical vision. Here, the Goddess is the three-faced, eight-armed Guhyakālī, worshipped along with other fearsome goddesses. Its scriptures include the *Jayadrathatantra* and the *Kālīkulakramārcana*, which is also transmitted in a variant form known as the *Mahākālasaṃhitā*. This tradition is still very much alive in the Kathmandu Valley (Bhaktapur[15]) in Nepal, where it is commonly known as the worship of Guhyeśvarī.

Because the goddess of the Paścimāmnāya system is Kubjikā, the doctrine of this āmnāya is called Kubjikāmata. It is linked with the Trika, from which it has borrowed many elements. The humpbacked Kubjikā is black, fat, adorned with snakes, and ugly—she is to be visualized embracing her consort, the god Navātman ("Ninefold"). He embodies the nine-part mantra *HSKṢMLVYRŪṂ*, a black but beautiful youth dancing in cremation grounds, surrounded by gods, on a lotus that grows from the navel of Agni, the god of Fire, which the worshipper must visualize on his cranial aperture (*brahmarandhra*) at the summit of an axis of light rising from his genital region (*svādhiṣṭhāna*). This reference to the tiered six power-centers (*cakra* or *ādhāra*), which was to become a common element of *kuṇḍalinī*-yoga in India, is interesting because it is the first we know of historically. These *cakras* may have first appeared in the Kubjikāmata. Navātman is sometimes worshipped alone as the Solitary Hero (*ekavīra*). Its scriptures include the *Kubjikāmatatantra* of the *Kulakālīkāmnaya* and a *Kubjikā Upaniṣad*. The cult of Kubjikā is still alive today in Nepal, where she is the secret goddess of the Newars, the ancient population of the valley of Kathmandu.

The main deity of the Dakṣiṇāmnāya is Tripurasundarī (the Beautiful Goddess of the Three Worlds), with Bhairava as a consort. (She is also called Kāmeśvarī, with Kāmeśvara as consort.) She is shown as peaceful, clad in red, one-faced, with four arms holding her "weapons" (*āyudha*[16]), seated on a lotus placed above the gods Brahmā, Viṣṇu, Rudra, Īśvara and Sadāśiva. She is also embodied as a fifteen-syllable mantra (*HASAKALAHR̥ĪṂ, HASAKAHALAHR̥ĪṂ, SAKALAHR̥ĪṂ*), the *śrīvidyā*. The basic scriptures of this comparatively late (tenth-century) tradition, perhaps born in Kashmir, are the *Vāmakeśvarīmata*, also called *Nityāṣoḍaśikārṇava*, and the *Yoginīhr̥daya*. She is worshipped in and as the nine-triangle *śrīcakra*, her diagrammatical aspect, which symbolically embodies her cosmic activity of creating the universe (*sr̥ṣṭi*)—maintaining (*sthiti*) and pervading it with her power and resorbing it (*saṃhāra*) in herself. She abides in its central triangle, surrounded by deities emanating from her that are concentrically placed in the nine constitutive parts of the *cakra*, where they are tiered hierarchically from the supreme plane in the center down to the level of the earth on the outer square. Tripurasundarī's worship is performed not on but with the *srīcakra* as a geometrically drawn consecrated area whereon all the deities abiding in the *śrīcakra* are to be ritually placed by their mantras and mentally visualized. The offerings include pieces of meat and alcohol, but there is no sexual union in spite of the character of erotic magic this tradition sometimes has. Meditating on the *śrīcakra* and worshipping its deities from the center to its outer limit (or conversely from the outside to the center), the adept follows and identifies himself with the cosmic creative and destructive flow of the activity of the Goddess.

The Śrīvidyā tradition is still active in India and Nepal. In its South Indian, "de-Tantricized" Vedic form—under the spiritual guidance of the Śaṅkarācāryas, which appeared around the sixteenth century—the goddess is more commonly referred to as Lalitā.

The Goddess

Although the Kula Tantric traditions we have seen are classified as Śaiva, all have a great, all-powerful goddess as their main deity. It is therefore apposite to say a few words on the theme of the Goddess. Because the Goddess is Śakti, these systems could well be called Śākta—which they are, since goddesses are individualized forms of this omnipresent divine energy (*śakti*), incarnations of the power of the godhead. However, following a common use among Sanskritists, I call them Śaiva because, for these traditions, a form of Śiva usually remains metaphysically—if not theologically—supreme, and because the exegeses of these traditions were essentially Śaiva in spirit and practices. The Tantric period of the history of India was (as I have already said) a "Śaiva age."

The divine power (*śakti*) is one—omnipresent, supreme, auspicious, and also fearsome. The goddesses worshipped in domestic or temple cults, in spite of their differences, are but different aspects or forms of the one Goddess: *ek hi mātā hain*, "all the Mothers are One," to use a current Hindi formula. This is why one may speak of "the Goddess," with a capital *G*. This is a fundamental, characteristic trait of Tantric Hinduism, going back arguably to the Yoginī cults. In fact, this trait is not merely Tantric but generally Hindu, as is shown by the *Devīmahātmya*—a portion of the *Mārkaṇḍeya Purāṇa*, dating perhaps from the sixth century—which extols Durgā as an incarnation of the power of all the gods, not as a Tantric goddess (though she is sometimes regarded in Tantric circles as being so described there). According to Thomas Coburn, the work is "surely the earliest [literary work] in which the object of worship is conceptualized as Goddess, with a capital G."[17]

The presence of the Goddess in her various aspects (Tantric or not Tantric) is very visible today in India (and in Nepal), where goddess temples and cults are very numerous (and where new goddess sanctuaries, and also new goddesses, go on appearing). Tantric goddess sanctuaries, or power seats (*pīṭhas*) can be found all over India. Providing a living presence of the divine power, they form, as it were, a sacred geography that the Tantric adept or devotee can follow in pilgrimage or experience as present in his body (see chapter 10). In addition to the great goddesses Pārvatī, Kālī, Durgā, Caṇḍī, and so on, Tantric or not Tantric, there are many regional, local, or clan goddesses, often of popular Hinduisms, some attended by large numbers of devotees.

Sanskrit texts sometimes also reflect this religious notion of feminine omnipresence. There are hymns (*stotra*) to her glory, poems extolling her "play" with Śiva, collections of the "thousand names" (*sahasranāma*) given to her—and therefore of the thousand aspects she may assume—metaphysical treatises on her divine and cosmic role, and so on. Even in the Pāñcarātra the Goddess is worshipped, as shown by the *Lakṣmītantra*. The ambiguous character of the Goddess in all her aspects should also be noted. She is alluring, auspicious, but also capricious and unpredictable, sometimes fearsome. Because the Śākta texts were, like all Tantras, written by men, they reflect the Indian male vision of women—attractive, a source of power, but also drawing out her male partner's semen and therefore dangerous. I must add that although she sometimes appears in the form of the Mother (Ambikā) or invoked as Mother by her devotees, the Goddess (in all her aspects) is not properly a mother goddess. She is a cosmic creator but she is not procreative. She has no children (except as Pārvatī, consort of Śiva and mother of Gaṇeśa and Skanda, but this is an exception). The Tantric Mothers (Mātṛs; often referred to as Mātṛkās) are anything but maternal.[18] I will review similar goddesses in chapter 10.

Śaiva Postscriptural Works and Exegeses

The Śaiva scriptures we have seen included few theoretical developments. Being sacred revealed texts, they contained mostly mythical and metaphysicotheological elements, together with much ritual (often magical)—as well as some socioreligious—prescriptions, and yoga. They did propound important theoretical notions, but the more important and interesting philosophical, mystical, as well as ritual developments were to be found in another category of works: the commentarial and exegetical literature that was to follow them. This literature was produced from approximately the ninth to the fourteenth century, a few important works written even into to the eighteenth and nineteenth century. Its most noteworthy texts came from Kashmir and later from South India. In Kashmir, one finds several of the most interesting and original aspects of Tantric thought, as well as ritual and spiritual notions and practices, some of its main authors being among the most brilliant of Indian thinkers. One finds there all that the Tantric vision has produced to renovate and enliven the ancient Vedic Upaniṣadic base. This literature spread the Tantric teaching out of the limited circle of ascetic renouncers to a wider circle of married householders, who became the main recipients (and practitioners) of Tantra. Another reason to examine this literature is because much of it continues to be in use today—compendiums, mantraśāstra, iconographic treatises, and ritual manuals are still being consulted and, although most cults have disappeared, some still exist, and their theological doctrines have continued to enrich Indian philosophical debate (or are now transposed in the West as systems of thought or mystical ways).

This postscriptural literature falls into two philosophical categories. On one side are the commentaries of the dualist Śaiva Siddhānta. On the other side are those of the nondualist āmnāyas—including the Trika, Krama, Spanda, and Pratyabhijñā.[19] These different bodies of exegetical literature had a common point in that they were not meant for ascetics seeking supernatural powers (*siddhi*), as the Tantras typically were, but for those seeking liberation (*mukti*) or self-perfection by following the physical, mental/spiritual, and ritual teachings of Śaivism. The latter, forming the broad social base of the Śaiva traditions, were married householders. For them, Śaivism was, to use Sanderson's words, "not merely a system of doctrines but first and foremost a set of social facts independent of or presupposed by a doctrine." Sanderson also notes that in spite of fundamental differences in theology, there is a basic notion that it is enough to be a Śaiva in the ritual sense to seek (and perhaps attain) liberation at death. If we look at Abhinavagupta's vast treatise, the *Tantrāloka*, the first five chapters on mystic or spiritual ways or means (*upāya*) to reach liberation and the next five on cosmogonical subjects are followed by one on grace, then by twenty dealing all with ritual practices.

The antignostic and ritualistic bias of the Śaivasiddhānta was naturally taken up and developed in its exegeses of ritual as a way to liberation. One of its main authors, Rāmakaṇṭha (fl. c. 950–1000), underlined the necessity of the daily or occasional ritual practices after the initiation (*dīkṣā*) by which one enters on the path to liberation. Ritual treatises were very important in this ritual perspective. The best-known treatise on ritual is probably the eleventh-century *Somaśambhupaddhati*.[20] There is also the *Kriyākramadyotikā* of Aghoraśiva (twelfth century), the author of many works. Philosophically, Sadyojyotih's works, in particular the *Nareśvaraparīkṣa*, are especially worth mentioning, for they mark the beginning of the dualistic Śaiva exegetical tradition (insofar as it is accessible to us today).

Infinitely more important, abundant, and interesting are the nondualistic Śaiva exegeses, those of four Kashmirian schools of thought: Trika, Spanda, Krama, and Pratyabhijñā.

Ritual remains important for these systems because through it, when intensely "lived" in body and in soul and associated with meditation and yogic elements, the self can break through its limits. But in all cases, the self is, in essence, an absolute omnipotent consciousness—part of the divine one—which only appears to be individuated as discrete selves.

This is the doctrine of nonduality of consciousness (*saṃvidadvaya*), which affirms that the deity is a nondual omnipresent dynamic consciousness, a consciousness that is the very nature of the apparently separate individual consciousness. This doctrine has its roots in the Kāpālika Kaula scriptures. The first exegetical developments of this doctrine are the ninth-century *Śivasūtra*—the "Aphorisms of Śiva" and the "Stanzas on Vibration"—and the *Spandakārikā*. The first text is deemed to have been "discovered" by Vasugupta, while the other is said to have been composed by him. They are two fundamental works that are often edited, translated, and commented.[21] The *Śivasūtra* includes seventy-six aphorisms, the longest of which is six words long. It is too brief and allusory for one to find a coherent philosophical doctrine. It has to be interpreted, a task taken up by commentaries. The best known are a brief one by Bhāskara (c. 925–75) and a longer examination by Kṣemarāja (c. 1000–1050), a follower of Abhinavagupta and a prolific and important author in his own right. His rich and insightful commentary stresses the *Śivasūtra*'s mystical aspects; deals with meditation, mantras, and *kuṇḍalinī*; and quotes a number of other texts.

The other main work is the *Spandakārikā*, which comprises fifty-two stanzas. Four commentaries on it survive.[22] It is more explicit than the *Śivasūtra* and is considered the basic text of the so-called Spanda School. According to this school, the godhead, Śiva, an all-inclusive single omnipresent consciousness, is animated by a vibrating dynamism (*spanda*), which is its essential nature. To mystically realize that this vibration is the essential nature of all human states of consciousness is to gain liberation. The first mention of *spanda* as the dynamism of consciousness is, in fact, in the *Jayadrathayāmalatantra*. The passages of this text on mantras, their nature, and how they work are very illuminating.

Another exegetical tradition—more philosophical and less heterodox than the former, though keeping a dynamic ontology—is the Pratyabhijñā (the Recognition). Śiva, rather than a goddess, is the main deity of this tradition. It began in the tenth century with the "Perception of Śiva" (*Śivadṛṣṭi*) of Somānanda (c. 900–50). It was followed by the "Stanzas on the Recognition of the Lord" (*Īśvarapratyabhijñākārikā*), an exceptionally interesting work by his pupil Utpaladeva (c. 925–75), who was also a master of the Krama and the Trika. Abhinavagupta, Utpaladeva's indirect disciple, wrote two vast commentaries on the work, the "Examination of the Recognition of the Lord" (*Īś varapratyabhijñāvimarśinī*) and then a longer one on Utpaladeva's exegesis of his own text, the "Examination of the commentary on the Recognition of the Lord" (*Īśvarapratyabhijñā-vivṛtivimarśinī*). They are two subtle and difficult texts that are among the most original works of the Indian philosophical tradition. According to the Pratyābhijñā, "A new and easy path to salvation" is the recognition (*pratyabhijñā*) of the identity of one's own self and Śiva, the Great Lord (Maheśvara). Thus realized, the transpersonal self (*ātmeśvara*) contains the totality of all phenomena, objective or subjective. It is a nondual synthesis where the distinction between here and there, the self and others, is transcended in the absolute bliss of a fusion with the total fullness of the Absolute—an Absolute that is not a static substance but an infinite living consciousness that is also pure autonomy (*svātantrya*). It is also the Great Being (*mahāsatta*), the supreme Absolute, which brings everything to existence by appearing as different from itself without losing its total fullness (*pūrṇatā*).

Some themes of the philosophy of the Pratyabhijñā were taken over and developed by Abhinavagupta in his two commentaries on Utpaladeva's *Īs'varapratyabhijñākārikā*, which are—along with his *Tantrāloka*, *Tantrasāra*, *Mālinīvijayavārttikā*, and *Parātrīśikāvivaraṇa*—the main works of the Kaśmirian system of the Trika, whose ritual and doctrine are said to be based on the *Mālinīvijayottaratantra*. The Trika evolved over the course of time, beginning with the cult of the three goddesses as propounded in such texts as the *Siddhayogeśvarīmata*, then giving more place to the cult of Kālī, and finally to the Pratyabhijñā-based Trika of Abhinavagupta, who formulated a Kālī-based cult in the *Tantrāloka* and a cult of Parā as the Solitary Heroine (*ekavīrā*).

The Trika thus appears as one of the richest Śaiva Tantric traditions—all the more so because of its main author, Abhinavagupta (fl. c. 975–1025). He is one of the most remarkable Indian personalities (yogin, mystic, metaphysician, the main Indian aesthetician[23]), who, borrowing for his Trika elements from other nondualistic traditions, appears as a central and exemplary figure. His exegesis is based on the Pratyabhijñā. The supreme deity is Śiva, conceived as pure consciousness (*saṃvit*, *cit*) manifesting itself by its own power (*śakti*) as the totality of the cosmos, which, while different from it, is not outside it—all is in God. It is a "nondualism of consciousness" (*saṃvidadvaita*). In truth, individual consciousnesses are but aspects of the one divine consciousness—only God acts in (and as) ourselves.[24] The Goddess is unlimited power (*śakti*). She is also the Word (*vāc*). The deity is active and dynamic, pouring out generosity, a spontaneous effervescence expressed notably by the term *spanda*. This Absolute is defined as light (*prakāśa*) and self-cognition (*vimarśa*), being indissolubly both light and consciousness (*prakāśavimarśamaya*). It is also absolute freedom, autonomy (*svātantrya*).

Therefore, the Trika is sometimes called "the doctrine of autonomy" (*svātantryavāda*). Without losing its absolute oneness and purity, the omnipresent Supreme Reality, or Supreme Consciousness, both transcendent and immanent, causes limitations to appear in itself so as to bring the world and living beings—who do not differ from it in essence but, blinded by their innate ignorance (*avidyā, ajñāna*), do not realize their true nature—into existence. However, once humans free themselves from this ignorance by recognizing (*pratyabhijñā*) that their true nature is that of the Absolute Consciousness, of Śiva, these bound, limited creatures will escape transmigration and attain liberation (*mokṣa/mukti*). This condition—which some will attain during their lifetime (*jīvanmukti*)—is identification with the deity, a mystical fusion (*samāveśa*)[25] with it. The fully liberated is truly identified with Śiva or the (ontologically identical) Goddess, transcending the world while dominating it. So many themes differentiate this Tantric tradition of nondualism from that of Śaṅkara's Vedānta.

Abhinavagupta also incorporated some elements from the Krama in his synthesis. He adopts the system of five stages (*krama*) of that tradition, which considers that human bodily and mental existence is an emanation of a set of five goddesses representing the cycle of cognition, so that the body is the true site of worship and a seat of power (*pīṭha*), the cult of each goddess corresponding to a stage of consciousness. Abhinavagupta considers that the four stages of emission (*sṛṣṭi*), maintenance (*sthiti*), resorption or retraction (*saṃhāra*), and the Nameless (*anākhya*) appear in that order first in the field of the object of knowledge (*prameya*), then in that of cognition (*pramāṇa*), and finally in that of the cognizing subject (*pramātṛ*), on whose plane of subjectivity the adept is united with the Nameless—the infinite consciousness that is the Goddess. However, according to Abhinavagupta, this is realized by the play of twelve Kālīs, from Sṛṣṭi-Kālī—the Kālī of emission, where appears a first consciousness of the objective world—through ten other Kālīs with whom the consciousness of the world appears. It is then dissolved in successive stages, each of these Kālīs being more fearsome, culminating with the twelfth, Mahābhairavacaṇḍograghora-Kālī ("The Kālī of the Most Terrible, the Fierce, the Violent, and Fearsome"). This plane of total void is reached when the adept transcends all sequences and all dichotomy by fusion into the absolute autonomy (*svātantrya*) of the Goddess, thus attaining liberation. This play of the twelve Kālīs is described, or rather extolled, by Abhinavagupta in his *Kramastotra*.[26]

Because the Trika is an exegesis of Tantras that consider the world to be a transformation (*parināma*) of *brahman*, and because it incorporates Pratyabhijñā notions, it considers the cosmos to be a luminous projection or apparition (*ābhāsa*). The cosmos consists of luminous images that the Supreme Godhead, which is consciousness (*samvit*) and light (*prakāśa*), projects onto itself as onto a screen, or like a reflection in a mirror. Thus, the universe is a luminous play of the godhead, a manifested form of its power that pervades and animates it. As the divine substrate, the essence, of the world, it quite naturally offers humans the means to reach the divinity. This is one of the justifications of the Tantric principle that one may use the means of the world (body, senses, and notably sex) to progress toward liberation.

In the Trika, one also finds the most important and subtle speculations (and practices) on *vāc*, the feminine power of speech, which all Tantras regard as the source and substrate of everything—as we shall see in chapter 7.

In this exegetical system, where—as for all the others (and as for the *darśanas* generally)—the ultimate aim of philosophy is to offer an experience of truth as a way toward salvation, the role of divine grace (*anugraha*), or descent of power (*śaktipāta*), is fundamental. It is one of the five cosmic actions or functions (*karmapañcaka*) of Śiva, and our salvation depends on it. Thus, in the *Tantrāloka*, Abhinavagupta ranks the ways (*upāya*) to liberation according to the intensity of the grace received by the adept, the highest way being where grace is the most intense. In that case, liberation is immediately gained without any spiritual or ritual access being necessary. The adept may not even survive its impact. Characteristic in this respect is the fact that, in the Trika, the most eminent spiritual master (*guru*) is the one spontaneously initiated by his chosen deity (*iṣṭadevatā*)—the deity of his consciousness (*svasaṃviddevatā*)—without any ritual consecration being necessary. (One sees here once more an instance of the tension common to the Hindu world between ritual or yoga on the one hand and devotion, spiritual search, or grace, on the other.)

The reader will perhaps find this section on exegeses too long and sometimes difficult to grasp, but it could not be much shorter considering the textual bulk and the intellectual importance of the subject, elements of which one will often find underlying passages of the chapters of part 2 of this book.

The Nāthas

The philosophy or religious position of the Nāthas, insofar as it can be ascertained from different works—generally attributed to the more or less mythical Matsyendranātha/Mīnanātha/Macchanda (also sometimes named Lui-pāda) and to Gorakṣanātha/Gorakhnāth—appears to be a particular brand of *advaita*, since it considers itself as transcending both dualism and nondualism. Śiva and Śakti are described as sexually united, with Śiva dominating. *Śakti* is merely Śiva's power; she is never worshipped as the Goddess. Śiva is the supreme consciousness (*parāsaṃvit*). The world results from a self-manifestation of Śiva, an effect of the play of consciousness (*cidvilāsa*); it is the cosmic body of Śiva, the "Great Being" (*mahāpuruṣa*), or the "Primordial Body" (*ādyapiṇḍa*). The human body is seen as a microcosm, and its control and transformation through yoga practices (*layayoga*) with meditation (*dhyāna*)—including the ascent of *kuṇḍalinī*, with concentration on the inner subtle sound (*nāda*)—is the way toward spiritual perfection, or liberation (*mokṣa*). This is a state of perfect purity, where all empirical dualities—pleasure and pain, good and bad—are transcended. It is sometimes called the state of *kula*, or of *avadhūta*. There are also developments on the role of mantric practices. On the whole, the Nātha conception of the yogic body, with its *cakras* and *nāḍīs*, is the one usually found in Tantric traditions. This is to be expected because these traditions borrowed such notions from the Nāthas. There are no transgressive ritual practices, though ritual offerings are nonvegetarian. Śiva is often worshipped as Bhairava. Yoginīs, too, are worshipped.

But in fact, Nātha elements can be found in different Tantric texts. Nātha works such as the *Haṭhayogapradīpa* are classic Tantric yoga works. The Nāthas are considered the main proponents of haṭhayoga, which differs from the yoga propounded in some Śaivasiddhānta āgamas, but hardly from the yoga of various Śaiva Kaula traditions. We have also seen that Nātha elements were used for drafting or redrafting Tantric Upaniṣads. To posit Nāthism as different from "mainstream" Tantra (if there is such a thing) is, therefore, problematic.

The Nātha tradition has survived until today, as we shall see in chapter 11.

Vaiṣṇava Pāñcarātra Developments

As I have already said, there is much less to say about Pāñcarātra than about Śaiva postscriptural developments. The Tantric world is first and foremost a Śaiva world. Its Vaiṣṇava side is less original and inventive. On many counts, it does not differ greatly from the Śaiva traditions. When the two are compared, it often appears as derivative. Both traditions were born in similar milieus, both with a similar Vedic-brahmanical origin, and both were influenced by similar local factors, but Śaivism predominated.

The surviving Pāñcarātra religious and philosophical works are not as varied as the Śaiva ones. Its deities are more peaceful. It is also nearer to Purāṇic Hinduism and is more Veda-congruent. The main deity, Viṣṇu/Nārāyaṇa, is worshipped as Vasudeva. He is the supreme *brahman*, Consciousness (*cit*, *samvit*) without duality—stable, pure, and spotless (*nirañjana*). Three hypostases, known as Vyūhas, emanate from him. These are named Saṃkarṣaṇa, Pradyumna, and Aniruddha, or Acyuta, Satya, and Puruṣa. The next stage of manifestation (*prādhānikasarga*)—which is the work of Māyā, who is Śakti, the divine energy, sometimes worshipped as Lakṣmī—issues from them. Then, from Matter or Nature (*prakṛti*), come the other constitutive elements of the cosmos, the *tattvas*. However, these only number twenty-four. In other words, they are simply the principles of the Sāṃkhyas (without *puruṣa*). This cosmogonic pattern does not differ very much from that of the Śaiva systems. Some saṃhitās describe a manifestation of the cosmos through phonemes of the Sanskrit alphabet, as in the Trika. However, the phonemes issue from *bindu*. The role ascribed to ritual, to mantras or to yoga, as well as to mental and spiritual practices—visualizations (*dhyāna*) and the like—do not differ greatly from those of Śaivism, as we shall see in the next chapters on the various aspects of the Tantric world.

The Pāñcarātra is, however, not the only form of Tantric Vaiṣṇavism. There were also other developments of a more popular character, such as the Vaiṣṇava Sahajiyā tradition of Bengal. Its mystical *sādhana* is based on the eternal love dalliance of Kṛṣṇa and Rādhā, which the worshipper is to emulate, for he is to realize himself as Kṛṣṇa and to see his partner as Rādhā. This love—in spite of its physical aspect—is not erotic desire (*kāma*) but true pure love (*prema*). It is also a love in separation from a god who is "near but difficult to reach," and is therefore a longing for the absent (*viraha-bhakti.*)[27] This love is to be lived, body and soul, in a particular intense spiritual atmosphere (*bhāva*) with a partner who is not one's wife but another woman (*parakīya*). One finds there an interesting case of "imaginative structuring of experience," an interaction between the body and the cosmos where the reality of the body—always present and experienced (notably in sexual intercourse)—is also transcended. The Vaiṣṇava Sahajiyā's is, I believe, a very interesting case.[28]

We might mention here the Vaikhanāsa tradition whose priests are present in many Vaiṣṇava temples of Southern India. Though it considers itself "Vedic," its ritual practices include a number of Tantric elements (as I have noted above).

Magic

Throughout the course of centuries, magic has been a fundamental, constitutive trait of Indian thought and life. It is arguably at the heart and the origin of the Tantric traditions, which can be traced on the Buddhist side to the growth of a literature of spell-like formulae called *dhāraṇīs* and, on the Śaiva side, to the use of mantras as spells not just for this-worldly magical attainments but also for the highest spiritual attainment of all—namely, that of liberation.

Because of the continued importance of religion in Indian civilization—and also because of the way its great philosophical works were discovered by Western scholars, influenced as they were by German idealist philosophy—India was (and still often is) considered fundamentally "mystical," renunciant, otherworldly. In many ways, this rings true. But it is also, probably more fundamentally, "magical,"[29] looking for freedom from the limitations or fetters of this world but not forsaking it—on the contrary, wishing to dominate it, participating in the divine play that animates it both as a performer/player and as an active participant. The wish to gain magical control of this world (if possible, of the whole cosmos) appears always to have been very much a part of the Indian thought-world.

Magic is pervasive in Tantra. It is already present in the Veda and remains so in its brahmanical sequel. The first Indian magical text we know of is the *Atharvaveda* (c. tenth century BC). The Vedic god Indra is characterized by the fact that he envelops the world as in a net (*jāla*) by his powers (*indrajāla*), a term that has come to mean "illusion," "delusion," "magic," or "the art of magic." Admittedly, the frontier between magic and religion is blurred not only in India; the category of magic is not easy to define. Typical of the Indian case is the fact that there is no term for magic or for a magical act in Sanskrit.[30] The nearest equivalent perhaps, at least for hostile magic, is *abhicāra* ("inimical action"), which is often taken as meaning "black magic." In a world that is not "disenchanted," where deities are believed and felt as actively omnipresent—as India was and still is to a certain extent today—supernatural action and power (*siddhis*) are just another, albeit less frequent, category of powers or actions.

In India, in the past and today, all spiritual masters or "saints" are believed to have supernatural powers. Yogis, too, are believed to enjoy them. The third section of Patañjali's *Yogasūtra* deals with the supernormal powers (*vibhūti*) of the yogi, some (if not most) of which might well be called magical—for instance, the power to enter another person's body (*paraśarīrāveśa*; a power even such a person as the great Vedānta master Śaṅkarācārya is said to have once made use of[31]). In Tantra, supernatural power (*siddhi*) is typically paired with liberation (*mukti*), which can be obtained with Tantric practice. Sometimes *mukti* is presented as the highest among the *siddhis*. The use of such powers may be frowned upon by some, but they are there. In the stages of the "classical" Śaiva Siddhānta system of salvific initiations (*dīkṣā*), in the *sādhaka-dīkṣā*, the initiated adept (*sādhaka*) is so called because he is deemed to obtain supernatural powers (*siddhis*), the main power being the power to master a mantra and use it to different ends, spiritual or mundane, including those we would call magical. There are two categories of *sādhakas*: those looking for rewards, mundane or supernatural (*bhukti*)—in Sanskrit, they are said to be *bubhukṣus*, wishing for *bhukti*—and those looking for liberation (*mukti*). These are called *mumukṣus*, wishing for *mukti*. Extolling their own teachings, Tantric texts often claim that they can bestow both *bhukti* and *mukti*. Interesting to note is the fact that these texts put women and children among those qualified merely for wishing to become a *mumukṣu*. This is perhaps because, according to the texts, only male adults can be trusted to use magical powers.

Mantras, which are words of power, are much more than mere magical formulas. In the texts I refer to here, their use is mainly spiritual or ritual, as performative forms of the Word (*vāc*). However, they are used profusely in magic. They can be either uttered—flung out orally like an arrow at their target—written on amulets (*kavaca*, in Sanskrit), included in the pattern of magical diagrams (*yantras*), placed by *nyāsa* so as to give objects (weapons or drugs, for instance) "magical" efficiency, or placed on the body to protect it.[32] Mantras are the active element in the well-known Tantric "six [magical] actions," which we shall see in chapter 9 about the Tantric Word. In Tantra, magical actions are innumerable and can be simplistic or complex. Often, complex hostile rites involve corpses and the accoutrements of the cremation-ground. Some of these are described already in the fifth- through seventh-century Saiddhāntika *Niśvāsatattvasaṃhitā*. There is a pervasive presence of magic in Tantra.

Bhakti

Bhakti, devotion, may well be considered as antithetical both to the essentially ritual Vedic and early brahmanical approach of the divine and to the dominant Śaiva Tantric school of thought. But *bhakti* is present in such ancient texts as the *Mahābhārata* (in the *Bhagavadgītā*, a "classical" work on the subject), and it is present in Tantra. Tāntrikas are devotees of their chosen deity. In many texts, both liberation (*mukti*) and rewards (*bhukti*) are described as the result of the correct ritual use of mantras, but they are also described as the fruit of devotion to the chosen deity. As I will show in chapter 9 on the spiritual aspect of Tantra, it is also present in Sanskrit scriptures and exegetical works, this even in a nondualist (*advaita*) context. For instance, Abhinavagupta sometimes says that the adept is to act with devotion (*bhaktyā*).

In the *Tantrāloka* (13), he appears to identify the work of the descent of Śiva's energy (*śaktipāta*) with devotion to Śiva (*śive bhaktiḥ*). To mention another, older case, in chapter 2 of the *Mālinīvijayottaratantra*, possession of an adept by the power of Rudra (*rudraśaktisamāveśa*) is detected first by his obtaining a firm devotion to this god (*rudre bhaktiḥ suniścalā*) and second by his mastery of mantras (*mantrasiddhi*). In this case, contrary to the general view, *bhakti* is first to produce an effect, acting before the more "technical" action of mantras.

The importance of *bhakti* is especially clear in the Tantric works in vernacular tongues (as we shall see in chapter 9), since these works, written later, appeared in times when *bhakti* tended to prevail. In those times, *bhakti* remained present in Sanskrit texts of all sorts, scriptures or works of exegesis. If not exactly a constitutive trait of Tantra, *bhakti* is nevertheless of such importance that it must be mentioned here.

PART II

The Tantric World

After an overview of the history and expansion of Tantra and of the texts of its main currents and doctrines, we must now look at the different aspects of the Tantric world as it existed in practice in India for centuries and as it survives today.

The Tantric world is, first and foremost, a world of ritual. Tāntrikas, as I have already said, are "hyperritualists." However, rites are actions done bodily—a body that is sexed—as well as mentally. They consist mainly of words or speech, whether expressed or mentally evoked. This is an essential point, for there is no ritual without some form of word. Therefore, I will begin this section by considering first the body, then sex, followed by the Tantric aspects of the Word, especially mantras. There is also the world of ritual action, and the spiritual or devotional aspect of Tantra. As already noted, ritual, temples, images, or bodily practice are always organized, oriented, explained, or justified by an ideology—by beliefs. One does not perform a ritual or practice yoga without knowing what one is doing and why. There are no ritual rules without (some) meaning. While describing practices, I will also quote doctrines and notions—rites are actions to be consciously performed and understood, "lived" in body and mind. Also fundamental is the particular Tantric experience and vision of the human body. There is, too, the transgressive aspect of Tantra, as well as an important spiritual or mystical side. Finally, I will consider how Tantra appears materially on the ground in pilgrimages, temples, and iconography—all cases where the power of the Word also plays a role.

5

The Tantric Body

My body is the portion of the universe which my thought can modify at will.

G. C. ICHTENBERG

Dear pursuing presence,
dear body:
you brought me
do not leave me
behind . . .
A Hindu to his body

A. K. RAMANUJAN

To live, to be present in the world as a Tāntrika, is to live in a universe pervaded by divine powers, by the power (*śakti*) of the deity—a universe experienced as a field of energy in which the body is immersed. The body is part of the universe, reflecting its structure. Supernatural forces and deities are present, animating the body and connecting it with the cosmos. A body whose structure and life are simultaneously human, cosmic, and divine is also a yogic body. The place and the role of the human body in Tantra are such that most aspects of the Tantric domain could be studied from the body's point of view.[1]

From its earliest period, India gave the body a particular importance in its vision of the world and of human beings. Yoga is proof of this fact. Only a being having a body can gain salvation, says an ancient text. Tantra, which considers that the means of this world can be used to gain liberation, emphasizes this view. In many ways, the body is given the pride of place.

In all Tantric traditions, deities are present in the human body, which they inhabit and animate. Cosmic divisions, mystical geography, are present or reflected in the body. In one of his poems, Saraha (twelfth century) said, "Here [in my body] are the Gaṅgā and the Yamunā . . . here are Prayāga and Varaṇāsī, here the Sun and the Moon. Here are the sacred places, the *pīṭhas* . . . Never have I seen a place of pilgrimage and an abode of bliss like my body." True, he was a Buddhist Tāntrika. But a Hindu Tāntrika would have said as much, for the Tantric path toward liberation is practically always a bodily and mental ascetic process linked to the cosmos.

Though innovative in many ways, the Tantric conception of the human body is no more than a very intense, ritualized, sometimes strange, variety of an ancient, traditional Indian conception of the body. "Gods abide in the body as cows in a cow-pen," the *Atharvaveda* said. Two thousand years ago, the earlier Upaniṣads (*Bṛhadāraṇyaka*, *Chāndogya*, *Maitri*) described the movements of breath and of vital force in the body as linked to the cosmos, a point further developed in more recent Upaniṣads—the *Praśna*, for instance. The cosmos itself was sometimes conceived of or depicted as a huge body.[2] In the Hindu world, body and cosmos are closely linked.

A practicing Tāntrika is nearly always a yogi, for his ascesis (*sādhana*) most often includes somatopsychic practices that are yogic. Many rites, notably the worship of deities (*pūjā*) but also a number of ritual, magical, or spiritual practices, include yogic elements. These practices are usually "undergirded" by, or even patterned according to, a yogic experience of the body. Tantric texts, when describing rites or practices to be performed, very often call the person who is to perform them "yogi." This almost continuous presence of yoga is an important point. (However, I must note that from early times, there were bodily ascetic practices [*tapas*], which were not part of yoga.)

Tantric Yoga, the Yogic Body

There is no so-called Tantric yoga, for the yogic practices and theoretical constructions of the various Tantric traditions differ on several counts. However, they have a number of common traits, notably that they evolved from an ancient, pre-Tantric source different from Pātañjali's *Yogasūtra* and the series of commentaries on that work. Some have labelled it *kuṇḍalinī*-yoga because of the role played in it by *kuṇḍalinī*, the divine cosmic power abiding in the body while transforming it. The practices of this "Tantric yoga" rest on an imaginary structure that is conceived as present in the body (sometimes overstepping its limits) and made up of an ensemble of centers or nodal points. These points are named knot (*granthi*), wheel (*cakra*), or lotus (*padma*). They are connected by a network of tubes or channels (*nāḍīs*), where the vital breath (*prāṇa*; as well as mantras or supernatural powers) circulates. These channels are said to be seventy-two thousand in number. Three are considered as more important, the main one being the *suṣumnā*, a vertical axis extending from the perineum to the top of the head, along which the *kuṇḍalinī* moves up, leading the adept toward liberation. The two other *nāḍīs* stretch along or around *suṣumnā*. The yogic body's main *cakras*, from the *mūlādhāra* in the perineum to the *brahmarandhra* on the top of the head, are tiered along it and even above it. All this is well known.[3] I do not need to describe it here. It is worth pointing out, however, that *suṣumnā*'s central position in the body gives it a special place among the *nāḍīs* not only as the path followed by *kuṇḍalinī* but also as the "central abode" (*madhyadhāman*), sometimes identified with the "heart"—the place where the adept may experience high spiritual or mystical states bodily.

This inner bodily structure, being entirely imaginary, is usually called the "subtle body." This is an unfortunate misnomer, for the subtle body, called *sūkṣmadeha* or *sūkṣmaśarīra* in Sanskrit, is something else. It is the entity that transmigrates from body to body after death, made up of a group of *tattvas*, and therefore without any shape that one could visualize. It is not an inner structure "intraposed" within the physical body that one can visualize mentally (and even feel within oneself). It is better to call the visualizable inner bodily structure (as I will do here) the yogic (or imaginal) body—a designation all the more justified because it is a development of an image of the body and of a "mystic physiology" that go back to very ancient times and was taken over and further elaborated in yogic, chiefly haṭhayogic, circles. Oversimplifying perhaps, I could say that Tantric yoga is haṭhayoga.

The internalized image of the yogic body is a fundamental element, for nearly all meditative and ritual Tantric practices are meant to give supernatural and magical powers or to lead the adept to the highest levels of consciousness and liberation. Rites of initiation (*dīkṣā*), the practice of mantras, and even some stages of ritual worship are also based on this structure. There are devotional and mystical ways to liberation, as we shall see, where yogic elements play no role. They are the highest paths, meant for a small minority of spiritually gifted devotees benefitting from divine grace. But all other practices, mental and spiritual, magical, or ritual, have a psychosomatic, and therefore yogic, side. These activate different centers, or channels, of the yogic body according to the aim of the practice. When the attainment of higher states of consciousness, spiritual perfection and, still more, liberation, is the aim, the internal bodily energy ascends vertically and is linked to the ascent of *kuṇḍalinī*.[4] The path to liberation is always an ascending one. This is not only the case in India; ascent is one of the "metaphors we live by."[5]

The varieties of Tantric yoga differ from the so-called classical yoga based, in principle, on Patañjali's *Yogasūtra* and on its commentaries[6] not only in that its practice rests on the internalized image of the yogic body, which is not to be found in the *Yogasūtra*, but also in that it is usually not an "eight-limbed" yoga (*aṣṭāṅgayoga*) comprising eight elements, *yama* and so forth, but a "six-limbed" yoga (*ṣaḍaṅgayoga*). This system was, in fact, already described (not as yogic) in the ancient ("Vedic") *Maitri* Upaniṣad (6.18). It does not include the two preliminary "limbs," *yama* and *niyama*, or *āsana*—(which does not mean that it excludes them but simply that it does not count them as "limbs"). These three limbs play a larger role in Tantra than in the

Yogasūtra. In fact, the *āsanas* (on which Patañjali does not expatiate) are particularly important in Tantric yoga, marked as it is by haṭhayoga. It adds, however, another (ancient) element—namely, reasoning (*tarka*).[7] Meditative fixation (*dhāraṇā*) takes on a different character, since it consists, in most cases, in focusing attention on a point of the yogic body while concentrating on one of the five gross constitutive elements (*bhūta*) of the cosmos (earth, water, air, fire, and *ākāśa*). Tantric yoga thus acquires a cosmic dimension experienced by the body, while its efficacy is increased by the mental exertion of *tarka*.

Contrary to what is often believed, the *cakras* of the yogic body are not always six in number. Their number varies according to traditions, to texts, and even to needs. The *dvādaśānta*, as its name indicates, is twelve (*dvādaśa*) finger-breadths above the *brahmarandhra*, which is the highest point of the ascent of *kuṇḍalinī* (and therefore of the *prāṇa* and of the *uccāra* of mantras[8]) for most Tantric traditions. In this example, they number seven. The Śrīvidyā tradition has nine *cakras*, for their number must tally with the nine sections of the *śrīcakra*. The *Kaulajñānanirṇaya* has eleven and the *Kubjikāmata* has a system of five. When the ascent of *prāṇa* or of the *kuṇḍalinī* is shown as starting from the heart, there are sometimes only four active *cakras*. In all traditions, there are also secondary *cakras*, or nodal points, varying in number and in location, ranging along the *suṣumnā* or placed in various places in or around the body. They are given such names as support (*ādhāra*), knot (*granthi*), void (*śūnya*), target (*lakṣya*), space (*vyoman*), and luminary (*dhāman*).

This pattern is the one contemporary practitioners of haṭhayoga usually refer to without knowing its Tantric origin and without realizing how much today's conceptions and practices of yoga differ from their preceding forms.[9] Modern yoga (even as propounded by Indian masters) owes, in this respect, probably as much to the "nature cure" elaborated in Europe in the nineteenth century as it does to Patañjali, and also to how his Sūtra was interpreted over the course of centuries by Indian authors of different philosophical persuasions.

Some Yogic Practices

A hundred instances of ritual or meditative practices based on the yogic imaginary body could be quoted, not to mention *nyāsa*, *mudrā* and other Tantric psychosomatic practices. Most of these are well known and do not need to be recalled here. They are described in a number of works, some of which were quoted in chapter 3, as well as in modern Indian or Western books. I would therefore rather mention merely two meditative practices from two different Tantric traditions, which I choose because of their complexity and of the intense mental exertion they require. One case comes from an arcane but important work not translated into English. The other case comes from a little-known work, though it is now available in English.

The first is taken from chapter 15 of Abhinavagupta's *Tantrāloka*, which deals with the "regular"—that is, common or preliminary—initiation (*samayadīkṣā*), through which the disciple of a spiritual master becomes an adept of the Śaiva Trika tradition. During this ritual, the adept will experience a cosmic, transformative purification of his body-mind through his imagination.[10] The practice outlined there (TĀ 15, 295–328) is only a part of a long ritual process (this chapter is 612 stanzas long).

It begins with various preliminary purificatory rites done with mantras placed by *nyāsa* on the body of the initiate, which is thus "burnt out" and consubstantiated with Śiva and Śakti, his consciousness being fused with that of the supreme deity. The initiate must then proceed by first worshipping his body, which is now identified with Śiva—a transformation shown by the fact that the movement of his breath becomes so faint that it becomes an infinitely subtle throbbing to be dissolved in the "fire of the rising breath," which then ascends along the *suṣumnā* up to the *brahmarandhra* and culminates as "Śiva consciousness" in the *dvādaśāntacakra*, twelve finger-breadths above his head.

The adept, now fused with the Absolute, is nevertheless to continue. He is now to identify himself with the *maṇḍala* of the three goddesses of the Trika, which are to be visualized as present in his body. To do this, he must visualize Śiva's trident extending in his body from below his navel to his palate, all the constitutive principles of the cosmos—the *tattvas* (with their deities)—being tiered along this axis, from the Earth to *māyā*, which is visualized as above the palate. All the *tattvas* that constitute the lower, impure universe (together with *māyā*, their material cause) are thus tiered in his yogic body. Above *māyā*, he now visualizes the plinth of the trident and, layered above it, the three next *tattvas*, which form the "pure universe." On the highest of these he installs the twenty-fourth *tattva*, the god Sadāśiva, visualizing him as a blazing corpse, "resonant with the mad laughter of destruction," gazing upward at the light of the Absolute. He is then to visualize the three prongs of the trident rising up through his cranial aperture from the navel of Sadāśiva and extending out and up to the *dvādaśānta*. Ranged in tiers along these prongs, the adept imagines the presence of ever subtler levels (the *kalās*[11]) of the Word (and of higher consciousness), which eventually fuse into a transcendent consciousness. On the apex of the three prongs, he is to visualize the three supreme goddesses of the Trika, each seated on a Bhairava that lies on a white lotus. In the center is Parā, the Supreme—white, peaceful, auspicious. On her right is Parāparā, the Supreme-Non-Supreme—red, active. On her left is Aparā, the Non-Supreme—black, furious. These goddesses are themselves emanations from the absolute supreme goddess Kalāsaṃkarṣiṇī, the Destroyer of Time, who cannot be visualized because she is totally transcendent. The yogi to be initiated thus sees, mentally ranged along and above his body, the whole cosmic manifestation as existing in Śiva. Since the trident reaches above his head, he mentally follows an ascending movement going infinitely above his body up to the point where the cosmos dissolves in the Absolute with which he is connected. He is carried out in the infinite movement of the divine cosmic energy, which both pervades and transcends him. Insofar as this is possible, he exists cosmically (see figure 1). A similar bodily cosmic pattern is to be found in other, less complex, initiation rituals, where one uses mantras to place cosmic divisions on the body of the initiate who—thus "mantrified" and identified with sections of the cosmos—transcends his normal human condition for as long as the ritual lasts.

The other instance of a Tantric mental projection experienced in the body comes from a Śrīvidyā work, the *Yoginīhṛdaya*, whose main deity is Tripurasundarī. The ritual worship of this goddess ends, like all Tantric *pūjās*, with the recitation (*japa*) of the deity's mantra, the *śrīvidyā*, which consists of fifteen syllables divided into three clusters, all ending with *HRĪṂ*. This *japa* is not a mere vocal (audible or inaudible) enunciation of the mantra but a yogic practice linked to the ascent of *kuṇḍalinī* in the officiating adept's (yogic) body. Thus, the adept is to imagine the five syllables of the first part of the *śrīvidyā* (*HA SA KA LA HRĪṂ*) as present in his lowest *cakra* (*mūlādhāra*). He is then to imagine the second cluster (*HA SA KA HA LA HRĪṂ*) in the heart *cakra* and the third cluster (*SA KA LA HRĪṂ*) in the *cakra* between his eyebrows (*bhrūmadhya*). The enunciation of these three *HRĪṂ*, like that of all mantras ending with *Ṃ*, is deemed to be prolonged by a subtle phonic vibration (*nāda*), which goes through eight ever-subtler stages, called *kalās*. The highest and subtlest of these stages, the "transmental" (*unmanā*), finally dissolves in the silence of the Absolute.

This being so, the *japa* consists of the mental utterance (*uccāra*) of the three parts of the *śrīvidyā*. The adept first enunciates their phonemes in each of the *cakras*—in each case from *HA* or *SA* to the *bindu*, *Ṃ*—then lengthens the mental pronunciation (*uccāra*) of *Ṃ* by the eight *kalās* of *HRĪṂ*, from *bindu* to *samanā*. This subtle vibration ascends from *mūlādhāra* to the heart for the first cluster, from the heart to the *bhrūmadhya* for the second cluster, and from *bhrūmadhya* to the *dvādaśānta* for the third, where it reaches its

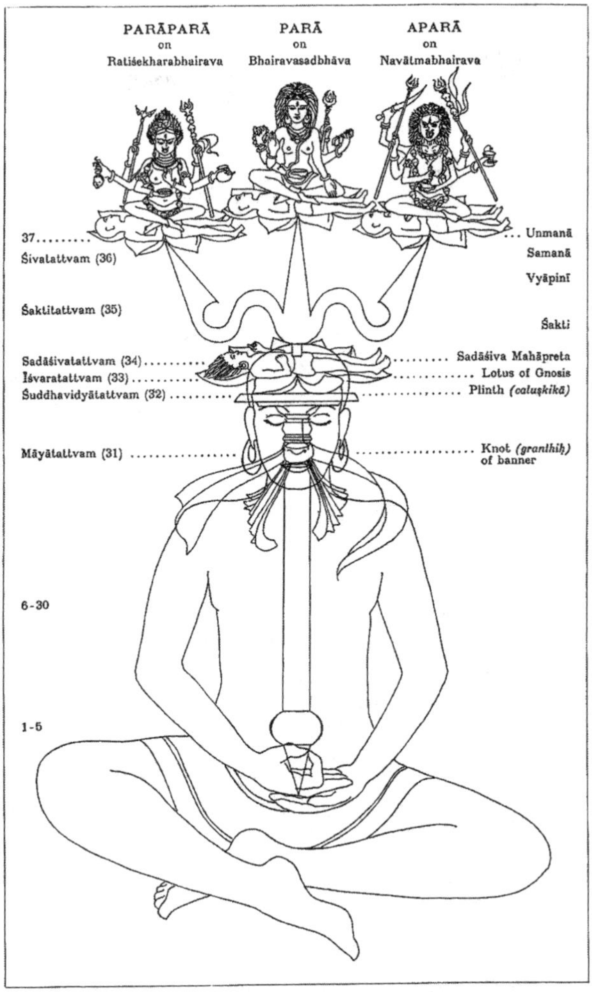

The maṇḍala throne and the three goddesses enthroned upon it, as visualised along the axis of internal sensation during internal worship. See TĀ 15.295c-328b.

FIGURE 1

ultimate level. It does this together with the last *kalā* (*unmanā*), the transmental vibration of the two first *HRĪṂ*s, with which it intermingles. There, the phonic vibration unites with and disappears into the Absolute together with the consciousness of the adept, who will unite with the godhead. Thus, the adept goes through a liberating spiritual experience with the ascent of the mantra in the *suṣumnā*.[12]

Practices of this kind, where mantras are imagined and mentally seen as travelling along the *nāḍīs* of the yogic body so as to divinize it and lead the adept toward salvation, are found in a large number of Kaula and Nātha texts, as well as in saṃhitās of the Pāñcarātra.

Mudrās

Mudrā, divine seal imprinted on the world.
B. BÄUMER

The literal meaning of the Sanskrit term *mudrā* is seal. A *mudrā* is thus that which "seals," that which confirms or supports an utterance (or an action). This is how mudrās are usually understood or made use of. When a mantra is placed by *nyāsa,* it is placed with a *mudrā,* which is a hand gesture supporting and reinforcing the efficacy of an utterance. A *mudrā* is always a conventional gesture—it is not any spontaneous or arbitrary movement or bodily stance. It is a rule-governed action: the finger or hand positions that make up a *mudrā* are carefully described in ritual manuals, for they have a meaning and a symbolic value and are considered to have a ritual efficacy. Like mantras, they are only effective when performed as prescribed, in the proper circumstances.

The symbolic role of mudrās in classical Indian dance (then often named *hasta*) is well known. Mudrās are, however, used in all kinds of Hindu rites. Their role and forms are markedly important in Tantra, where their function is not merely symbolic. They are ritually performative elements of a ritual action. Because they are consciously and bodily performed, they identify the officiating adept with the action he is performing and thus with the power or deity being invoked or manipulated. In Nātha haṭhayoga, too, there are mudrās that assist in the preservation and raising of the essence of life (*bindu*),[13] in other words, of semen.

During the Tantric worship of deities (*pūjā*), mudrās are often displayed by the officiant. Some merely accompany the utterance of a mantra, "sealing"—that is, confirming—its efficacy. However, they are more than mere gestures accompanying the utterance. They corporally express the action being performed, thus implicating the body and mind of the performer in what he is not simply doing but vitally experiencing. A *mudrā* can also be considered as a gesture that does something, produces an effect, by itself. For instance (in a Śaiva cult), the officiating adept would attract the purificatory power embodied by an (imagined) river with the hook *mudrā,* then fasten it to its place with the resorption *mudrā.* These two actions are achieved by ritual gestures. In a similar ritual, the *liṅgamudrā,* a gesture made with both hands intertwined is deemed to "affect" the sexual union of Śiva and Śakti—a symbolical action, of course, but actually realized through bodily movements.

According to the *Tantrāloka*, mudrās performed during *pūjā* reinforce the presence of the deity. At the end of worship, a *mudrā* is used to resorb the deity being worshipped into the worshipper, thus reinforcing his unity with it. All this shows the efficacy of Tantric mudrās.

Different instances of such mudrās can be found in the *Vijñānabhairava*, where mere bodily postures, or the fact of looking intently on a precise point together with mental concentration, are described as mudrās fusing the performer with the Absolute. The most extreme form of this mystical view of mudrās is probably found in *Tantrāloka* 4, 200: "The yogi immersed in Kula"—in divine energy, that is—"who staggers inebriated by the essence of Bhairava which pervades him entirely, whatever posture his body assumes is a *mudrā*." In the same way, Kṣemarāja, commenting on *Śivasūtra* 3.26, says, "The Sage constantly sealed by mudrās born spontaneously from his body is a 'bearer of mudrās.' All others bear merely their bones." In such cases, we may well consider there is no real *mudrā* but merely the way the liberated in life "lives" his body. This transcendence of the body through the body is a very typical feature of the Tantric vision.

The case of the mudrās of the *Yoginīhṛdaya* (1.56–71) is especially interesting. The commentary describes the ten mudrās the adept is to display as hand gestures symbolizing ten goddesses—the Mudrās—as well as *being* these deities at the same time. The deities that will be worshipped during the *pūjā* are first to be made present, the adept visualizing them in ten different places of his yogic body, identifying with them by intense meditation (*bhāvanā*). These mudrās, therefore, are not only displayed, acted out, but "lived."

The term *mudrā* is also used (in the *Tantrāloka*, for instance) for the sexual union of a yogi with his female ritual partner, a bodily activity that is believed to "seal" him with the Absolute. The ten mudrās described in the *Haṭhayogapradīpikā* are also bodily attitudes meant to bring about a transcendental experience. Particularly interesting is the meaning and scope ascribed to mudrās in the thirty-second chapter of *Tantrāloka*. According to this text, there are four kinds of mudrās: hand gestures, bodily postures or movements, the act of maintaining a state of identity with a mantra, or a mental state (*citta*) consisting of a state of identification with the deity visualized or meditated upon. Abhinavagupta says that in this last case, the *mudrā* appears from the deity, arising from an original divine image, and causes the yogi to reproduce the appearance and nature of the deity. Also described in that chapter are notably different forms of *khecarīmudrās*, which are complex and bizarre yogic practices combining hand gestures, strange facial expressions, and the utterance of sounds such as *hā-hā* together with mental concentration and visualizations. These practices "cause the presence of deity" wherever one may be and bring about an identification of the adept with the deity.

Nyāsa

Nyāsa, the ritual placing or depositing on the body of a mantra (of a supernatural power, that is) or of some other element, divine or mundane, is a frequent and important practice in Tantra. It is done according to precise rules given in Tantras and ritual works. It is made use of in most (not necessarily Tantric) Hindu rituals. The practice goes back to ancient forms of ritual, where touching meant transmitting a supernatural power, practices also found outside Hinduism. It consists of placing, with one-pointed attention, a mantra on the body with a *mudrā*, while uttering it vocally or mentally and mentally evoking (or visualizing) the aspect (or sometimes the written form) of the mantra, supernatural entity, or power being placed. It is both a bodily and a mental action—the mental aspect being sometimes considered as the more important and effective one.[14]

Nyāsas are made use of in many circumstances. A common use is during *pūjā*, which, even when non-Tantric, begins by assigning mantras to the body and hands of the officiant so as to purify—to divinize—him. This preliminary rite is necessary because one cannot approach a deity or touch any object used during worship if one is not pure—and even, for the Tantric *pūjā*, divinized[15]—a state that lasts only during the ritual action. To this effect, ritual manuals prescribe a number of *nyāsas*. One of the most important is on the hand (the *karanyāsa*), which transforms it into the "hand of Śiva" (*śivahasta*). With this *śivahasta*, one transforms the whole body into Śiva. This process is called *sakalīkaraṇa*, a transformation of the body of the officiant into the Sakala deity.

Such *nyāsas* can be very numerous. The *Yoginīhṛdaya*, for instance, prescribes four series of preliminary ritual placings, which is modest when compared to modern ritual handbooks, which may prescribe twenty series of *nyāsas* on different parts of the body, some including up to fifty different placings. Thus one places the root mantra of the deity (*mantranyāsa*), the mantra of the divine image (*mūrtinyāsa*), the so-called members and faces of the deity (*aṅga* and *vaktra-nyāsa*), the mantras of ancillary deities and of their seats or thrones (*devatānyāsa, pīṭha-/āsananyāsa*), and so on. The assigning of letters (*mātṛkānyāsa*)—that is, the *mātṛkās*, the phonemes not as mere letters but as aspects of the power of the Word—on the body, either on its surface (*bahir-mātṛkānyāsa*; "outer letter-placement") or on points of the inner yogic body (*antar*; "inner"), of which there are different sorts, is an important form of *nyāsa*. A particular form of this placing of phonemes of the alphabet is the *mālinīnyāsa*, where the phonemes are listed in apparent disorder, going from *NA* to *PHA* (see chapter 7). Even a *cakra* or *maṇḍala* can be placed by *nyāsa* on the body of the officiant—as, for instance, the *śrīcakra* at the outset of the *pūjā* of Tripurasundarī. Deities, spiritual forces, or cosmic divisions are placed on icons or on ritual diagrams (*maṇḍalas*) used for worship, or on objects to be sanctified or divinized, by *nyāsa*, too. For example, one consecrates a rosary by placing its mantra on it and infusing it with the power of the deity.

Nyāsas are not necessarily made on a precise, limited part of the body. They may also be spread out on the whole body by one ritual gesture. This is called a spreading (*vyāpaka*) *nyāsa*.

The practice of *nyāsa* in its more complex forms is perhaps comparatively recent, but it goes back to an ancient past and, above all, it is founded on an ancient way of conceiving, apprehending, and "living" the body in religion and asceticism (a case of what T. J. Csordas calls "embodied knowledge"). India has always invested the religious and the cosmic in the body, and *nyāsa*—placing cosmic elements in the body—actualizes its cosmic potentialities and correspondences, an actualization that is the very goal of Tantric practices. Hence its importance.

Other bodily mental practices could be cited. In effect, all ritual practices are, in some respect, somatopsychic (bodily and mental), since they consist of actions and gestures mentally followed and vitally experienced by the officiant. In India, as elsewhere, there is no discontinuity between body and mind in action. In Tantric *pūjā*, as we shall see (and as we saw about mudrās), many actions are accompanied by (or even sometimes consist of) visualizations, which are sometimes bodily acted out. In Tantric initiation (*dīkṣā*), cosmic divisions mentally imagined by the initiate, are assigned to parts of his body. In the initiation by penetration (*vedhadīkṣe*), the initiating guru, tightly embracing his disciple mouth to mouth, transfers his breath, which is charged with the initiatory mantra, to the disciple who inhales it. All sexual ritual practices are both bodily and mental, including mantras, mental concentration, and visualizations, which give their "mystical" value to the bodily actions being performed and are therefore inseparable from them. The yogin often acts while being in what one may call an "altered state of consciousness." But in many cultures, prayer, which is mental, is associated with bodily attitudes or gesture. Mystical experience goes through the body, as Marcel Mauss noted.[16] In Tantra, *bhāvanā* (from the Sanskrit root *BHŪ*; "to become," "to come into being"), a deep, intense meditation—which both creates images in the mind and identifies the meditator with this creation—brings him to feel such mental images as present in himself and plays (as we have already seen) a great role in a number of circumstances. It is an important form of action of mind on body—or rather, of the interaction or interpenetration of the body and the mind. In the following sections, we shall see its importance in ritual as well as in the spiritual domain.

Tantra Alchemy and Medicine

Alchemy (*rasaśāstra* or *rasāyana*), the "science" or the "way" of humors (or bodily fluids), has held a significant place among Indian magical or religious speculations and practices from ancient times down to our days. Its origins are pre-Tantric, going back as far as the *Atharvaveda*, and it is present outside of the Tantric field. But it developed as an aspect of Tantra. The oldest alchemical texts we know of are Tantric. One such work prescribes the use of Tantric mantras and of *maṇḍalas* for the initiation of alchemists. Tantric formulas bestowing supernatural powers (*siddhi*) are used to consecrate alchemical instruments and substances. Like the Tantras, alchemical texts inextricably mix together cosmic, mental, spiritual, and bodily yogic elements. However, their ideology and aim are different, the main concern of Indian alchemy being this-worldly—bodily perfection, the mastery of bodily fluids, immortality gained through the use of drugs (notably by the calcination of metals, especially mercury). Its aim is not, as often in Tantra, transcendentally oriented—that is to say, aimed at spiritual progress or liberation (even if this sometimes includes the quest for mundane satisfactions and of supernatural powers). In Tantra (couldn't one say in India?), spiritual perfection entails the presence of such powers.[17] But the two domains sometimes intermingle. The Nātha Siddhas are proponents of alchemy; Tantric deities, aspects of Śiva (notably Maheśvara), and goddesses such as Kubjikā are evoked or described as to be propitiated in the *Rasārṇava*, one of the main alchemical treatises. The subject is complex and interesting, but I cannot expatiate on it in this overview.[18]

Traditional Indian medicine (*āyurveda*), whose sources go back to post-Vedic times—its classical texts dating from the first century CE—is basically a rational system, but it includes magicoreligious elements coming from popular beliefs and from Tantra. This medicine, being essentially psychosomatic and linked in some respects to yoga and alchemy, includes quite naturally the use of mantras (Vedic or Tantric), ritual diagrams (*yantra*, *mantra*), mudrās, and alchemical drugs and remedies. Today, there are, as in the past, Tantric medical practitioners. Medical (Tantric) mantras of various kinds are used in placing (*nyāsa*), in charms or protective amulets (*kavaca*, *rakṣa*), or in formulas (*dhāraṇī*). Exorcism by Tāntrikas is also used medically to fight possession by hostile powers, demons, or deities.[19]

These few instances show the main role of the body—or rather, of the body-mind—in Tantra. In later sections I will discuss other instances of the role of the body in ritual, meditation, and spiritual experience. The body one refers to here is (as I have said) not the physical, concrete one, limited by our skin, but the body with whose image we live, the "dear pursuing presence,"[20] with which we "exist" and interact with the world. The Tāntrika's body-mind image is merely more complicated.

The Tāntrika, like everyone else, has a body and limbs, but he is also sexed. Sex and sexuality as a vital fact and as a notion plays a central role in Tantra, and I will explain a number of sex-related speculations and practices in the next chapter.

6

Sex

Else a great prince in prison lies
To our bodies turne we then.

JOHN DONNE, *The Extasie*

In the West, Tantra is nearly always associated with sex, which is widely considered its main aspect. This is a misunderstanding, for though the place of sex in Tantra is ideologically essential, it is not always so in action and ritual. Sexual practices do exist and were, as we have seen in chapter 2, very important in the beginnings of Tantra. Ritual sex was, it seems, one of the main traits of the earlier small Kāpālika groups, but they lost their prevalence when Tantra spread to other larger social groups. I must also add that the place of sex in Tantra is nothing else than a more intense, systematic, and diversified version of a very ancient Indian perception of sex.

The sexual differentiation is a basic element in the Indian vision of the cosmos and in its conception of human beings and of their place in the universe. From the Vedic period, all creation was understood as resulting from a sexual union or from the conjunction of two sexually different elements. The sexual metaphor is pervasively present. It is sometimes found in what are, for us, unexpected cases. For instance, in a passage of the *Śatapathabrāhmaṇa*, one of the main texts of the ancient brahmanical exegetical tradition, the Mīmāṃsā, speech is described as born from the sexual conjunction (*mithunā*) of the two lips. The *Brāhmana* also says that speech may come out silently, as sperm is emitted silently. In Sāṃkhya, cosmic manifestation results from the conjunction of the male Puruṣa with the female Prakṛti. And there is a remarkable passage on the cosmic aspect of human sexual union in the *Bṛhadāraṇyaka-upaniṣad* (6. 4, 3). The Sanskrit term *vīrya* means "force," "power," as well as "sperm." This presence of the sexual element, or of the sexual metaphor, was taken over and infinitely developed—in myth, metaphysics, and theology (deities usually have a consort of the opposite sex), and therefore in ritual, as well as in ascesis and yoga—in the Tantric domain, where a principal means for transcending the empirical self and uniting with the Absolute is through the use of *kāma* (Eros; passion). Tantra made use of one of the main human urges while also stressing its transgressive side, Tantric sexual ritual practices being contrary to Hindu orthodox rules of purity.

Tantric ritual sexual practices, or, more generally, the transgression of brahmanical norms of behavior, explain the bad image Tantra often has in India. Many Sanskrit literary works are proof of this critical attitude—some instances were quoted in chapter 3. In the nineteenth and early twentieth centuries, those in India who wished to reform Hinduism by ridding it of its "superstitions and impurities," influenced as they often were by the British prejudices of those times, strongly condemned Tantric practices. Orientalists in the West, after first being shocked by the sexual side of Tantra, now tend to look at it mainly from that angle. This, I feel, is a rather biased view, for although sex, whether as a metaphor or as founding and patterning ritual practices, is in many ways at the very heart of the Tantric vision of man and of his presence in the world, I believe it never had more than a limited place in the Tāntrika's religious experience and practices.[1] This view, of course, presupposes seeing (as I do here) Tantra as it is—that is, as permeating the whole Hindu domain, not as limited to the teachings of the Kula.

Kāma, which is central to Tantra, is not merely sex or desire but passion, a joyful, receptive opening to and enjoying of the beauty, fullness, and infinite diversity of the world, knowing how to live in it while also transcending it. Sex is just a part of this. Moreover, the ritual uses of sex as described in Tantras are usually said to be secret, taking place only during particular rites and practiced only by a few initiated and fully qualified adepts. The guiding rules for such practices are binding, precise, and complicated. Sexual union is a means to overstep the limits of the empirical self, to unite with the godhead—it is not to be enjoyed for pleasure. For the male practitioner, there is also the search for power or for a greater vital force drawn from the feminine partner, since power, energy (*śakti*), is feminine, and therefore is possessed by women.

This view of the feminine is not peculiar to Tantra; it is a generally Indian trait. Woman holds the power, which man can draw from her, but he might lose it when emitting his seed (an ever present fear). Hence the ambiguous Indian view of woman: the source of power, she is also the cause of its loss. Protective, maternal, she is also dangerous. Testimonies to this attitude can be found in a number of Indian texts, and even more so in masculine behavior, from post-Vedic times to the present day. In India, woman may be divinized, but in practice, in social life, she is often considered and treated as inferior—"Déesse et esclave" (goddess and slave), as a French scholar of Indian anthropology once said.[2]

Tantric traditions or systems do not all give the same importance and role to sexual practices. There are none in the Pāñcarātra—among Vaiṣṇavas, only the Sahajiyās of Bengal include any. Among the Śaiva traditions, the sexual union of the yogi with a female partner (*dūtī*) is considered a characteristic trait of Kaula systems. It is not a general rule. And when there are such practices, they are far from prominent. One finds them in the older saṃhitās of the Śaivasiddhānta, but not in the more recent, "classical" āgamas, which expound the basic and generally practiced Śaiva teachings.

If Tantric sex is criticized in India, it is because it is transgressive, since it violates the very strict brahmanical rules of behavior and ritual purity. Not because it is "sinful." The Christian prejudice against sex remained unknown to India, whether Hindu, Buddhist, or Jain, until colonial times. In India, sex is seen as a natural human activity of great importance and consequence. It is submitted to precise rules but devoid by itself of moral connotations. Its practice and the attachment to it, however, binds human beings to the pleasures and pains of this world and is also a waste of a power that could more usefully be stored, increased, and/or used for higher transcendental aims. The Tantric view of sex is a particular form of this general Indian view.

A "Sexed" Theology, Sex and Metaphysics

A characteristic trait of Tantric pantheons, as we have seen, is that deities go by sexed pairs: Śiva and Pārvatī, Bhairava and Kālī, Tripurasundarī and Bhairava, Viṣṇu and Lakṣmī, and so forth. In Yāmala Śākta Tantras, the different forms of the Goddess dominate their male consort and are often depicted as seated on his shoulder. When a deity has a Tantric and a non-Tantric form, the Tantric one has a consort of the opposite sex. For instance, Gaṇeśa (or the Gaṇeśas; they may number fifty-one[3]), when Tantric, is generally shown as ithyphallic, a goddess seated on his left thigh holding his phallus.

We also saw that, in Tantra, the supreme godhead is deemed to be polarized as masculine and feminine, the male principle being metaphysically (if not always theologically and ritually) above the female one, which is, however, the pole of power (*śakti*). There are bisexual divine forms (*ardhanarīśvara*), "the Lord half woman"—Śiva, for instance. In the Trika, the Kashmirian school of nondualistic Śaivism, the godhead, metaphysically conceived as the Supreme Consciousness—unique, nondual—is also, inseparably, conscious light (*prakāśa*; masculine) and self-awareness (*vimarśa*; feminine), which is its aspect of life, power, and Word.[4] Other instances of the pervasiveness of sexual symbolism and metaphors could easily be adduced.

The reader knows, of course, that the usual icon of Śiva, in temples and elsewhere, is the *liṅga*, which, though in practice most often a mere column, is a phallic symbol. Its base is inserted in a more or less triangular plinth, conceived of as a *yoni*, a female sexual organ. The sexual symbolism of this icon is clear (though usually not perceived by devotees, while some Indian scholars persist in denying the fact).

The *kuṇḍalinī*, very important in Tantra, is also symbolically sexual. It is the (female) divine energy as present in the yogic body, which ascends along the *suṣumnā* to unite with Śiva above the yogi's head. This ascent is sometimes described as resulting from a tight contact or embracing (*saṃghaṭṭa*; a term that has a sexual connotation in Sanskrit) with Śiva.[5]

Obviously, sex is present in Tantric ritual when symbolized or depicted by the icon used for worship (Kālī united with Śiva, or the Goddess's *yoni* in the Kāmākhyā temple in Assam, for instance), when evoked by mantras or mantric practices, or symbolically embodied in a *mudrā*. The *śrīcakra*'s and the *śrīvidyā*'s salvific efficacy, when meditated on and ritually worshipped, is due to the fact that these two symbols embody the creative union of Tripurasundarī and Bhairava.

More explicitly sexual is another diagram of the Śrīvidyā tradition, the *kāmakalā*, made up of two superimposed triangles. The upturned triangle symbolizes Śiva, while the downturned triangle symbolizes his consort, Śakti. Of this six-pointed figure, the upper apex is the face or mouth of Śakti and is also the first letter of the alphabet, *A* (and the Sun, which is male). It is passion (*kāma*). The lower point of the feminine triangle is the sexual organ (*yoni*) of Śakti, which is the letter *HA*, the last letter of the alphabet.[6] On the ends of the lower horizontal line of the figure are the breasts of Śakti, one with Fire, the other with Moon. They are both *kalā* (limiting power). In the center of the diagram is *kuṇḍalinī* in the form of the Sanskrit letter *Ī*, or, more exactly, the *bījamantra ĪṂ*. Erect, she extends from the lowest to the topmost part of the figure, which can thus be meditatively seen as the body of the goddess, composed of head, breasts, and *yoni*—which is her "nether mouth" (*adhovaktra*), whence comes initiatory wisdom (see figure 2).[7] According to some iconographical treatises, the *kāmakalā* diagram is the pattern underlying some erotic temple sculptures showing a male and a female figure in sexual union.

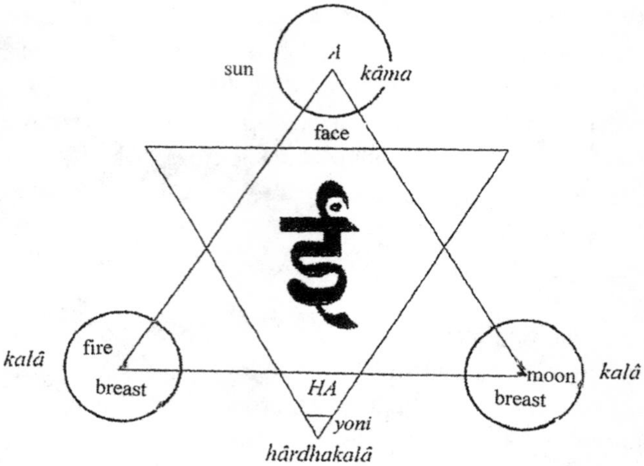

The *kāmakalā* diagram

FIGURE 2

Ritual Sex

Sexual symbolism plays a role in a number of Tantric rites, which sometimes also include sexual practices. These are certainly very ancient, but we do not know how and where they appeared. There are no such rites in the Veda.[8] They would therefore be autochthonous, born from the Indian soil. But the sexual metaphor is also Vedic. The conjunction of these two sources may have given birth to Tantric ritual sex—it being however understood that action does not originally follow thought: it appears as a spontaneous gesture of the body, which afterwards is explained, enriched, and further developed by theoretical thought.

Be that as it may, the first such rites we believe we know of were arguably those of small ascetic groups, worshippers of fearsome, sometimes theriomorphic (or "therianthropic") female deities, Yoginīs. In these ecstatic rites, the sexual unions of devotees of both sexes provided fluids that were first offered in oblation to the deities and then partaken of by the worshippers. Such groups tended to disappear in the course of time, but their practices have survived. Prescribed in particular rituals and meant for initiates, such practices are not likely to have been very widespread. Their importance is essentially symbolic, for the point in their case is for the practitioner to acquire a power whose source is feminine and is all the more powerful because, in orgasm, female fluid is mixed with male sperm (*vīrya*) and is therefore part of the creative power of the sexual conjunction: force and the overstepping of all limitations. Such oblations are prescribed in the cults of feminine deities, high or low, in those of the different aspects of Śiva, and are used in some initiations. In oblations, these sexual fluids are usually mixed with some alcoholic beverage and/or with flesh (animal or human), as well as (in the most transgressive cults) with other excretions (including excrement). They are used as excipients and also to intensify the bodily, vital, and transgressive side of the practice. According to Kaula texts, the best chalice for such oblations is a human skull adorned with incisions (*tūra*). The oblation is sometimes a small ball made with such elements, called *kuṇḍagola* or *kuṇḍagolaka*, "a small ball (*gola*) coming from a ritual pit (*kuṇḍa*)," the pit being the *yoni* of the feminine partner of the ritual.

A common practice in Tantra is the worship of the feminine sexual organ (*yoni*). To worship it is to worship the source of the universe, the mouthpiece of Revelation, the place where one fuses with the Absolute—the mouth of the Yoginī (*yoginīvaktra*). This cult is described in a short text, the *Yonitantra*.[9] According to this Tantra, the *yoni* must be that of a loose woman, or prostitute,[10] or of the beloved of the performer. She is not described except that she must have pubic hair. She is to be seated on the yogi's left thigh. He adorns her, paints her *yoni* with sandal paste, makes her drink an alcoholic beverage, paints a red crescent on her forehead, recites a mantra 108 times, kisses her, then unites with her. The discharges then emitted from the so-called *yonitattva*, the supreme essence (*uttamatattva*) are offered to the Goddess, for she is the one really being worshipped. This mixture is also ingested by the adept, who will thus gain power and sanctification. According to the Tantra, the adept who continually recites "*yoni, yoni*" will gain favor with the Goddess and obtain both supernatural powers and liberation. This simple rite is described somewhat differently and sometimes with more details (there is a veritable vaginal cartography) in other texts, but the pattern and the meaning of the ritual is always the same.

The *Yonitantra* is a Vaiṣṇava text from Bengal, a part of India where Tantric worship of the Goddess remains most alive. Not far is Assam (*Kāmarūpa*, in Sanskrit) where a temple has been built in Kāmākhyā (near Gauhati) where it is said that the *yoni* of the progressively dismembered body of Pārvatī, Śiva's spouse, fell as he roamed across India bearing the body on his shoulders. Its carved stone representation in the temple "bleeds" once each year.

A particularly transgressive (because of its setting and its nature) sort of sexual union, prescribed in some Tantras, is performed at night in a burning ground, the officiating partners resting on a corpse.[11]

The most detailed description of a ritual sexual union that I know of is that of the so-called Sacrifice of Kula (*kulayāga*), or Primordial Sacrifice (*ādiyāga*), for it is deemed to be the main ritual of the Kula tradition, expounded in the first 166 stanzas of the twenty-ninth chapter of Abhinavagupta's *Tantrāloka*. The description is based on the teachings of ancient nondualistic Tantras (*Brahmayāmala, Jayadrathayāmala, Triśirobhairava, Mālinīvijaya*, etc.), which are also abundantly quoted in Jayaratha's commentary. It is a "secret ceremony," "suited only to the most advanced gurus and disciples." However, I cannot give more than a brief survey of this complex ritual.[12]

The practitioner of such a ritual—totally involved, body and mind, in what he is doing, or rather, experiencing—is to be a perfect, accomplished being (a *siddha*), endowed with supernatural faculties, a "hero" (*vīra*) mastering his *kuṇḍalinī*, in full control of his sexuality. The female partner of the ritual (*dūtī*), the "messenger," is supposed to be endowed with the same degree of excellence as the yogi. In his commentary, Jayaratha says she is not to be chosen "because of lust" but "for the sake of achieving steadiness [of mind]." The practicing pair is aiming at liberation, not looking for pleasure. She is also to be chosen "without regard to caste, etc." (29, 101).[13]

To begin the ritual, the initiated and fully qualified adept is to enter with his *śakti*, his *dūtī*, into the "hall of sacrifice"—a consecrated area or pavilion perfumed with incense and "decorated with flowers, etc." He purifies first himself, then the instruments for the rite, with the main mantras of the Kula tradition, and he prepares the chalice (preferably a *tūra*) for the oblations, which include alcohol and flesh. He then draws and places the support of the worship on the ground, a square cloth and a *maṇḍala* on which gods will be placed (*nyāsa*) by their mantras, as well as *śaktis* with whom he is mentally to unite. The ritual, consisting mainly of mental visualizations created by creative meditation (*bhāvanā*), is basically a mental, spiritual action—a manipulation of supernatural entities for which one may consider the bodies of the acting partners as merely concrete supports.

This being so, the yogi, holding his *śakti*, the *dūtī*, close to himself, begins the ritual. The two partners are first to worship each other, to awaken their "wheels of power" (*cakras*), to create a mutually shared state of sensory and spiritual—bodily and mental—rapture and exaltation. States of consciousness are experienced, "lived," with and through the body.[14] Circles of deities are invoked, made mentally present and animated, and worshipped. In addition to kisses, fondling and other preliminaries are added so as to bring about this state of emotional rapture. The beauty of the place, which is adorned with flowers, perfumed by incense, furnished with food, and so on, demonstrates the essential aesthetic side of Tantric rites.[15] The yogi and his partner are thus deemed to become intensely conscious of their inner essence, together with the circles of goddesses mentally made present, which "expands" thanks to these sensory elements. They reach a state of blissful vibration (*spanda*) where their sense of personal bodily identity disappears in the bliss (*ānanda*) of other-worldly consciousness, a bliss both sensuous and beyond all sensation.

The adept is now to worship the "main wheel" of his partner, the "mouth of the Yoginī" (*yoginīvaktra*)—her sexual organ, that is—"from which knowledge is obtained," "the essence of bliss" (Jayaratha, *ad* 29, 127). He is to unite with her, the ejaculated sperm and her vaginal secretions "reciprocally passed from mouth to mouth." The commentary explains that, after having "agitated" his partner (by having sexual intercourse, that is), the yogi is to offer the mixture to "the circle of the deities of Kula, Gaṇeśa, etc."—who are as much actors of the ritual process as the yogi and his *dūtī*—and drink the substances they have thus produced (mixed with water and an alcoholic beverage[16]) with them. The deities are then worshipped, first before the "mouth of the Yoginī," then on the yogi's body. These ejaculates, it is said, are "a most pure substance since it is identical with consciousness" (29, 128); they are *kula*, the Supreme. The partners now reach a state of absorption in peaceful bliss tending toward union with the divine, then they experience an "outpouring of fully surging consciousness" (29, 139). The *Tantrāloka* and the commentary explain that though the body, with its centers and its seventy-two thousand *nāḍis*, is wholly involved in the process, the sexual actions and their products are of a supernatural, divine nature. The acting partners, as I have said, are not (in their minds, as they imagine it) dealing with human, natural substances and actions and living altered states of consciousness but with supernatural elements and deities deemed to be ever present. This is the essential aspect of the process that creates and "satiates" them, a process that takes place and is psychologically "lived" on a supernatural, divine plane by the officiating partners. For them, it is a play of deities and divine powers, not a mere human ritual action. Of course, we do not know how far, how deeply, their bodies—the images of their bodies—are actually penetrated, transformed by the Other they invoke and wish to fuse with. But that is another question.

In this respect, I will also note the essentially "technical" nature of the process as it is described by Abhinavagupta and Jayaratha. It is a work of the yogi who mentally manipulates supernatural powers. There is, it seems, no descent from above, no divine grace (*śaktipāta*), but an upward-tending human action. Though, of course, the reference to the Supreme is always there.

At the end of the ritual, a ritual recitation of a mantra (*japa*) is performed

(300,000 times), which is also an intense meditative process. It is followed by another worship at the "mouth of the Yoginī." Then another sexual union is to take place, where the two partners make all their powers unite and interpenetrate. This ends with the total fusion of the yogi's consciousness with the Supreme. He enters in the ever peaceful state of Śiva, described as "a luminous sea of subsiding waves." He is "liberated while living," identified with the supreme Bhairava (*id.* 162). If a child is conceived during this last ritual intercourse, it is said to be "Yoginī-born" (*yoginībhū*). He is "a repository of knowledge, a Rudra. Even in the womb . . . he is a form of Śiva." (According to Jayaratha, Abhinavagupta was such a child.)

We see that, as in most Tantric rites, this ritual is continuously carried out with the utterance of mantras and, more important, with a continual succession of mental visualizations (of deities and of the yogic body), all of which are the essential constitutive parts of the process, which is efficacious only insofar as deities are made present by being mentally created and "perceived." The ritual is a bodily, sexual action, but performed and "lived" by the acting pair on a spiritual, divine plane, resulting in a fusing experience of the Absolute.[17]

Because Abhinavagupta's and Jayaratha's descriptions are based on several Tantras of the Kula, we may assume that in those times (tenth through the twelfth centuries), it was fairly well known in Kaula circles and put into practice by a few ascetic *virtuosi.* The last prescribed conjunction would give birth to a child, which does not seem to be the usual case in other such Tantric rites, whether ancient or modern, where the act appears to end with some sort of *coitus interruptus*—in most cases, ejaculation was carefully avoided. This is because the aim of the ritual is to increase the power of the male actor to obtain either supernatural powers (*siddhis*) or more energy to seek liberation. In such cases, avoiding seminal loss would be essential. (This, as I have already said, is an ancient, basic concern of the Indian male.) The sterility of the union may also result from the fact that, in some traditions, coition takes place during the menses of the female partner.[18] The yogi is thus to experience the full intensity of orgasm and feel united with the godhead but, by exercising mental control, he does not ejaculate. Moreover, he can increase his power by drawing in his partner's secretions.[19] If he ejaculates, he can also draw back the mingled products of the intercourse through his urethra using a particular physiological technique called *vajrolimudrā*, prescribed in such Nātha works as the *Haṭhapradīpikā* (2. 83–91) and aiming mainly at preserving the yogi's semen (*bindu*).[20] I believe that ancient texts such as the *Jayadrathayāmala* prescribe the same practice (which is still being used by some yogis in India today). It is also described in more recent works—for instance, the *Kaulāvalinirṇaya* or *Kaujñānanirṇaya*—which often show a remarkable inventiveness in this rather peculiar domain.[21] There are also Kubjikā texts that have a particular system of five *cakras* (of the yogic body and of Yoginīs) and works from the Krama tradition of Kashmir.

Whether of this kind or another, Tantric sexual ritual practices seem to have been more often used to gain supernatural or magical powers (*siddhis*) than to reach liberation.[22]

Those I have described or alluded to are meant for individual yogis or adepts. But there were (and are) also collective sexual rites—the "orgies" denounced by British missionaries—where the participating pairs of worshippers are placed in a circle around their guru on a consecrated area and have sex together. These rituals have a ritual ascetic *mise en scène* and are of the mental concentration and spiritual intensity we have seen. Because the female participants are considered ritual incarnations of Yoginīs (the male ones being *siddhas* because deemed to be spiritually "perfect"), such collective religious acts were called *yoginī-melana* or *yoginī-melaka*. These took place in various circumstances.[23]

Sex and Mystique

The ritual sex notions and actions we have seen, though transcendental in their aim, are essentially yogic, "technical," in practice. The ritual practitioners are devotees of their chosen deity. Theirs being usually a nondualistic context, they believe themselves to be "fragments," or "parts" (*aṃśa*) of Śiva or of the Goddess who are, in essence, absolute, all-embracing, pervasive Consciousness. They live "divinely." But gifted yogis as they are, they manipulate the divine forces they invoke and worship. In this respect, they are more ritual technicians (or perhaps magicians) than devotees. However, there is also devotion in Tantra (*bhakti*), even with sex.

Such is the case of the Vaiṣṇava Sahajiyā tradition of Bengal, with the cult of Kṛṣṇa and Rādhā. Its atmosphere, if very erotic, is intensely devotional. It is more a case of erotic mysticism than of ritual sex. It appeared and spread within Vaiṣṇavism as a development of the ancient—first Buddhist then Hindu—local Sahajiyā cult, while also being marked by the extremely devotional atmosphere of the local cult of Kṛṣṇa (illustrated in the same period by the famous devotee-saint Caitanya [1486–1533 CE], a Gauḍīya-vaiṣṇava—an exceptionally intense but not Tantric figure). I mentioned a few main traits of this tradition in chapter 4. I will add here that the devotee of Kṛṣṇa and Rādhā, wishing to identify with this divine pair of lovers, would replay their amorous *līlā* with a female partner. But he could also identify with the god's lover, Rādhā, a feminine role. He would then behave as a madly loving woman not only spiritually but at least in some aspects of his everyday life. This is another form—not limited to Tantra—of Indian erotic mysticism. Transvestism is mentioned in several Tantric texts, which often prescribe that the worshipper of a deity should dress like the deity he worships so as to better identify with that deity. This sometimes requires the officiating male to dress like a woman.[24]

All the cases we have seen are so many instances of the basic place given in Indian culture and, more specially, in Tantra to sex—whether as a bodily and mental action or as symbolically, metaphorically present. In most of these cases, sex is transcended because it opens a way to something that is very much "beyond the pleasure principle." It seems that Indians were more aware than other peoples of the fact that sex, love, passion is simultaneously pleasure, joy, *and* an opening to another, "higher" plane, so that one "lives" it while transcending it. In Tantra, sex is an aspect of the creative "agitation"—effervescence—of divine energy (*śaktikṣobha*). The yogi experiencing the "agitation" of sex participates, as it were, in the divine cosmic creative *kṣobha*, thus transcending his limitations. It is a mystical experience leading not to pleasure but to bliss (*ānanda*)—*brahman*, as one knows, is *ānanda*. For a yogi, pleasure, delight (*sukha*), can also lead to bliss. This is said in the *Vijñānabhairava* (68): "[The yogi] should project [concentrate, that is] his mind, which is pure delight (*sukha*), onto the middle point between fire and poison. It is then either isolated or filled with vital breath. [The yogi, then] is united with the bliss of sexual love (*smarānanda*)."

This stanza is understandable if one knows that "fire" and "poison" are technical terms for the beginning and the end of the sexual conjunction. They also refer to the contraction of *prāṇa* when entering the central tube (*suṣumnā*) at its base and then to its expansion at the apex; what takes place in the "middle," between these two points, is the ascent along the *suṣumnā* of *kuṇḍalinī*, the divine energy present in the human body. Thus, rising during the sexual conjunction, *kuṇḍalinī* reaches her terminal point together with the orgasm and then the yogi fuses with the Absolute.

Stanza 70 of the *Vijñānabhairava* is also worth quoting here: "O Goddess! even in the absence of a *śakti* (a woman), a flood of bliss appears by intensely calling to mind the pleasure [experienced with] a woman when kissing, caressing, embracing."

This should not be understood as erotic dreaming. The power of creative imagination is not at play here; it is the power of remembrance (*smr̥ti* or *smaraṇa*, in Sanskrit). For Śaiva nondualistic traditions, memory—bringing together a past event and a present one—is a transcending of time.[25] By destroying time's binding flow, remembrance bestows liberation from the fetters of this world. This calling to mind is so powerful that Abhinavagupta could say that remembrance "is at the root of all the modes of existence" and that "he who remembers is none other than the Supreme Lord." This is why remembering sex with the beloved—which is a mundane reproduction of a divine, cosmic activity—can open the path, for a yogi, to the Supreme.

7

The Tantric Word: Mantras

Car la parole est le Verbe et le Verbe est Dieu.
VICTOR HUGO

Vāc is the imperishable one, the first-born of the cosmic order, the Mother of the Vedas, the navel of immortality.
Taittirīyabrāhmaṇa 2.8.8,5

The belief that words are not merely names for different things or notions but that they may have a power or an efficacy of their own when uttered, spoken, or written by humans—that there are "performative utterances," "speech acts," or "illocutionary acts"[1]—is (with nuances) a universal fact. Poetry, too, may open new vistas, exude a creative power. The poets who "saw" the Vedas were seers (*rishis*) whose hymns, in their phonetic pattern, were powerful mantras.[2] The notion that poetry may have an evocative, eye-opening power is not uncommon nowadays. More specifically, the belief in the ritual and/or magical efficacy of stereotyped formulas such as mantras is found in all cultures. In India (and still more in Tantra), this belief gives rise to particularly varied and interesting developments.

Tantra having appeared—if marginally—within the brahmanical tradition, its conception and speculations on the Word (*vāc*), if not its practices and its ritual, are but developments of ancient Vedic notions, drawing them, however, to extremes. The identification of *brahman* and *vāc* is Vedic, as are the notions of the creative cosmic power of *vāc*; of its oral, phonic nature; of the importance of stereotyped formulas (utterances, rather) such as *OṂ*; of their presence in the body, and so forth. The fact that *vāc* is feminine was also early underlined. The wealth of speculations and of ritual practices bringing into play such "metalinguistic" elements goes back also to Vedic or early brahmanical times.[3] From such a starting point in the fifth century, Tantra built a huge, new, and infinitely diverse ensemble of notions and practices, forming one of the main aspects of Hindu Tantra as it existed and has survived into our time. These teachings are so important in Tantra that the term (in effect, a modern one) currently used to name them when taken all together, *mantraśāstra* ("the teaching of the mantras"), is often taken as synonymous with *tantraśāstra* ("the teaching of the Tantras"). Though modern and arbitrary in some respects, this identification is not entirely unfounded, for one of the characteristic traits of Tantra is that liberation as well as mundane or supernatural goals can only be reached through the power of mantras.

Of such a vast subject, I cannot but give a very cursory view, starting with metaphysical-mystical notions. I will then look at the role and place of *vāc*, or of phonetic elements, in the human (yogic) body, then take up the subject of mantras, which is the most important aspect—both theoretically and practically—of Tantric speculation. Finally, I will discuss the ritual, mystical, and spiritual practices on the powers of the Word.

Before tackling the subject, I would like to draw the reader's attention to the fact that in all these notions and practices, from Vedic times down to the present time, the word (the Word) was conceived as verbal, oral/aural, not written. In India, Revelation is "what is heard" (*śruti*)[4] and is to be transmitted orally—"from ear to ear," as one says in Sanskrit. It is not scripture, as we would say.

Indians are known for ascribing a particular importance to grammar. They are historically the first grammarians we know of. They are, however, also and mainly phoneticians—the first ones, too, and very remarkable ones. For them, only the eternally enunciated speaking Word (*vāc vadantī*) is divine, valid, and powerful. Admittedly, Tantras were written, but as mere transcriptions on a lower level of an oral revelation, spoken in heaven by a deity and therefore heard, then orally transmitted by a first master to a first disciple, and so forth down to our time. There is, of course, a wealth of written texts in India, sacred and profane. Sanskrit literature is probably the largest body of ancient texts in existence. Writing appeared in India before our era and was abundantly made use of, but merely for mundane, practical ends. The oral nature of the Word is the rule, even if (as we already saw) there are a few—religious or magical—written exceptions.

Another ancient and basic trait of *vāc* is that it is feminine and therefore innately a power (*śakti*). However, as we shall see, this does not prevent her from being presented in theological traditions as appearing first as an aspect of Śiva, and then as mantras, which are also masculine.

Not to be forgotten is that, for all Hindu traditions the Word is creative; objects exist only insofar as they are named. God brings the world into existence by naming it, which is precisely what we shall see presently.

The power and cosmic role of the Word—extolled in hymn 1.124 of *Ṛgveda*, which divides it into four—are extolled or described in many Tantric texts, Śaiva and Vaiṣṇava, the main metaphysical developments on the subject being those of the Śaiva traditions of Kashmir. Whatever their religious bias, however, the metalinguistic theories of all these traditions are based on the structure and rules of Sanskrit.

Bhartṛhari lived in Kashmir during the fifth century. A Śaiva, he is probably the most original Indian philosopher of language and religion. In his treatise "On the Sentence and the Word [*Vākyapadīya*]," he extolled grammar as first among all the sciences and the gateway to liberation. But one of the main and most important views of this philosophical semanticist—who followed the Veda in believing that *vāc* was the first source of everything divine or mundane that exists—was that the Absolute, *brahman*, was in essence "word-*brahman*" (*śabdabrahman*), the substrate and essence of all that exists (which became the common Tantric view), and therefore the inherent primordial ground of all human cognitions. He thus stated, "In this world, there is no idea that is not formulated by words. All knowledge appears as permeated by speech" (*Vākyapadīya*, 1.131). For him, all discursive knowledge or thought is necessarily expressed in and consists of speech (*śabda*), whose essence is the Word. Most of the notions or constructions underlying the Tantric philosophical or psychological notions we shall see in this chapter rest in some respect on the views of Bhartṛhari.

The Metaphysics of *Vāc*: Word and Cosmos

Many readers will surely be more interested in Tantric ritual or meditative uses of the Word or of language than in the philosophical aspects of *vāc*. However, these aspects will be looked at first because they underlay, or pattern, the other (more easily understandable) forms of Tantric word—mantras, notably. They are basic notions going back to Vedic times, present throughout Indian culture. More fundamentally, they are based on the grammatical structure and characteristics of Sanskrit, which is the "language of the gods," of Revelation, but also the language of Indian literate culture. For Indians of traditional Sanskrit culture, which is steeped in grammar, many aspects of their philosophical or literary discourse include, or are based on, grammatical notions or grammatical ways of thinking. Only in India could a poet, such as Kālidāsa, evoke the inseparable bond of lovers (Śiva and Pārvatī, in this case) by assimilating it to the link between a word and its meaning.[5]

A particular—and, for a Western mind, a surprising—trait of many of these metalinguistic speculations is their tendency to mix metaphysical constructions or cosmic elements with corporeal ones. Such an interweaving is not surprising, since (as we have seen) from early times, the human body was correlated with the cosmos in metaphysical constructions and cosmic visions (the *tattva* system, for instance) as well as in ritual—its structure being seen as corresponding with, or as analogous to, that of the cosmos, the deities residing in it, the divine forces animating it. *Vāc*, supremely divine, is first spoken (*vadantī*) cosmically and then by humans on a lower level.

But to be spoken is to be articulated, and Indian Tāntrikas were all the more conscious of this because they were not only grammarians but—I would say mainly—phoneticians, and therefore conscious of the way linguistic sounds are bodily produced. The letters of the Sanskrit alphabet, on which rest all these speculations and practices, are not enumerated in phonetic disorder, as our own alphabet is, but enumerated according to their nature and their basis of articulation. This being a natural, not an arbitrary, order, a philosophical construction could easily be elaborated combining phonetics—the sound and bodily element—and cosmic-metaphysical notions. Many Tantric texts describe or allude to the coincidence or interplay of these two levels, describing this as a phonic process going from its original transcendental source down to the spoken word—in Sanskrit, of course—either as the alphabet in its traditional order or as stages (both cosmic-metaphysical and lived in the human body-mind) of sound or as those nonlinguistic powerful utterances, the mantras.

Very typical of this interweaving of levels is a passage from the *Tantrasadbhāva*,[6] which runs,

> This *śakti* is called supreme, subtle, above all rules of conduct. Enclosing within herself the *bindu* of the heart,[7] her aspect is that of a serpent lying in deep sleep, O Umā. Sleeping there, O Illustrious One, she is not conscious of anything. Having cast within her womb moon, fire, sun, the planets, and the fourteen worlds,[8] this goddess is in a swoon as if poisoned. Then, O Fair One, she is awakened by the supreme sound[9] whose nature is gnosis, being churned[10] by the *bindu* resting in her belly. This whirling churning movement goes on in the body of Śakti, this cleaving in herself resulting first in very brilliant light-drops (*bindus*). Once awakened by this, [she becomes] the force (*kalā*), Kuṇḍalinī, the Supreme One, the *bindu*, staying in her belly, being possessed of a fourfold [limiting] force (*kalā*).[11] By the union of the Churner and of Her that is being churned,[12] this [*Kuṇḍalinī*] becomes straight, O Dear One. This [Śakti], when she abides between two *bindus* is called Jyeṣṭhā. Being agitated (*kṣobha*) by the *bindu*, the immortal Kuṇḍalinī becomes straight and is then known as Rekhinī (Straight), having a *bindu* at each of her two ends.[13] She is also known as Tripathā ("the Threefold Path") and is celebrated under the name of Raudrī. She is [also] called Rodhinī because she obstructs the path of liberation; she is shaped like a crescent-moon; Ambikā being like a half-moon (*ardhacandrikā*). The supreme Śakti who is one thus takes on three forms. Through their conjunction and disjunction are born the nine classes of [Sanskrit] phonemes. She is called Ninefold when considered as made up

> of these nine classes. When, O Goddess, she resides, in their order, in the five mantras Sadyojāta etc, she is called Fivefold,[14] O Guide of all Gods! Staying in the twelve vowels, she is called "She who Stays in the Twelve." When divided into fifty, she resides in the phonemes from *A* to *KṢA*. In the heart, she is said to be of one atom. In the throat, she is of two atoms. At the root of the tongue, she consists permanently of three atoms; at its tip, without doubt, the birth of the phonemes is accomplished. Thus is described the coming forth of the [divine] sound (*śabda*), by which [all that exists,] movable and unmovable, is pervaded.

This myth expounds the birth of speech as an "anthropocosmic"—both human and cosmic—process. *Kuṇḍalinī*, an aspect of Śakti, divine Energy, becomes straight by her union with the *bindu*, which is Śiva and then appears as various deities: this happens on the divine plane. She then manifests as five mantras that are both deities and linguistic utterances, thus both divine and humanly produced. Then she becomes the phonemes of the Sanskrit alphabet—a human element—but phonemes as forms of *vāc* are divine and, as such, cosmically creative while *also* resulting from the contact of breath with the organs of phonation in the body. The process is irreducibly both human and divine.

There are other similar phonically or alphabetically based cosmogonies in Śaiva as well as in Vaiṣṇava texts. In the Pāñcarātra, for instance, we find two such cosmogonies: in the *Ahirbudhnyasaṃhitā* (chapters 16 and 17) and in the *Lakṣmītantra* (chapters 18 to 20). The process they expound is also "anthropocosmic," but less mythic (one could say less irrational)—more phonetic and metaphysical than in the account of the *Tantrasadbhāva* we have just seen. In the *Ahirbudhnyasaṃhitā*, for instance, the process begins with the awakening of Viṣṇu's willpower assuming the form of supreme subtle sound (*nāda*) then evolving into a "drop" of sound-energy (*bindu*), which, dividing itself into *brahman*-sound (*śabdabrahman*) and into the "root" of the objective world, initiates a complex process through which the phonemes of the Sanskrit alphabet manifest themselves in the traditional order. This "garland of mother-phonemes" (*mātr̥kāvarṇamālinī*), as a great goddess, will create the cosmos.

Such phoneticometaphysical constructions are more numerous, more varied, and infinitely more complex and subtle in the Śaiva traditions, especially among those from Kashmir, where they were developed mainly in the Pratyābhijñā system expounded by Somānanda, Utpaladeva, and Abhinavagupta, followed by Kṣemarāja.[15] They are all built on the same pattern: the Supreme Godhead, the Absolute, is the Word (*vāc*). It is one and infinitely subtle—pure energy (*śakti*). This then progressively materializes, becoming a subtle form of phonic vibration (*nāda*), which then concentrates into a drop (*bindu*) of phonic energy. It then evolves through different processes and takes on the form of *kuṇḍalinī*, who gives birth to the Sanskrit alphabet and eventually to the world—a world permeated and animated by the omnipresent power of *vāc*. Such a process is not unique to Kaśmirian Śaiva traditions; it is also found elsewhere—in the first chapter of such a mantric digest as Lakṣmana Deśikendra's *Śāradātilaka*, for instance. It is alluded to in the *Netra* and *Svacchanda* Tantras, and in other texts.[16]

The most philosophically and phonetically elaborate linguistic cosmogony is that of the third chapter (*śl.* 66 ff.) of Abhinavagupta's *Tantrāloka*,[17] which describes one of the means (*upāya*) for gaining liberation—this way being through a mystical union of the adept's consciousness with the precognitive impulse of the deity, who creates the cosmos by becoming conscious of the appearance in itself of the phonemes of the Sanskrit alphabet. Each of these phonemes appears in the Supreme Śiva, Paramaśiva, each bringing about the birth of each of the constitutive categories of reality, the *tattvas*, first as stages in the deity tending toward cosmic creation[18] then creating the cosmos. This process takes place in the deity, out of time. It also goes on ceaselessly as the source and omnipresent substrate of the universe, which would disappear if the deity ceased to create and animate it.

Śiva, holding thus in himself the archetype of the Sanskrit alphabet and of the cosmos, which the alphabet causes to appear, will create—on the supreme (*para*) plane of divine energy—a paradigm or archetype of this alphabet in himself, then (but always out of time) project these elements by shining them forth onto the other, lower planes of cosmic energy corresponding to the three levels of *vāc*—namely, *paśyantī* ("she who sees"; "the visionary"), to *madhyamā* ("the middle one"), to *vaikharī* ("the gross")—as first described by Bhartṛhari. He will do this through successive (but out of time) acts of creative consciousness (*parāmarśa*), which appear following the order of the Sanskrit alphabet, from *A* to *KṢA*. Thus Śiva has a synthetic vision of the cosmos as a "mass of sound" (*śabdarāśi*) made of *vāc*. This plane is therefore called the visionary (*paśyantī*). This *paśyantī*, which is an infinitely subtle form of the cosmos, will be projected on a lower, intermediate, middle (*madhyamā*) plane of energy where it is reflected, appearing as the first lineaments of cosmic manifestation. This is now projected on and reflected by the last, lowest plane—called the "displayed" or "corporeal" (*vaikharī*)—where not only phonemes but words, the whole (Sanskrit) language, will appear in Śiva and, with and thanks to it, the paradigm of the cosmos in its infinite diversity. These levels of *vāc* from *paśyantī* to *vaikharī* exist only insofar as they rest on, and are pervaded by, *parā vāc*, the Supreme Word, without which neither they (nor the world) would exist. For Indian traditions since Vedic times, Tantric or non-Tantric, all divine forms are lower than the Absolute (*brahman*), who is the omnipresent source of all that exists, but infinitely beyond it.

Vāc in the Human Being: Word and Consciousness

The complex cosmological system of levels and aspects of *vāc* we have just seen is expounded by Abhinavagupta as a means (*upāya*) to gain liberation—as an inner, spiritual process the adept must go through. But there is more to it for Abhinavagupta. By extending Bhartṛhari's psycholinguistic conception metaphysically, grounding it in *parā vāc*, he wishes to show that the supreme plane of the Word is basically present in human consciousness. On this basis, speech (*vāc*) appears and develops in human consciousness together with this being's own consciousness while also causing the consciousness of the world to appear. As the world in him/her is born from *vāc*, so is human awareness and consciousness of the world. *Vāc*, in these Tantric traditions, is the life of consciousness; speech and consciousness are indissolubly linked. Because human nature mirrors the structure of the cosmos, *vāc* plays the same role in humans as in the cosmos. It is the source and ultimate nature of human consciousness, this pervasion being not merely by speech and language (as it was for Bhartṛhari) but also by all the levels of the Word, including the supreme one (*parā*). In the Hindu, and notably Tantric, metaphysical view, the presence of *parā* in our consciousness is necessary, for all aspects of the Word, however explicit, cannot have any reality and therefore any validity as means of knowledge if they do not rest on the absolute, eternal basis of the supreme consciousness, which is also the Word.

All this has been summarized all too briefly, but I hope the reader can see that these are not just foreign and sometimes arcane conceptions but elements worth considering as approaches to some aspects of the human condition.[19]

Word and Life-Breath—*Prāṇa*

Less esoteric than these psycho-linguistic metaphysical constructions and more generally present in Tantra are other, more concrete, largely yogic views and practices concerning the Word as associated with the vital or respiratory breath (*prāṇa*), which from early times was seen as an important vital force located in the human body that also had a supernatural character.[20]

Such notions are found as far back as Vedic Upaniṣads, in the *Maitri*

Upaniṣad, for instance, where breath ascends along the *suṣumnā* together with the syllable *OṂ*, whose nature is divine. Breaths also played a role in Āyurveda and still more in yoga, with *prāṇāyāma*. All such elements were taken over in Tantra, where they were considerably developed. They are one of the aspects of the structure and "functioning" of the yogic body. For instance, in mantric practices where mantras are visualized as moving along its channels together with *prāṇa*, wherever aspects of *vāc*—as mantras or otherwise—move in the body, a form of *prāṇa* is there (we will see instances of such practices further on when looking at mantras). Traveling along such channels, breaths tend to multiply. To the first three "basic" ones, *prāṇa*, *apāna*, and *udāna*, others were added, spreading over the whole body, sometimes overstepping their limits. Each had a particular role, was associated with different aspects of *vāc* (letters, alphabet, mantras), and filled the body of the adept with the power and activity of *vāc*. As we will see when looking at mantras, when in the body, these phonemes or mantras are usually to be visualized (sometimes even to be somehow felt) by the adept as deities or as written sounds (in Devanāgarī script). A curious case of the latter instance is that of the so-called *mālinī*, an order of the alphabet (which is the phonematic form of the goddess Mālinī) whose fifty phonemes, arranged in this order in an ancient scripture, are to be visually realized so as to represent the (anthropomorphic) body of that goddess.

Mantras

The medium is the message.
MARSHAL MCLUHAN

The role of mantras in Tantra, their theory and practice, is so important—overwhelming, in effect—that a whole book, rather than a mere chapter, should be allotted to them. This is therefore a most cursory overview of the subject.[21]

Mantras are not proper to Tantra. In the Veda, there are already mantras, the term denoting the hymns (but hymns that, as mantras, act through their content, not through their meaning). The aspects and uses of mantras then evolved in Brahmanism and Hinduism, the term coming to mean a stereotyped, usually brief, phonetically efficacious ritual formula used to evoke or invoke deities, having also other various—especially magical—uses. Mantras then became a general presence in texts and practices. However, the main development of mantras was in Tantra, where they infinitely multiplied and diversified, becoming omnipresent salvific, magical, or ritual formulas, often without discursive meaning but teeming with power, including (or consisting of) monosyllabic nonlinguistic elements such as *OṂ*, *HRĪṂ*, and so on.

DIVERSITY OF MANTRAS

Mantras, I must first say, are always in Sanskrit. Never in another tongue. They are conventional formulas, proper to each tradition, of supposedly divine origin, which are formally transmitted, never personally drafted. One is given a mantra; one does not freely choose, still less compose it. This is the field of tradition, of revelation, not of personal fancy.[22] This being so, Tantric mantras are of a great diversity of form. Very often, especially when they invoke or evoke a deity, they consist first of *OṂ*, then of the name of the deity (in the dative case), followed by an exclamation, called a *jāti*, which is an originally Vedic formula.[23] A mantra invoking Śiva would thus be *OṂ Śivāya namaḥ* or *OṂ HAUṂ Śivāya namaḥ* (*Śivāya namaḥ* means "homage to Śiva"). Such mantras are very common.

There are, however, a great many different Tantric mantras. Some mantras, especially when of Vedic origin, may include or consist of a sentence, brief or long, which has a specific meaning. In Tantra, syllables (*bījas*) tend to precede and/or follow the central formula and even to replace it. Thus *OṂ* may be used alone, as well as *HRĪṂ*, *ŚRĪṂ*, *HAIṂ*, and so on, but it may also precede one or several such *bījas*—*OṂ ṢAUḤ*, for instance, or *OṂ JUṂ SAḤ*, which is the *netramantra*, the mantra of the Eye (*netra*) of Śiva. The mantra of Tripurasundarī, the *śrīvidyā*, consists usually of fifteen syllables in three clusters: *HA SA KA LA HRĪṂ HA SA HA KA LA HRĪṂ SA KA LA HRĪṂ*. The mantra called *vidyārāja* is made up of nine groups of nine syllables—eighty-one syllables in all (usually shown in diagrammatic form). Such syllabic groups have no evident meaning. They may even be impossible to pronounce. Such is the case of the *piṇḍanātha*, the *Śaiva* mantra of cosmic destruction: *KHPHREṂ* or *HSHPHREṂ*, or the *navātmamantra HSKṢMLRVYŪṂ*, and so on. The Sanskrit alphabet (called in this case *mātṛkā*, a name also used for each of its fifty phonemes) may also be used as a mantra (for *nyāsas*, notably), each phoneme being the *bījamantra* of a deity. Other alphabetical ensembles may be used in the same way, such as the "script of the elements" (*bhūtalipi*), an alphabetical ensemble of forty-two phonemes, from *A* to *SA*, placed into nine groups. Or consider the *mālinī*, an alphabet going from *ṆA* to *PHA*, where vowels and consonants are in apparent complete disorder—Mālinī is also a goddess, an alphabetical deity,[24] as are also other deities, called "letter/alphabetic deities" (*varṇadevatās*).

Many other instances could be cited. But whatever the phoneticolinguistic content of a mantra, it is always to be exactly respected. A mantra may be without meaning, but it has a role as a form of verbal metalinguistic power that can be put into action only if it is correctly uttered and made use of as prescribed, for this action is accomplished through the power of its syllables.[25] When a mantra is not uttered correctly, exactly, and when prescribed, it is powerless and can be dangerous for the performer. Even when impossible to pronounce, as it is made up of sounds (vocally or mentally uttered), it acts. A written mantra is powerless—at least in principle.

Mantras given in initiation (*dīkṣā*), and those used for worship of a deity or for some other ritual or magical purpose, that are to be mastered through a particular (and often very long and complex) ritual practice are always secret, being transmitted confidentially by word of mouth. If such a mantra happens to be overheard, or is found in a book, it is powerless. This, however, does not apply to mantras currently used in ritual, which one can find in ritual handbooks or treatises.

Given that a mantra consists of words or sentences as well as of (often meaningless) groups of phonemes or syllables, how does one recognize such phonetic, linguistic (or quasi-linguistic) ensembles as being mantras? Can one refer to a generally valid criterion? Unfortunately, no. It is sometimes said that one recognizes mantras by some phonetic or linguistic traits—their ending in *OṂ*, for instance. But this is not true. Mantras end in various ways, notably in *Ṃ* or in *Ḥ*, as in Śiva's mantra *SAUḤ*. Mantras are power-words proper to a tradition or a system, phonetic groups designated as such by each tradition in its sacred scriptures or ritual treatises. Each tradition has its own mantras (and is often disparaging of the mantras of other traditions). There are, however, mantras used in all traditions—*OṂ*, for instance. Tantric mantras are traditionally said to be seventy million in number. Though they are very numerous and diverse, one may well doubt they reach such a number, but nobody has ever attempted to count them.

There are classifications of mantras. They are either masculine, when referring to male deities or entities, or feminine, when referring to female ones. These feminine mantras are called *vidyā* ("wisdom"). Monosyllabic mantras are called "seeds" (*bīja* or *bījamantra*). A deity can be invoked by a whole, more or less long, mantra or, more briefly, by his or her *bīja*. Mantras are sometimes classified according to their syllabic length. There are, indeed, a number of compendiums or repertoires of mantras published in India by various religious groups.[26] However, the choice and classifications of mantras reflect their own preferences or prejudices and are of little help to outside observers.

ON THE NATURE OF MANTRAS

A number of theories and interpretations were put forward in India over the centuries, as well as (more recently) in the West, on the nature of that particular use of linguistic elements, mantra. For many in the West, evidently, mantras are merely "nonsense syllables" (*pace* Farquwar), a (mis)use of language for magical ends, instances of which are especially frequent and developed in Indian culture. But from the Indian, and particularly the Tantric, point of view, the nature of mantras is of importance and is all the more problematic because they are considered as being in essence aspects of *vāc*, the eternal divine original Word—transcendental, immortal, all-powerful, all-pervading—while being also linguistic (or quasi-linguistic) utterances. They are empirically perceptible, used in current ritual, spiritual, or magical practice on the level of everyday human life.[27] In this respect, mantras are very different from the divine *vāc*, which is their essence, their basic nature.

When considered from the transcendental point of view, mantras are the phonic, highest aspect of deities. They are the aspect of deities (or of other supernatural entities or cosmic elements) evoked and/or made present in worship or manipulated in rituals, whether one places them ritually on the body or on some support (icon, vessel, *liṅga*, etc.) into which the deity is to be made present for its "external" worship. Mantras may also be sent like missiles toward some goal, acting then like a weapon (this is one of the uses of the *bīja PHAṬ*).

When a mantra is used in this way, the performer is to imagine it mentally. What is visualized is the deity, whose essential nature is the mantra. Mantra and deity are thus identical, a point sometimes mentioned in ritual treatises, especially when they give the syllabic content of the mantra of a deity. Such verses are called *dhyānaślokas*—that is, verses of visualizing meditation. This being so, it is often said that Tantric pantheons are, in truth, pantheons of mantras.[28]

That there are such verses as well as repertoires of mantras may appear to contradict the principle that mantras are secret formulas. But as I have said previously, only certain mantras are secret and are to be transmitted by word of mouth—namely, those of initiation, those given to invoke deities or supernatural powers, or those to manipulate for religious, spiritual, or magical reasons. Mantras used in this way are necessarily given by a spiritual master, a guru, and are then mastered by the initiated adept, who performs a number of often complex rites to propitiate the mantra (*mantrasādhana*) before being permitted (having the ritual ability [*adhikāra*]) to use it. Ritual texts also protect the secrecy of mantras either by giving their syllabic content indirectly by using conventional secret terms for each letter involved or by the use of diagrams where the letters of the Sanskrit alphabet (and therefore those constituting the mantra) are displayed in a particular order that only an initiated adept can discover.[29] Such diagrams are also used to compare the letters of the mantra with those of the name of the user or of the person attempting to use the mantra to see if they are compatible. If not, particular rites, some involving a sacrifice—even, according to the ninth-century *Netratantra*, the offering of human flesh—are to be practiced to attain this compatibility.

Mantras are not only the phonic, highest form of deities; the body parts and the attributes held by the deities may also have (or be) mantras, as may be elements or divisions of the cosmos. Mantras are therefore used in ritual whenever these entities are invoked and/or ritually placed on the body or on supports, which are then permeated with, purified by, or transformed by their power (water becoming nectar [*amṛta*], for instance). Mantras thus accomplish a number of actions. They are "performative utterances" that "do what they say" in ritual. One thus cuts or divides two elements with the sword (*astra*) mantra, one protects or delimits a ritual area with the cuirass (*kavaca*) mantra, and so forth. As ritually active elements, mantras are especially present in rituals and magic. In this respect, they are supernatural forces rather than deities—these two aspects being sometimes difficult to differentiate, for mantras are always divine in essence. Mantras, one must add, though forms of *vāc*, also have a visible aspect, human or written, often visualized in ritual.

MANTRIC PRACTICES, THE USES OF MANTRAS

Only a very brief overview can be given of the vast number of mantric practices in Tantric ritual, yoga, and spiritual life.

Being vocal, phonic entities, mantras are by nature linked to breath—the vital breath (*prāṇa*) mainly, but also to physical breathing. They are, therefore, naturally present in the body. A living body is a body that breathes, a breath where mantras may be present. The utterance of a mantra in Sanskrit is called (*uccāra*), which can mean both an utterance and an ascent, and therefore describes the ascending thrust of a mantra in the body. The *uccāra* may be vocal. It may also consist of the silent inner ascent of a mantra in the yogic body of the adept, following the way of the *suṣumnā*, the path by which the *kuṇḍalinī* ascends up to the *dvādaśānta* above the body. By nature, mantras tend toward the suprahuman.

This natural connection between mantras and breath, and the way mantras "function," appears clearly in the practice of the "unrecited recitation" (*ajapājapā*), where not a mantra but the respiratory breath is recited or rather not recited—no word is uttered. The practice is mentioned or described in a number of texts, notably in Tantric Upaniṣads such as the *Dhyānabindu*, *Haṃsa*, and *Yogaśikhā* Upaniṣads (and in the *Vijñānabhairava*, 156). One considers that the mantra *haṃsa*, made up of the two sounds *ha* and *sa*, is spontaneously produced and is then understood as *ahaṃ saḥ* ("I am Him") and, conversely, as *so'ham* ("He is me")—two imaginary syllables, each associated with the ingoing and the outgoing of the breath. Mere breathing becomes the repetition of a formula of identification with Śiva, this being repeated twenty-one thousand times every twenty-four hours.[30] Thus a natural bodily, physiological motion becomes a religious utterance. By merely breathing while concentrating on his or her breath, the adept experiences a fusion with the deity.

This is a special case. The presence of mantras in the (yogic) body usually takes on different forms. They are placed on the body or on *cakras* by *nyāsa*, pervading them with their power. They also travel in the body; for instance, when they travel up from the *mūlādhāra* or from the heart *cakra* to the *brahmarandhra* or to the *dvādaśānta* with their *uccāra*. We have seen this in chapter 5 with the *japa* of the *śrīvidyā*. This also happens with the mantra *OṂ* when its *uccāra*, proceeding beyond its final *M*, by way of an after-resonance called *bindu* (Ṃ), followed by eight ever subtler stages of phonic vibration named *kalās*—in other words, from the *kalā* named *ardhacandra* ("crescent moon") to *unmanā* ("beyond mind")—until it dissolves finally in the silence of the Absolute. This process is to be imagined as taking place in the yogic body, where *OṂ* rises from the *mūlādhāra* (or from the heart) up to the *brahmarandhra* or to the *dvādaśānta*. Mantras can also circulate like a fluid in the channels (*nāḍīs*) of the yogic body, permeating it with their power. Thus in chapter 7 of the *Netratantra*, the mantra of the Eye of Śiva goes up with the ascending vital breath, pierces the *cakras* tiered along the *suṣumnā*, then pierces secondary centers and eventually reaches the *dvādaśānta*, where it flows down to the heart *cakra* of the adept, filling it with nectar of immortality (*amṛta*), which suffuses the body and makes it immortal.

JAPA

The ritual repetition of a mantra is one of the most important mantric practices, since it is by repeatedly reciting a mantra that one puts it into action. Mantras are thus sometimes to be repeated a million times!

Japa is an ancient common Hindu practice. It goes back to Vedic times and is found everywhere in India today. It is not specifically Tantric (or Hindu) but its most varied and peculiar forms are found in Tantra, where it is often associated with other elements such as mudrās, visualizations, or other rites, or linked to *prāṇa* (in the *ajapājapa*) so as to make it spiritually, religiously, or magically more effective. To keep count of the repetitions, *japa* is practiced using a rosary (*akṣamālā*), which is used according to precise rules. Some of these (on the use of particular fingers of the hand, for instance) are simple. Others meant for practicing Tāntrikas are complex and binding, going from how to choose the beads and assemble them to how to dispose of the rosary. The assembling of the rosary is a precise ritual action concluded by the consecration of the object, which is henceforth considered an icon in which the deity is present and which must therefore be treated as such.[31]

Japa is practiced in a number of cases. It is often a daily practice; for instance, as the last item of the Tantric *pūjā*. It is also part of many rites. For example, it is part of the *mantrasādhana*, where long repetitions of the mantra given by the master helps the *sādhaka* to master it, permeating his body-mind with its power. The ritual of initiation (*dīkṣā*) also includes *japas.*

In magical rites, the role of *japa* is all the more important because repetition increases the power of the magical formula. *Japa* may, of course, also be a simple act of devotion to the deity, a "prayer of the heart." It is like this for the majority of Hindus; Tantric rites merely add their own greater efficacy to the utterance. For instance, the repetition of the name of god (*nāmajapa*), is an ancient and still ever-present devotional Hindu practice. However, to translate *japa* to "prayer," as is sometimes done, is misleading—especially in Tantra, where *japa* is, in most cases, a ritual operation associated with psychosomatic and/or spiritual elements or a with a mystical practice. (Tāntrikas, naturally, also "pray," as everybody does. However, their prayer consists more of visualizations than of vocal or mental utterances.)

Thus in chapter 3 of the Yoginīhṛdaya (stanzas 6–7), on the "supreme form" of worship of the Goddess, the *japa* to be done is described by the commentary as being not a mere "external" (*bāhya*) *japa* but an inner (*āntara*) one consisting of fixing one's attention on the subtle phonic vibration perceived in the heart (*nāda*), the mystical center of the human being. "This," says Amṛtānanda, "is indeed what is called *japa.* The external *japa* is not a real *japa.*"

Another Tantric *japa*, particularly subtle and complex and very much worth describing, is the meditative realization of the *bījamantra SAUḤ*, the so-called Seed of the Heart (*hṛdayabīja*), which symbolizes the creative power of the deity taken at its source. It is described in Abhinavagupta's *Parātriṃṣakavivaraṇa* and *Tantrāloka.*

SAUḤ is made up of three phonemes: *S*, *AU*, and *Ḥ*. *S* is understood as the word *sat*, the Supreme Being, the Absolute that holds within itself the germ of the whole cosmos. *AU* is, in the phonetic emanation we have seen above, the conjunction of the three basic powers of Śiva. It symbolizes the divine energy that animates the cosmos. *Ḥ* is the emission (*visarga*)—it represents the cosmic creative power of Śiva. *SAUḤ* is thus, to quote Abhinavagupta, "the cosmos (*S*) that, thanks to the creative awareness (*vimarśa*) of the three powers of Śiva (*AU*), becomes the germ of the cosmos to be emitted (*Ḥ*) within Bhairava." *SAUḤ* thus symbolizes the germ of the cosmos as present in Śiva, as well as the pervasive presence of Śiva in the cosmos—God as holding the universe in Himself, the universe *in statu nascendi* in God. *SAUḤ* is thus truly the "Germ of the Heart," the *hṛdayabīja*, the *bīja* of Śiva—heart, center, and origin of everything.

This is to be "realized"—spiritually assimilated by the adept. For this, the adept is to visualize, to experiment within himself, while uttering (*uccāra*) the three phonemes of the mantra—the ascent of power (*kuṇḍalinī*) going up to *dvādaśānta* where he will fuse spiritually with the supreme deity, which holds within itself the whole cosmos. It is a cosmic saving experience combining a bodily mental cosmic experience of the power of the Word together with an intellectual understanding of a metaphysical system—a Tantric *japa*, therefore, that is much more than a mere repetitive utterance of a mantra.

8

Tantric Ritual

In a book on Tantra, the chapter on ritual perhaps ought to be the longest, for the Tantric world is a world of ritual. As we saw in the introduction, some authors define Tantra by reference to its ritual aspects and, truly, if one considers the whole Tantric world—Hindu and Buddhist, as it is in Asia from India to Japan—the only common trait is in ritual. But the very abundance and variety of Tantric rites make it impossible to give more than the merest overview of the subject here. I will therefore describe mainly two rites, those of ritual worship (*pūjā*) and of initiation (*dīkṣā*), both chosen because they are important and common rites, and because these two rites are to be "lived" (existentially participated in) by the actor. They are thus typically Tantric in the role given to the body-mind and to meditative visualizing experience. Ritual, especially when Tantric, is a *mise en scène* organized by the officiating adept, who is its main character, as he goes both bodily and mentally through the ritual process by creating mental images visualized as present in his yogic body, while being also projected mentally onto icons or other ritual supports. This is done together with the constant use of mantras.

The importance given to ritual is not a solely Tantric trait. It goes back to Vedic times, when certain sacrificial rites were long and complex. The ancient traditional brahmanical orthodox system of Mīmāṃsā is primarily devoted to the exegesis of ritual. But soon, with yoga and the (Veda-based) Upaniṣads, the transcendence of ritual was extolled and the spiritual-religious quest was considered higher and capable of leading more directly to liberation. This view was kept alive down to the present time by the so-called *śramanic* traditions, notably Buddhism and Jainism, and later by the devotional movement (*bhakti*).

Note that the rituals we shall see are private, domestic rites practiced by devotees in their homes or in selected auspicious places, on their own behalf or for others. They are not temple rites, which are more visible and accessible for outsiders and optional—one only attends if one wishes to. On the contrary, the performance of private rites, whether daily or occasional, is mandatory. Not to perform them is a fault. Private rites may happen to be performed in a sanctuary, but a sanctuary or a temple is not the main place for their practice (even if performing them for others is—at least today—the main activity of temple priests, who get from this their main income). Rites are normally performed in a consecrated place, a purified area that may be a room in a house, a pavilion erected for the occasion, or a particular auspicious or sacred place: a cremation ground, a riverbank, a crossroads, and so on. These are common Hindu rules, of which those of Tantra are only a more intense variant.

Mainstream Hindu temple rites (especially if they are Śaiva) are, like private rites, expounded in āgamas or Tantras and are therefore formally Tantric. They are performed by priests who are Tantric initiates. The ritual daily service of the main deity keeps the temple active from morning to evening. In larger temples, other deities are also worshipped in separate shrines. There are also a number of other rites, daily or occasional, organized following a precise ritual lunisolar calendar, to which private worship is to be added. There are also festivals, some of which draw large numbers of devotees.[1]

The Spirit of Tantric Rites

The Tantric world is a world of power, a world pervaded by the power of the deity who manifests and animates it, a power that can be mastered and manipulated through ritual. Ritual produces effects because it puts this power into action. Because rites are prescribed in Tantras that are revealed by the deity and so are of divine origin, they are to be performed by humans animated by divine power (*śakti*). Ancient kāpālikas performed transgressive cults including sexual rites to gain access to the supernatural powers of Yoginīs. Even now, Tāntrikas often go on wishing to have access through ritual to dark but powerful natural or cosmic forces. Hence rites are performed at night, using sometimes a corpse, in cremation grounds inhabited by dangerous spirits and vampires. Another example is the possession (*āveśa*) of the officiating person by the powers or deities that are ritually invoked.[2]

Even if "possessed," however, the officiating Tāntrika is always to act according to precise injunctions. Rites, like mantras (of whose mere utterance rites sometimes consist), are efficacious insofar as they are used according to very precise and strict rules. Ritual mistakes are carefully avoided, for they may have dire consequences. When a ritual fault is committed, it is to be atoned for by expiatory rites called *prāyaścitta*, a particular category of rites all the more important considering the abundance and complexity of Tantric ritual. From a certain time onward, the importance of ritual exactitude diminished under the influence of popular devotion (*bhakti*), the spiritual, devotional attitude of the performer coming to be considered more important than ritual precision. Nevertheless, ritual precision remains important even today.

Tantras often say that rites are to be done as lavishly as possible. To spend lavishly on costly rituals is meritorious—it is even a religious duty. One must never be stingy in one's relations with the deity.[3] Hindu rites are often expensive. A pavilion may have to be erected and adorned with a variety of offerings such as flowers, jewels, and so forth. The officiating Brahmin is entitled to a ritual gift (*dakṣiṇā*), to which various gifts may be added, as well as gifts to the temple. Indian temples sometimes received large grants of land (the property is often controlled by the state since British times). This spending is seen as spiritually meritorious, as help toward liberation, even. However, such expenses may be difficult to bear. These days, temple priests are sometimes not fully initiated because they cannot afford the cost of an initiation ritual. To us, all this may seem unjustified. But we must never forget that in India, poverty was not meritorious; it was an imperfection, a stigma, the result of the play of karma and therefore, in the opinion of many, never unmerited. As for the sumptuousness of the ritual, it is a token of respect to the deity. In the Tantric view, the beauty of rites and ceremonies is considered as a spiritual help for the officiating person insofar as it fosters a feeling of joy, of wonder, that opens the mind to the divine.

In addition to these traits, a salient characteristic of Tantric ritual is the fundamental role of the mental activity of the ritual performer. He is not merely to do a number of bodily and vocal actions; he is to imagine and visualize a number of elements that accompany these actions, while mentally projecting them onto a support—an icon, a ritual instrument or vessel, a diagram, or other consecrated item or area. This mental activity is continuous and is so important that one may well say that (at least in some rites) the ritual performer lives (or is supposed to live) in a veritable visual imaginary world. For instance, in the Śrīvidyā *pūjā*, performed using a ritual diagram, all the deities to be worshipped are to be mentally placed on the diagram by their mantras while visualizing them as described in the *dhyānaślokas* of Tantric texts. This also happens when icons or ritual vessels are used. Furthermore, in some cases, the ritual performer is to imagine mental elements as present in his (yogic imaginary) body—in his "heart" or on a *cakra*—

that he then transfers mentally from his body onto an icon or other support. That in actual practice such mental exercises are not intensely "lived" is likely. Nevertheless, the theory is there, very clearly expressed in Tantric texts. For instance, in an initiation rite described in the *Tantrāloka*, when the initiate is brought blindfolded before the altar where deities have been placed by their mantras, he is suddenly to see this (invisible to a noninitiated) display, and he is deemed to be so struck by the splendor revealed to him that he falls in a swoon—the power of imagination!

Worship—*Pūjā*

The ritual worship of deities (*pūjā*) is a particularly interesting instance of this complex ensemble of bodily actions and mental images. This practice is all the more complex because Tantric *pūjā* aims at identifying the ritual performer with the deity he worships. This ritual worship is traditionally composed of two parts. The first, "inner" (*āntara*), part is entirely mental, resting on the image of the body. The second, "external" (*bāhya*), part is the visible, concrete worship using material supports such as icons, vessels, or diagrams, and the accomplishment of physical ritual actions.[4]

The first part, often considered the main one because it aims at divinizing the performer, is entirely a work of creative (or rather evocative, for only prescribed images are to be visualized) imagination. It is also an imagination working on the body. It begins with a purification of the body of the worshipper, which aims at creating a "divine body" that will replace his ordinary, impure one for the duration of the *pūjā*. This is necessary because, as the saying goes, "one who is not god cannot worship God."[5] Only a pure, divine being can approach the deity. To this end, the worshipper, who has already been submitted to seven different "baths"—of water, fire, mantras, and so on—will (in the Śaiva case) enter the consecrated area for worship and mentally burn his body with the fire of the *astra* mantra, then scatter the ashes by blowing on them "a wind made of *śakti*." Because he is deemed to have no body at this point, using mantras he will replace it by the different parts of Sadāśiva's (the "Eternal Śiva") body—luminous, with five heads, with all his "members" and ornaments—to whom he is to offer a throne in his heart. He is then to bathe and to clothe this new body with garments adorned with jewels. All this is done mentally while uttering the mantras that represent and symbolize all that he is to "see." One can easily realize the difficulty of such a virtuosic mental exercise, unless it is lazily done by merely reciting mantras, without any attempts at mental concentration, as is often likely to be the case.[6] However, even if it is not performed with the intense mental concentration theoretically needed, the worshipper must feel somehow "transformed," since the deity he worships is imagined as present in him, body and soul, taking his place, as it were. Of course, this does not give immediate liberation, but by purifying the soul of the officiant, it somehow opens the way toward it.

The previous paragraphs summarize all too briefly a long description given in the *Mṛgendrāgama*. There are other descriptions of this process in other texts, with variants, but they all aim at first purifying and thus "destroying," then at "reconstructing" the body of the performer. I would like to mention here a picturesque variant of the process described by the twelfth-century Southern author Aghoraśivācārya. There, the adept imagines his body as a banyan tree, which he plants and makes to grow. It bears flowers, then fruit, then withers. It is eventually burnt, and its ashes are scattered by "the wind of Śakti."

In whatever way this first imaginative process is followed, the adept then performs the "inner" cult consisting of mentally carrying out all the ritual actions of the "external" worship. He is to imagine the deity he is worshipping as present in the lotus of his heart. He proffers a throne, places the deity on it, and induces the deity to stay there using the appropriate mantras and mudrās. He then offers, in imagination, all the services (*upacāra*; variously numbering from five to sixteen) that are usually offered to a respected guest: bath, anointment, dress, ornaments, food, perfumes, betel, incense, lights, and so forth. He then mentally evokes the "faces" and "members" of the main deity and of the ancillary deities surrounding it—those being imagined "as having different aspects according to the aim of the ritual," says the *Mṛgendrāgama*.[7] The process ends with a (mental) liquid offering (*arghya*), followed by the *japa* of the *mūlamantra* of the deity.

Only then is the actual, "external" *pūjā* to be performed, during which the officiating adept will materially accomplish the same acts of reception and homage to the deity, all accompanied by a number of imaginary visualizations. In Śiva's cult, for instance, if a *liṅga* is being used, what the performer is to "see" in front of him is not a cylindrical icon that symbolizes Śiva and to which offerings are made; he is instead to consider this object as the throne of the deity, a throne to be built by mentally piling up along the *liṅga* all the elements that constitute it and that are the totality of the cosmos. He must therefore visualize all the elements that compose the cosmos, from the Basal Power (*ādhāraśakti*) all the way up to the deity, with all the other thirty-five *tattvas* from the earth to *śuddhavidyā* ranged in between.[8] Thus, the officiant is to "see" the whole universe with the deities abiding in it instead of the mere objects in front of him. He will then mentally install the "body of wisdom" (*vidyādeha*) of the god on this throne, "transparent as a crystal, having ten arms, three eyes on each of his five faces, a crescent moon shining on the crown of his head."

The god being thus imagined is now worshipped with mantras. He is invoked, then conceived of as being made up of a mantra that the adept brings to his forehead, where it will become shaped like a *bindu* and "shining like the moon." He is then transferred in imagination by the officiant "in the flowery cup of his hands" and placed in and united with the cult icon where he will be ritually fastened. Śiva is henceforth present in the *liṅga*, and the adept will proceed with all the ritual actions of worship: bath, offering of flowers, incense, lights,[9] and so on, and the various substances that constitute the *arghya*. The *pūjā* ends with an oblation in the fire (*homa*), a last *japa*, and the ritual dismissal of the god.

The same pattern of *pūjā* is used for other icons, for other aspects of Śiva, as well as for other Śaiva gods or goddesses. This is also generally the pattern of the daily *pūjā* in Vaiṣṇava Pāñcarātra, with the purification of the officiant first, then the mental worship (*mānasayāga*), followed by the external one (*bāhyayāga*). Visualizations also play an essential role in these rituals; but there are, of course, differences due in part to different theologies.

Differences may also result from the use of particular supports for the cult. Thus, in the Śrīvidyā tradition, the worship of the goddess Tripurasundarī is performed (as I have said) with no image of that deity, using instead the *śrīcakra* diagram as support. This means that after the first "inner" *pūjā* is practiced mentally as described above, the worship consists of worshipping first the Goddess then all the deities of her retinue, conceived of as present in the series of triangles and circles encircling the central triangle. All are placed mentally and visualized as precisely as possible in the different parts of the diagram where they are deemed to abide, each deity (or group of deities) being separately worshipped. The mental effort of creative imagination is particularly great.[10] The worship ends with the *japa* of *śrīvidyā*, which, as we have seen above, is not the recitation of a mantra but a yogic mental and bodily action where the mantra ascends along the *suṣumnā* together with the adept's *kuṇḍalinī*.

From these examples, one realizes that, if practiced with all the prescribed singleness of mind and concentration, the Tantric *pūjā* entails an intense effort of visual imagination, all the more intense and difficult because many of the mental images are either to be felt as present in the officiant's body and/or placed on the support that is the locus of worship. One may well suspect that no such intense effort is actually applied in most current practice. But if it were to be, even feebly, its daily (mandatory) repetition could not but act on the performer. As said above, Tantric *pūjā* aims at identifying the officiant with the deity he worships. The process described should inevitably bring about some change in the practitioner's mind—in the way he goes on living and behaving in this world.[11] This is an interesting aspect of the subject.

Several particular traits typical of Tantric *pūjā* when the worship is that of fearsome deities are worth alluding to here. For Bhairava, for instance, the best *liṅga* is not the well-known cylindrical and more or less phallic icon[12] but a *tūra*, which, as we have seen above, is an incised human skull. It is important to note that the ritual offerings of a Tantric cult may be "nonvegetarian."[13] They include alcoholic beverages and a sacrifice—an animal or pieces of meat (or fish)—and sexual union is sometimes added (see chapter 6). These offerings are sometimes called *pañcamakāra*, "the five [offerings beginning with] the letter *ma*." These are *madya* (alcohol), *māṃsa* (flesh), *matsya* (fish), *mudrā* (grains),[14] and *maithuna* (sexual union). But this list of five is relatively modern. Ancient texts include only *madya*, *māṃsa*, and *maithuna*. The offerings, always mixed with some liquid or consecrated water, are the *arghya*, kept in a vessel. In the cult of Bhairava, according to the *Tantrāloka*, this vessel should always be full. If not, the god, voracious and hungry, would pounce on the devotee and devour him.

When rites are performed to obtain particular, unusual, or transgressive results, the offering of human flesh is sometimes prescribed in Tantras. Kaula texts prescribe the use of the so-called *kuladravya* (offerings of the Kula), which include bodily products and excretions together with sexual union (and sometimes the drinking of its products, male and female).[15] The greater the impurity and the transgression, the greater the power mastered through the ritual.

Initiations—*Dīkṣā*

The ritual of initiation is also, in principle, soul transforming. It is especially important in Tantra, for it is one of the elements that differentiates it from non-Tantric ("mainstream") Hinduism. It is not a mere "rite de passage," as are the brahmanical *saṃskāras* performed for all Hindus. These purificatory or perfecting rites mark stages in the religious and social life of caste Hindus, whereas *dīkṣā* transforms the initiate, purifies his soul, opens for him the way to liberation. The term *dīkṣā* is usually translated as "initiation," as is *upanayana*, the ceremony that introduces all male "twice-born" Hindus into their caste. But the two are not to be confused, for only *dīkṣā* allows the initiate to enter (or progress) into a Tantric tradition, linking him to a succession of spiritual masters he will invoke and honor before performing any ritual.

It goes without saying that not all those who worship Tantric deities (or who practice haṭhayoga) are initiated and they are not all necessarily practicing Tāntrikas. They are the Tantric majority, but true Tāntrikas, who are a minority, an active one, are initiates.

In the various Śaiva or Vaiṣṇava Tantric traditions, there are several degrees or levels of initiation, usually spaced out into three grades. The first one marks the entry into a tradition as an adept who is not permitted to perform rites. It is usually called "regular," or "common"—literally "rule-based initiation" (*samayadīkṣā*).[16] There are two initiations that confer powers and bring the initiate nearer to the deity: the *nirvāṇadīkṣā* ("liberating initiation"), which frees the initiate from all fetters, and the *sādhakadīkṣā*, which confers the possibility of having supernatural powers (*siddhis*) gained through the mastery of a mantra given in initiation. Also often classed as a type of initiation is the consecration or anointment (*abhiṣeka*) of the spiritual master, the guru; a few other initiations are mentioned.

There are different kinds of initiation rituals; some are simple, others are complex. However, whatever their kind, they always consist of a very important ritual ensemble—one could say a *mise en scène*—including a variety of ritual operations that can sometimes last several days. The importance of *dīkṣā* and of its ritual side is often underscored in Tantra. For instance, in Abhinavagupta's vast treatise, the *Tantrāloka*, twelve chapters (out of thirty-two) are devoted to the subject, dealing first with the nature of *dīkṣā*, then describing its different forms. Chapter 15, on *samayadīkṣā*, is the longest of that work.

The basic principle and organizing pattern of all initiations is the same. It consists in ritually destroying the empirical, imperfect personality of the initiate and replacing it with a new one—if not to make this personality appear immediately then at least to bring about the conditions for this to happen by transmitting the spiritual power of the initiating master to the initiate.

This, for instance, is how the *samayadīkṣa* is to be performed according to the Śaivasiddhānta. A pavilion is built for the purpose, its inner area is purified, an altar is erected with ritual vessels, and fire-pits are dug. Then, preliminary purification rites are performed. After two days of these rites, the master, having intensely meditated on his identification with the deity, covers the eyes of his disciple with a blindfold and brings him to the pavilion, an action symbolizing entry in the initiatory group. He then ritually places all the elements (*tattvas*) constituting the cosmos, elements that are then to be dissolved into each other, going from the lowest to the most subtle, on his disciple's body, from foot to head, by *nyāsas* of mantras. The ordinary body of the disciple is thus replaced by a body of mantras. He is henceforth qualified to approach and worship the deity. The master then puts his hand, which mantras have changed into the hand of Śiva, on the disciple's head. The god possesses the disciple, who is then brought blindfolded in front of a *maṇḍala* where Śiva and his pantheon are present in the guise of mantras (therefore not visible). The disciple's blindfold is then removed so that he may "see" Śiva and his pantheon. He throws a flower on the *maṇḍala*, the place where it falls deciding his initiatory name. The ritual ends with a few concluding rites. There are, naturally, different initiation rituals (for instance, when Śiva is deemed to move the initiate's hand when he throws the flower), but the general pattern and the spirit of the ritual are always the same.

The other initiations, allowing the performance of rites and giving access to higher spiritual planes, have other component rites, but they are organized along the same general pattern—the same symbolical movement—expressed by mental constructions applied on the body-mind, and their aim is to destroy a previous, inferior state so as to reach a higher, purer one.

First, there is the *nirvāṇadīkṣā*, which gives the initiate the qualification (*adhikāra*) to perform rites. It effectively opens the way to salvation, making him a spiritual son (*putraka*) of his master. A variant of this initiation is the *sādhakadīkṣā*, which gives the disciple possession of supernatural powers (*siddhis*), which he will obtain fully after mastering the mantra secretly given him by the initiating master. And, as we have seen above, there is also the initiation, or consecration (*abhiṣeka*) of the spiritual master, the guru (*ācārya*).

I cannot describe these initiations here, interesting as they may be, but can merely mention a few traits. For instance, in the Śaiva *nirvāṇadīkṣā*, as described in the *Somaśambhupaddhati*,[17] all the fetters binding the *ātman* of the initiate and binding him to this world (they are mainly constitutive elements of the cosmos [*tattvas*]) are transferred by mantras onto a string placed along his body, where they will each individually be destroyed. This is done on the string so as not to harm the initiate's *ātman*, which is carefully kept aside during the ritual. The next day, sections of the string are progressively cut off and burnt in the sacrificial fire, thus destroying the individual's bonds in each tranche of the universe. A union of Śiva and the Goddess now being imagined, the guru will deposit the resulting newly conceived *ātman* in the womb of the Goddess, whence it will be reborn totally purified. Because the burning ritual is to be performed separately for each of the many levels of the cosmos to be purged, one easily realizes the complexity of this ritual and the time it must require.

A few other cases would be worth mentioning, all showing the extraordinary ritual inventiveness of Tantric Hinduism in the way it stages and mentally manipulates images that are, in fact, mere abstractions but are dealt with as if they were concrete elements. These images are made effective by ritual.

They are remarkable instances of the effectiveness of symbolic efficacy when it is intensely "lived" by the ritual actor.

In this respect, I will mention the initiation by phonemes (*varṇamayī dīkṣā*), where the power of the Word acts, so to speak, by itself without any ritual. For, in this initiation, the phonemes of the Sanskrit alphabet are placed by *nyāsa* on the body of the initiate in their grammatical order, and then are taken out of it in the opposite order, beginning with the last one, each phoneme dissolving into the next up to *A*, traditionally considered as the supreme substrate of the whole alphabet (and therefore of the cosmos). The initiate's body, pervaded by these phonemes, is therefore symbolically dissolved—fused in the Absolute. The guru then identifies himself by mental concentration with his disciple and unites his *ātman* with the Supreme, from whence he mentally draws out the phonemes and then puts them back in the body of the disciple who, permeated with the omnipotence of the Word, enjoys the supreme bliss of union with the Absolute.

Also worth touching upon is the "initiation by penetration" (*vedhadīkṣā* or *vedhamayī dīkṣā*), which is a yogic bodily practice wherein the spiritual power of the master is transferred to his disciple using the structure of the yogic body. This initiation is important because it is used for the transmission of the secret teaching of the initiatory group concerned from master to master. It is used also for the consecration of a king (*rājābhiṣeka*). In Kula and Nātha traditions, it is considered as the highest of all initiations. There are different kinds of *vedhadīkṣā*; six are described in chapter 29 of the *Tantrāloka*.[18]

They are all basically the same. By a mental and bodily exertion, the spiritual master is to reinforce the power he possesses as much as possible, fusing it with the divine power. He then has it penetrate the body and the mind of his disciple, who reaches henceforth the highest spiritual planes, both human and divine. This introjection is associated with the ascent of *kuṇḍalinī*, the centers tiered along it being "pierced" by the power emanating from the guru—a power that, once entered in the disciple and ascending along the *suṣumnā*, fuses him totally with the Absolute, bestowing on him both supernatural powers and liberation. This penetration is realized in practice by the bodily interaction of the breaths of the guru and the disciple. These are to stay face to face, literally mouth to mouth, sharing the same respiratory and vital breathing. All their senses are to interpenetrate and unite, the powerful divine breath of the guru entering that of his disciple, who is thus initiated. There are variants of this penetration, with different results. The highest one, *paravedha*, causes a veritable divination.

Several other initiation rituals that are used in particular circumstances (absence, impending death, etc.) could be mentioned. In one initiation, the "initiation involving pair of scales" (*tulādīkṣā*), one judges the progress of purification of the initiate by the decrease of his weight brought about by the ritual.

A Few Other Rites

As I have said above, the life of a Tāntrika is a life of ritual. So too is, in principle, the life of any Hindu if he follows the rules that govern his social group (*varṇāśramadharma*). Some of these rules are, in fact, Tantric in form or in spirit.

After initiation, the Tantric adept is not only to worship his chosen deity (*iṣṭadevatā*) daily but also to perform several rites called *naimittika*, "due to a particular cause." These are to be accomplished regularly, notably on particular days called *parvan*, on which take place the meetings with Yoginīs we saw in chapter 6, where adepts assemble in pairs around their guru, worship the Goddess, and sometimes unite sexually. There are numerous other rites, of worship or atonement, and funeral (post mortem) rites, called *śrāddha*. In addition to such domestic/private rites, are those performed in temples, which are very numerous. Organized following a yearly (lunisolar) calendar, temple rites include several daily cults of the main deity (and of secondary ones), then cults performed on particular days of the week, and on some days of the lunisolar month. There are also annual cults, some of which are important feasts. Particular cults are also performed in temples for private persons, associations, guilds, and so on. A temple is thus kept active from dawn to dusk the whole year round. There are also rites of a political (civil or royal) nature performed to strengthen the power and prosperity of the monarch, increase the wealth of the kingdom, remove the obstacles to his power, and so on (see chapter 3). The chaplain of the monarch (*purohita*), his guru, as well as his ministers (called *mantrins*, which means both "minister" and "master of mantras") are there to help in the matter.

This, however, is not all. There are also all the mantric practices that usually include ritual portions where the powers of the Word are made present and effective through ritual—the ritual construction of a mantra with Sanskrit phonemes, or the checking of a mantra's suitability to the user's needs, as well as the *mantrasādhana* to master the mantra, and *japa*, which we have seen before, and so on. There are also all the innumerable rites, religious or magical, performed by means of these mantras, some of which we shall see further on.

I should perhaps underline here the fact that such rites are all *kāmya*—that is, undertaken to attain desired (*kāmya*) ends. When he is not performing obligatory, daily, or regular (*nitya* or *naimittika*) rites, the Hindu devotee or worshipper, Tāntrika or not, performs a rite because he expects from it some result (spiritual, religious, or mundane). This attitude, from the Hindu point of view, is entirely justified. *Kāmya* rites are not a lower category of rites. Like all rites, they aim at mastering a form of supernatural power (*śakti*), manipulating it ritually to reach some goal, interested or disinterested. The relationship of the Hindu devotee to the omnipresent deity who sustains and animates the cosmos with its power may very well be devotional, but it is also sometimes a pragmatic relation of power implying an identity with the deity (especially if she is a goddess).

Magical Rites, Supernatural Powers

I underlined the pervasiveness of magic in India in chapter 4. Indian gods act through magic. The world, insofar as it is the effect of *māyā*, is created as if by magic. In such a context, magical actions cannot but play an important role—a role particularly emphasized in Tantra, where ritual actions are always performed using mantras. I must reiterate that the category of magic is chiefly a Western one and that there is no word for "magic" in Sanskrit. The word *abhicāra* may correspond to "black magic" or "sorcery," but other "magical" (as we might call them) deeds are a variety of ritual actions that are not different in essence from other rites (indeed, why should we consider a ritual performed to make a weapon more effective "magical" and a ritual that, for the *pūjā*, transforms water into *amr̥ta* "religious"?). The dividing line between religion and magic is far from precise not only in Tantra (or only in India).[19]

We may, however, select a particular set of magical actions for particular attention. This is the *ṣaṭkarmāṇi* (or *ṣaṭkarman*), usually called "the six [magical] actions," in English, for they form a clearly distinguishable ensemble in Tantric texts. These actions are pacification (*śānti*), subjugation (*vaśīkaraṇa*), immobilization (*stambhana*), creation of hostility (*vidveṣaṇa*), driving away (*uccāṭana*), and killing (*māraṇa*). To these six (quoted here in the traditional order) are sometimes added causing bewilderment (*mohana*), attraction (*ākarṣaṇa*), and creation or augmentation of prosperity (*puṣṭi*). One of these actions may sometimes replace one of the six in the "classical" list. All these actions include or consist of the utterance of mantras. *Uccāṭana*, for instance, is to be performed (according to the *Mr̥gendrāgama*) by an oblation in the fire following a *pūjā* in which "destructive" mantras are used, the ritual being performed on a *maṇḍala* or on a *liṅga* where fearsome deities abide. According to another text, the oblation in the fire is made while uttering the *bījamantra* of Vāyu (the "Wind") followed by *PHAṬ* (a syllable usually uttered to expel). The utterance is then directed toward the oblation, which consists not of some liquid substance but of the feathers of a crow or of an owl, on which one imagines that the victim of this action is lying, and is thus driven away. Only initiated adepts (*sādhakas*) can perform such actions either for their own benefit or for others. Some were (or perhaps still are) performed by chaplains or yogis for the benefit of rulers, to give or increase the prosperity (*puṣṭi*) of the realm, to create peace (*śānti*), or to destroy (*maraṇa*) or drive away (*uccāṭana*) its enemies. Attraction (*ākarṣaṇa*) seems to be mainly used in an erotic context.

So-called magic is not the only case where power is used to particular ends. Power is constantly being ritually used and manipulated in Tantra. The Tantric initiate (*sādhaka*) is a holder of supernatural powers (*siddhis*). But so are all *siddhas*, "perfected" beings of all sorts. One also knows that Tantric texts very often say that their teaching leads both to liberation (*mukti*) and to the enjoyment of worldly or otherworldly rewards (*bhukti*). Tantric liberation in this life (*jīvanmukti*) is both the transcendence of our world and the "magical" domination of this world.[20] In fact, in India, not only in Tantra, today as in the past, a spiritual master is usually believed by his disciples to hold supernatural powers.

As well as the so-called six magical powers, there is also a traditional list of eight yogic accomplishments (*siddhi*), the first in the list being *aṇimā*, the power to become as small as an atom (*aṇu*).[21] There are many other such powers. More important, however, than the number of powers is the fact that they exist—the possibility of obtaining, mastering, and manipulating supernatural powers. But how supernatural are they really? For what is nature in Hindu India if not the work of the magic of the cosmos (*māyā*), a cosmos manifested by the deity and pervaded by its divine supernatural power (*śakti*)?[22] What is the world of Tantra if not a world, a work, of magic? It is an "enchanted" world, not a disenchanted one, as our Western world has become because it is considered as existing by itself, not as based on and ever linked with an otherworldly, transcendent source. But this is another question.

9

The Spiritual Aspect

Though fundamentally ritualistic, Tantra does not ignore other, more direct, ways to the divine. Devotion and mystical experience are also extolled in its literature. Tantra keeps a tradition that goes back to Vedic times alive while giving it a new life with new, often very interesting, developments. Thus ritual is sometimes decried,[1] given a secondary place below direct mystical experience, but it is also sometimes apotheosized, ascribed new, more intense spiritual aspects.

"Classical" Śaivasiddhānta claims that only rites can do away with the innate impurity (*āṇavamala*, in Sanskrit) of the limited human being (*paśu*) that binds him to this ever continuing empirical life. But as we have just seen, it is generally recognized that rituals are efficacious insofar as they go with an understanding of their nature and purpose (ritual is never without meaning[2] for those who perform it) and by devotion to the deity (*bhakti*), an element whose place and role went on increasing over the course of centuries in all Śaiva āgamic traditions. On the other hand, nondualist Śaivas (and especially Abhinavagupta) wholly condemn the Śaivasiddhānta view, since they claim that the root cause of human bondage is ignorance and that only knowledge, gnosis (*jñāna*), an understanding of the Supreme, can lead to liberation. Now, this knowledge, this "recognition" (*pratyabhijñā*) of our inner divine nature is first and foremost gained through spiritual quest. This is also, with nuances, the position of the Pāñcarātra and of other Vaiṣṇava Tantric traditions.

In Tantra, even in works with gnostic tendencies, ritual appears generally to have pride of place. In Abhinavagupta's *Tantrāloka*, more than twenty chapters out of thirty-seven deal directly or indirectly with ritual. However, when enumerating and describing the ways or means (*upāya*) to salvation, the lowest one—meant for less advanced yogis—is the way of ritual, while the higher ones are mystical and ranked according to the intensity of divine grace bestowed on the adept. Even in ritual action, devotion (*bhakti*) is often said to be necessary. All ways are to lead to salvation, liberation (*mukti*), which is union with the Absolute. Therefore, they are all mystical in different ways. Thus, what will be discussed here is what might be called the highest aspect of Tantra, an aspect that Tantra shares with the whole Hindu world, of which we must never forget that it is a part.

Tantric devotional or mystical notions or practices have, however, specific traits. If, for instance, Tantra uses the same spatial metaphors as Hinduism (as all religions, in fact)—notably, the "ascending" view of salvation—it qualifies it in a particular way. The Tantric liberation while living (*jīvanmukti*) is in large part experienced, lived in the body-mind that is part of this world, of its life, both acting on it and being influenced by it. The Tāntrika does not wish to escape it by merely transcending it mystically. His liberation takes place here—but it is a "here" pervaded by divine *śakti.*

The bodily, "lived," aspect of Tantric mystical experience appears notably in the role of possession by, or absorption into, the deity (*āveśa*). There are different kinds of *āveśa*, from unitive absorption in the divine to fusion with or possession by the deity. These existed in India from ancient times and continue existing today.[3] Tantra enriches them with different approaches and practices.

A characteristic trait of Tantric devotion and worship is also, as I have just said, the presence of visualizations. While worshipping a deity, the devotee should visualize its aspect as described in the *dhyānaślokas* of *mantraśāstra* manuals, a mental image that he can imagine as present in his heart or in a *cakra* of his yogic body. He thus identifies with it. Tantric prayer to a deity is also basically and primarily visual, calling forth images rather than notions.[4]

Mysticism in Ritual

Ritual activity and mystical states are not incompatible. A devotee may well worship his chosen deity and perform prescribed rites while being in a state of absorption (*āveśa*), feeling united with the deity. Tantric *pūjā* (as we have seen), implying the ritual divinization of the officiant, leads him, at least in principle, to a divine state that can be lived mystically. Kāpālika transgressive rites aimed at possession by the deity (as do many popular cults, in the past as well as today). Admittedly, possession is not mystical union, but the dividing line between the two is not very clear, nor is the Sanskrit terminology.[5]

Some Tantric *pūjās* include moments one may consider as being of a mystical character, moments of possession by the deity (*āveśa*) or of "penetration" or absorption (*samāveśa*) by it—be they spontaneous phenomena, brought about by the intense mental concentration (*bhāvanā*) of the officiating adept, or the effect of divine grace. In the ritual worship of the goddess Tripurasundarī, described in chapter 3 of the *Yoginīhṛdaya*, when worshipping the deities abiding in the *cakra* of fourteen triangles, the adept must cause his *kuṇḍalinī* to rise so that he feels united with the cosmic energy (*kulaśakti*). Then, as he concentrates on an inner phonic resonance (*nāda*), he raises again his *kuṇḍalinī* from the *mūlādhāra* to the *ājñācakra* and becomes "absorbed in his own essence." These are yogicomystical practices. The *japa* of the *śrīvidyā* ending this *pūjā* is of the same "unitive" sort, even more intense and "fusing" (see chapter 8). The sexual *kulayāga* we saw in chapter 6 ends with the total fusion with the Supreme of the consciousness of the yogi, who is identified with Bhairava.

I will add that Tantra always stresses the aesthetic aspect of ritual. The consecrated area of worship is to be as beautiful, as attractive to the senses, as possible. Flowers, incense, perfumes, and rich offerings create a scene of beauty that helps the spiritual élan or concentration of the officiating adept. As we have seen, in the Kaula initiation, the initiate is to be transported by the "beauty" of the mantras suddenly shown him. In the highest form of aesthetic experience, as expounded notably in nondualistic Śaiva works, the subject, immersed in this state of aesthetic experiences—of ecstatic wonder (*camatkāra*)—should be in a state of consciousness where time and space are abolished, a state of quiescence, of repose in one's essence (*svātmaviśrānti*), a condition one could well call mystical.

YOGIC ASPECTS

Mystical states being experienced by living humans inevitably have a bodily aspect, even if they are moments when the body is transcended—only the soul (*ātman*) is there. But this is experienced, "lived," by the adept in his body-mind. These altered states of consciousness are thus also bodily states. The mystical moments in ritual we have just seen were mostly associated with the ascent of *kuṇḍalinī*, which is the divine in the (yogic) body. Such states are constantly met with in Tantric (notably Śaiva) texts. Some deserve notice.

Those I will mention are from the fifth chapter of Abhinavagupta's *Tantrāloka*, which describes the ways toward salvation (*upāya*) open to yogis who are not fully detached from this world. There is, for instance, an intense meditation on the omnipresence of Bhairava flashing forth in the human and the divine heart, where the entire visible world dissolves. The yogi, identifying with it, realizes thus the one and threefold presence of the Supreme as the three supreme goddesses of the Trika: Parā, Parāparā, and Aparā. He may then experience in body and mind the madly twirling presence of the twelve Kalīs, becoming thus identified with the cosmic flashing forth of the deity in humans and in the universe—a veritable deification both cosmic and transcendental. There is also the identification of the yogi with the Supreme by mentally following the ascending thrust of *SAUḤ*, the "heart-mantra" associated with *kuṇḍalinī*, or identifying with the mantra *KHPHREṂ*, the "master of the cosmos," whose efficacy unites the yogi with the flow of the universe. Those (and other ones described in this chapter) are yogic practices that are mystically experienced, their efficacy ultimately depending on the grace of God (*anugraha*). They are also gnostic or metaphysical because they rest on a mystical apprehension of metaphysical notions. But all Indian philosophical systems aim at leading their adepts toward liberation, which is a mystical experience.

MYSTICAL WAYS—DIVINE GRACE

These diverse ways can be considered as more spiritual than the preceding ones although they also include bodily aspects—as does all mystical experience. The instances cited here are mostly Śaiva because the Śaiva systems (especially when nondualistic and Kashmirian) offer a larger choice of such meditative methods than other Tantric traditions. Śaiva traditions, especially those expounded by Abhinavagupta, underline the basic importance of the bestowing of divine grace (*anugraha*)[6] for humans, also called "descent of power" (*śaktipāta*). Śiva's power is described in the *Parātriṃśikāvivaraṇa* as having grace as its very nature.

The importance of grace is underscored in the *Tantrāloka*, where the means or ways (*upāya*) to liberation, all leading to mystical experience, are classified according to the intensity of divine grace. The highest one is the "non-way" (*an-upāya*), where the perfectly pure adept realizes at once this divine, "bhairavic" essence and is therefore at once and definitively liberated. This experience is so intense that sometimes the adept dies.

The next way, the first that is actually a path that can be followed, is the way of Śiva, here called Śambhu, the Benevolent (*śāṃbhavopāya*).[7] It is a very intense mystical way because the yogi is to realize spiritually and thus participate in the initial creative throbbing forth of the deity. This cosmic process unfolds (out of time) in the godhead as the apparition of the phonemes of the Sanskrit alphabet, the *varṇaparāmarśa* I described in chapter 7, a process the adept is to understand but, more essentially, to identify with by fusing mystically with the cosmic outflow of the deity in an illuminating and liberating experience. To quote four of the last stanzas of the chapter:

> "Manifesting the universe in myself in the ether of my conscience, I am the Creator, being made of the same substance as the cosmos": to realize this is to be identified with Bhairava. (283) "The universe dissolves in me, made as I am of the dishevelled flames of the fire of the supreme Consciousness": to see this is to find peace. "I am verily Śiva: such is the blazing fire that burns the House of so many rooms—the dream—of *saṃsāra*." "It rests in me and when it dissolves nothing remains": who understands creation, maintenance and resorption as indivisible, since unified, he flashes forth, having reached the highest state. (285–87)

The mystical experience of the fullness of cosmic flashing forth described in this chapter, far from being a simple and direct one, implies an understanding of complex metaphysical notions. Few adepts can attempt this way, even if guided by a guru steeped in this system. It is meant for mentally and spiritually gifted adepts.

More "intellectual" is the way of power (*śāktopāya*), for there the mystical vision where all duality disappears in the pure consciousness of the Supreme is based initially on a discursive intellectual approach, which is then transcended. This intellectual approach is pure discriminative discernment (*sat-tarka*), an intense intuitive awareness that, together with divine grace, leads to an illumination of pure gnosis—a mystical experience culminating in liberation. This is, however, a way of power that takes on the form of divine forces tiered from the highest plane down to that of humans. It is conceived as wheels of energy (*śakticakra*) whose innumerable rays animate the sense organs, their free play dominating the yogi who worships them and uniting him with Śiva. These wheels of power are the twelve Kālīs, powerful and fearsome goddesses with whose cosmic swirling the yogi is to identify until he attains the highest one, Mahābhairavacaṇḍograghorakālī, "Kalī the Terrible, Enormously Fearsome Terrifying Bhairava," the goddess who annihilates the cosmos into the void of the Absolute. Reaching this point, the yogi stays in the hub of this wheel of power, in the perfectly peaceful but vibrating center of the universe—pure divine Conscience—and he fuses with Bhairava.

When following this way, the yogi may also (as we have seen) reach the same cosmic liberating experience by a penetrating and identifying understanding of the constituent letters of the mantra *SAUH*, by which he will realize the perennial surging forth of Śiva's power, the creative throbbing flow of the divine Heart.[8] This is the same experience he may have with another mantra, *KHPHREṂ*. In both cases, the experience is both gnostic and yogic.

Similar yogic forms of identification with *śakti* using mantras are alluded to in *Śivasūtra* 21 and 22, their mystical interpretation given in Kṣemarāja's commentary.

I will also mention other practices of the same sort that are described in that very remarkable Tantric text, the *Vijñānabhairava*. From this work, we cited a case of fusion in the Absolute through sexual union in chapter 8. Here is a variant thereof, worth quoting because the spiritual experience of the absolute results not from the surging of power caused by actual coition but from the power of imagination or, more exactly, of remembrance (*smara/smṛti*). Especially in the Trika system, remembrance is given an important role, for it transcends time and thus opens a way to the Supreme by connecting the present with the past. "Memory," says Abhinavagupta, "is what brings about the apprehension of the deeper nature of the modalities of existence . . . It is consciousness in the highest sense" (*Tantrāloka* 5, 137–39). Remembrance is so divine in nature that Abhinavagupta goes so far as to write, "He who remembers is none other than the Supreme Lord." But here is the *Vijñānabhairava*, 69[9]: "O Goddess, even in the absence of a woman, there is a flow of delight due to the intensity of the memory of the sexual pleasure she gave by fondling, kisses and embracing."

This is evidently no mere erotic dreaming but the spiritual reactivation of a previous state of sensual intensity (the one described in stanza 68 we have seen in chapter 8). The power of image-creating imagination and its effect on the body (the body-mind, rather) is often referred to by Abhinavagupta in ritual, aesthetic, or mystical context.

In the following instances, also from the *Vijñānabhairava*, what operates is not the inner creative power of the mind but, conversely, its perception of the outside world—of the presence or absence of objects. Focusing the mind's attention on an object or on space while stopping all discursive thought brings about absorption in Bhairava, which is understood as the supreme, divine, pure Consciousness as related to the world. Thus: "If one focuses one's gaze on a jar or other [container] while disregarding its enclosing surface, one dissolves in this[void] and becomes identified with it" (59). Or: "If one casts his gaze on a place without trees, mountains, walls, etc., what constitutes the reality of a mental state is dissolved and the fluctuations of mind disappear" (60). Or, a variant: "One's gaze being focused on a portion of space variously lighted by the sun, a lamp, etc., there precisely the essence of one's Self shines forth" (75). Or, differently: "If, contemplating the pure sky, one concentrates firmly one's gaze on it, the body being completely motionless, at this very moment, O Goddess, the luminous nature of Bhairava is obtained" (84).

In the next two cases—perhaps more surprisingly for us—one-pointed attention on the body is used to reach absorption in the supreme: "Piercing some bodily part with a sharpened needle or some other [pointed object], if one then keeps one mind focused one-pointedly on that spot, access is given to Bhairava's immaculate purity" (93). Or, conversely: "All sensation, pleasant or painful, goes through the door of the senses. [Therefore] if one is detached from the senses, one abides in oneself and remains stable in his *ātman*" (136).

If one-pointed attention may bring about transcendence of the limited self, a loss of control, a sudden unexpected incident, or rapid bodily movements can also cause a brief loss of control of oneself and open a path to the Absolute: "If, having whirled round and round, one falls down suddenly, because of this sudden interruption of the effervescence of energy, the supreme state appears" (111). Or: "When sneezing starts or ends, in terror or anxiety, on the brink of a deep chasm, when fleeing from a battle, when one is taken over by intense curiosity, at the start or end of hunger, a state which is the essence of *brahman* occurs" (118).

In the *Vijñānabhairava*, there are 112 different methods for attaining (or attempting to attain) a mystical experience of the Absolute. These show that many elements or moments of current life can, if deeply understood, experienced, or somehow transcended, may—for a yogi—open the doors of perception.

Devotion—*Bhakti*

Authentic and deep as they may be, the spiritual experiences we have just seen may well be found lacking in feeling. They may be more metaphysical than properly "mystical," pertaining more to *śakti*—*śaktipāta*—than to *bhakti*. But *bhakti* is not foreign to all forms of Tantra.

Tantric texts often say that a given practice or rite is to be performed with devotion (*bhaktyā*), this even in nondualistic systems. The pervasive presence of the deity, the fact that we all are in God, does not preclude devotion. Far from it, it makes it easier because the devotee feels constantly "environed by God, capable of God, if he wants to" (to quote Pierre de Bérulle[10]). Possession by the deity can be devotional. The main effect of the fifty different forms of possession or penetration (*samāveśa*) by Rudra described in chapter 2 of the *Mālinīvijayottaratantra* is said to be that it bestows an unwavering devotion to Rudra. The role of devotion went on increasing over the course of centuries—in spite of the fact that a strong *bhakti* is necessarily at odds with the essential role given to ritual in Tantra, notably with the notion that *dīkṣā* is the necessary first step on the way to *mokṣa.*

In nondualistic Śaivism, two important mystical texts that give expression to *bhakti* should be mentioned: Utpaladeva's *Śivastotrāvali,* a "Collection of Hymns to Śiva," and the *Stavacintāmaṇi,* the "Jewel of Lauds" to Śiva by Bhaṭṭa Nārāyaṇa, both dating from the eighth/ninth century. Here are some verses from the twelfth song of Utpaladeva's *Śivastotrāvali* (in Constantina Rhodes Bailly's translation):

> Having completely entered
> Your lotus feet
> Having lost all desire,
> Let me consume the utmost bounteous honey
> And wander at will,
> Completely satisfied.
>
> Inundated with the pure,
> Endlessly flowing stream of nectar
> Of the supreme knowledge
> That all is one, When, O Lord, shall I realize absolute identification
> Between you and my physical form,
> And obtain never ending Bliss?
>
> Whatever is not,
> Let that be nothing to me.
> Whatever is
> Let that be something to me.
> In this way may it be
> That you be found and worshipped by me
> In all states.[11]

Other Tantric Śaiva mystical works could be cited. There are hymns to the Goddess, though these are more devotional than mystical. There are some hymns of Abhinavagupta, too. For instance, the "Offering of Inner Experience" (*Anubhavavedana*) or the "Hymn to [the Glory of] Bhairava" (*Bhairavastava*).[12] Such ancient works are not all in Sanskrit. I mentioned in chapter 4 the strange sepulchral poetry of Kāraikālammaiyār, and the Cittars, among them the famous Tirumūlar, author of the three-thousand-verse *Tirumantiram.* I will also mention the hymns of the Nāyaṉmārs, the Tamil Śaiva poet-saints whose songs, arranged in decades of verses, lay out a sacred geography of temples to Śiva in the Tamil-speaking south. There is also

Cekkiḷar's *Periya Purāṇam*, a work of unbelievable violence dating from the twelfth century but still read or recited today. Violent forms of religion are to be found in many Hindu traditions; however, they are aspects more of popular religion than of Tantra.[13] In Bengal, there is (as I have said previously) a vast collection of devotional hymns and poems to different forms of the Goddess, dating from the twelfth century down to modern times. Also to be cited is Lallā or Lalleśvari (also called Lal Ded), who lived in Kashmir between 1350 and 1400. Hers is an interesting case, for, a Brahmin Yoginī, she was also the disciple of a Sufi saint. She composed a number of very remarkable short poems in Kashmiri.[14] For instance,

> I saw He is in everything
> In everything I saw Him shine.
> Listen, pay attention, and you can see Hara.
> The house is totally His: who am I, Lallā?

and,

> I, Lallā, appeased in love the fire of love.
> Before dying, I died entirely.
> How many forms I saw in myself!
> When the I disappears; what shall I do? (136)

Naturally, there is also mystical experience on the Vaiṣṇava Pāñcarātra side, where the atmosphere is often more devotional than properly mystical. This latter form was especially present in South India with the Āḻvārs, the mystical Tamil poets. In Bengal, the important mystical tradition of the Sahajiyās, worshippers of Kṛṣṇa and Rādhā, whose love for Kṛṣṇa the devotees wish to live through mystically (and therefore, if male, transsexually) flourished too.

Some of the poet-saints of North India are also to be referred to in this context. (On these vernacular literatures, see chapter 3.)

In all such cases—but also, as we have seen, in Sanskrit traditions—*bhakti*, mystical effusion, is present in Tantra on the way to the divine or when reaching it. There are moments when metaphysical constructions, ritual or bodily techniques are to be discarded, transcended, yielding to devotion and divine grace.

Guru

In Hindu India, if devotion and mystical union are bestowed by God, his grace is generally transmitted through a spiritual master, a guru—"guru's grace." This is especially so in Tantra, where the guru, a consecrated initiate, is the first recipient of this power, which he then bestows upon his disciples. He is not merely respected but veritably divinized, considered sometimes as more important than the deity he serves. To quote the *Kulārṇavatantra*: "The guru is the father, the guru is the mother, the guru is God, the Supreme Lord. When Śiva is angry the guru saves [us from his wrath]. But when the guru is angry, nobody [can help]" (12, 49). This important fourteenth-century Tantra includes two chapters (of 129 and 133 stanzas) on the guru, the first extolling the guru, the second dealing with the qualities, good or bad, of guru and disciple. The disciple has to serve his master with absolute devotion and total submission. Another Tantric work, the *Yoginīhṛdaya*, prescribes that the adept should invoke and mentally perceive the presence of the "sandals" of his master (*gurupādukā*)—that is, the presence of his master—in a center of his yogic body. The text says that these sandals "pervade the universe and fill it with bliss," adding that "the nature of the guru is that of the supreme Śiva."

Tantric traditions are initiatory. They are all deemed to have been revealed (out of time) by a deity to a first master who, as a guru, transmitted it to a disciple, the second master, and so forth down to our time. This succession of masters (*guruparaṃparā*) is to be invoked and worshipped at the start of any ritual, an action that confirms, as it were, the divine origin and therefore the validity and efficacy of the tradition. This worship of the master (*gurupūjā*) as an annex to the worship of the deity is one of the obligatory rituals of Tantric adepts. "The Master is the way" (*gurur upāyaḥ*), says the *Śivasūtra* (2, 6). And on the Vaiṣṇava side, the *Jayākhyasaṃhitā*: "The All-knowing [God] takes on the form of the guru" (*sarvajño gurumūrtigaḥ*).

Nondualistic Śaiva Tantras distinguish between different sorts of gurus. Abhinavagupta states in the *Tantrāloka* (4.51–53) that the highest masters are those who reach perfection by an inner realization of truth together with a direct knowledge of the scriptures gained by intense mental concentration (*bhāvanā*), without any formal ritual initiation. Such masters are called *akalpita* ("not [ritually] made"). Only divine grace operates. So great is the divine power gained by the guru that it extends to his family, considered as also divinized by sharing his perfection.

10

Tantric Places or Practices

Sacred Geography

Born in the Indian subcontinent, Hinduism, whether Tantric or "mainstream," is deeply rooted in the Indian soil. The main deities—Śiva, Viṣṇu, the Goddess—are "pan-Indian," worshipped everywhere. These main figures have epiphanies, particular aspects that are worshipped all over the Indian subcontinent. There are also local forms of the main deities, as well as a number of local deities, linked to specific places in India or Nepal where they are deemed to have appeared, divinizing the region through their sanctuaries, which become so many places of pilgrimage (*tīrthas*), literally "fords." In effect, these are places where devotees cross over, as it were, to the beyond—places where they can go from this world to the Other one. They are sanctuaries where, during ritual commemorations, devotees participate intimately in the elements of the deity's life, even in their pains and problems, especially if it is a female goddess. Thus, in those places, there is a particularly emotional atmosphere.[1] These innumerable sacred places spreading over South Asia form the sacred geography of the Indian subcontinent—sacred geographies, rather, for they are not merely Tantric but Hindu (of different persuasions), as well as Jain and Buddhist. Sacred geography is especially important in Tantra, both because of the number and specificity of Tantric *tīrthas* and because this geography can be interiorized by the adept. Sacred geography is also politically significant, the Hindu realm being traditionally considered as ritually structured as a *maṇḍala* (see chapter 2).

The best known, and one of the most typical, aspects of this sacred geography is that of the *pīṭhas*, the sacred "seats" of the Goddess Satī (or Pārvatī), Śiva's consort. They are the places of the Indian soil where (after Dakṣa's sacrifice) the pieces of Satī's disintegrating body, which Śiva bore on his shoulders, fell to the ground while Śiva roamed all over India. The body is traditionally said to have been torn into fifty-one pieces. Hence the fifty-one sacred places, sanctuaries where different forms of the goddess, usually associated with Bhairava, are worshipped. In fact, there are different lists of *pīṭhas* ranging from 34 to 108 or 110. The locations of the places mentioned in the texts are often uncertain. They are, however, spread over the whole Indian subcontinent, forming a net that covers it with divine forces—a sacred universe superimposed (or metaphysically underpinning) the world humans live in. One may well believe that many such centers are more imaginary than real. But many do exist and can be located, some being important Hindu places of worship and pilgrimage still today.

There were and there still are other ensembles of *pīṭhas* that, like those of Satī, form nets of power. We saw that there were Tantric cults of fearsome feminine deities in ancient times, the Yoginīs, associated with Bhairava, whose ensemble was deemed to cover the Indian subcontinent with a net of power. Better known historically and still present today in several places in India and Nepal are those of the Kula traditions. Notably those of the Kubjikāmata and of Śrīvidyā, whose goddesses are (this even today) present in sanctuaries while being also bodily and mentally interiorized in spiritual-yogic practices. These traditions have a number of *pīṭhas*, the four main ones in the Kaula tradition being Oḍḍiyāna, Kāmarūpa, Pūrṇagiri, and Jālandhara. Oḍḍiyāna is especially important, for it is considered as the place of origin of the tradition. It is in the Swat Valley (today in Pakistan). Jālandhara is near the modern town of that name, in Panjab. The goddess Jvālāmukhī, "Of the Flaming Mouth," is also worshipped in Panjab, in a place where blazing flames of natural gas issue from the soil. Where Pūrṇagiri was is not known. Kāmarūpa/Kāmākhya is in Assam, not far from Guhawati. It is a particularly notable *pīṭha*, for it is the place where Satī's *yoni* fell, which "bleeds" once a year.

This sacred geography is all the more interesting and meaningful because it can be mentally interiorized, these two geographies, outer and inner, being closely linked. For the Śaiva systems of Kula, for instance, the bodily integration of the *pīṭhas*, which are penetrated by the power of the Goddess, is patterned according to their external "geographic" distribution. However, the texts consider the power of the "external" *pīṭhas* as derived from their "internal" counterparts, which are held to be more intensely divine. This inner net of power, centered on different points of the physical or imaginal body of the adept, can be "lived" as present in the respiratory or in the vital breath, especially when the *pīṭhas* are associated with mantras or other phonetic elements—the *mālinī* alphabet, for instance. Thus, the yogi "lives" a twofold identifying "geographization," since he mentally internalizes a sacred Indian landscape that he conceives as having its source in himself (for the Goddess abides in him), and as reflecting in outer space the landscape he imagines as present in his body.[2]

Pilgrimage

This sacred geography is mainly experienced exoterically by a Hindu devotee (Tantric or, more currently, "mainstream") when on pilgrimage. He would worship the Goddess's *yoni* and feel her power at Kāmākhyā. He would visit and worship the different forms of Śiva Mahādeva, the "Great God," in his city of Kāśī/Vārāṇasī (Varanasi, Benares, Banaras)—either as Lord of the Universe in the Viśvanātha temple or as Bhairava at Kapālamocana, where the head of Brahmā that he had cut off with his left hand and that remained stuck on it eventually dropped off. In Varanasi, there is also a Liṅga of Light (*jyotirliṅga*) symbolizing the manifestation of Śiva piercing the three worlds as a brilliant shaft of light.[3] In South India, at Chidambaram, he would worship a Liṅga of Space, all the more present for being invisible, and so forth in innumerable places of the Indian subcontinent and for innumerable divine forms.[4] Note that one may visit a Tantric deity as a pilgrim without being a Tāntrika. The main point in a pilgrimage is to approach a divine entity so as to benefit from its presence, hoping to have some wish fulfilled (for which a Tantric deity is often considered as especially efficacious). But visiting a deity, on pilgrimage or otherwise, is mainly to stand in the presence of the deity and to behold its image, both seeing and being seen by the deity. This vision (*darśan*), this interplay of vision where the devotee's vision is an act of love for the deity whose grace is bestowed by its gaze upon him or her, is an essential element of Hindu worship—without forgetting that there is also, perhaps more importantly, a physical feeling of the presence of the deity, often approached as living person, especially if the deity is a goddess.[5]

It sometimes happens, too, that deities are members of a group whose sanctuaries form a structured ensemble spreading across a whole district, considered as forming a *maṇḍala* that the pilgrim is to travel across in the prescribed order, worshipping them and benefiting from their power. This is the case of the pilgrimage to Vindhyavasinī, a local goddess of a mountainous district not far from Banaras. There, several sanctuaries to this deity delimit a sacred space, the Vindhyakṣetra, in the Vindhya Range. These mountains are considered to reproduce the triangle symbolic of the goddess (*trikoṇa*), who is thus worshipped by the ritual visitation of all these sanctuaries, on the ground.[6] In Banaras, Kāśī, the circuit around the sacred space formed by the city for pilgrimage—the so-called Pañcakrośī Yātrā, which includes 108 "stations"—is understood as a ritual circumambulation (*pradakṣiṇā*) around the *liṅga* of Śiva.[7] An analogous case, explicitly Tantric, is in Nepal, where the city of Bhaktapur is considered as a *yantra* divided into nine sections, each dedicated to one of the nine Mothers, guardian deities whose *pīṭhas* surround the city to form a protecting *maṇḍala*.[8] In the Himalayan region, sanctuaries to Tantric deities delimit the inhabited (or merely the cultivated) space, separating it symbolically from the outside world, which is felt to be inhabited by fearsome supernatural forces. The power of these protecting deities is reaffirmed and reinforced by their being carried in processions or in group pilgrimages.[9] In such cases, pilgrimage takes on a social as well as a religious importance. This importance of pilgrimage is not a specifically Tantric trait. Pilgrimage is an essential element, both socially and religiously, of mainstream Hinduism.

The reader might be surprised by the fact that, on *pīṭhas*, I referred to ancient texts while describing contemporary practices with which we are to deal in chapter 11. This confusion of periods is voluntary, for modern practices are based on ancient texts that are constantly being used. In India, the past is an aspect of the present. Down to recent times, India, as well as Nepal, remained untouched by modernity in many respects, escaping the disenchantment of the world (to speak like Max Weber). Politically, India is a democracy—the polity is without transcendental foundation, but socioreligiously India remains in touch with the divine, true to its Vedic origin. Gods, deities of all sorts, are present everywhere, rooted in the Indian soil, near to their devotees. Most of these deities are not Tantric, but many are. Āgamas and Tantras are the texts that rule many religious or socioreligious aspects. Down to modern times, they defined the relationship of the divine power with the political rule of the realm, a situation some aspects of which are still visible in temple festivals today.[10]

The Hindu Temple

A treatise on religious architecture is necessarily tantric.

JEAN FILLIOZAT

There were no temples in Vedic times, only consecrated areas for sacrifice. Such or similar areas went on being (and still are) used for specific ritual ends in Tantric practice (in *dīkṣā*, for instance, as we have seen). Temples seem to have appeared during the first centuries of our era. Their present architectural and iconographic traits mostly go back to the most active Tantric period, from the eighth to the twelfth century. Rules for their construction, decoration, and for their iconography are given in Tantras or āgamas and in their commentaries. They are also to be found in Purāṇas, in treatises on architecture, iconography, *mantraśāstra*, and so on—all of which are either Tantric texts or texts influenced by the ideology of Tantra. Besides temples, there are innumerable places dedicated to some divine manifestation, power or presence, scattered all over the Indian soil, all marked by an image or object that is the support of worship. Such sites are mostly aspects of so-called popular Hinduism, often modest in size but also sometimes important temples and places of pilgrimage.[11] Some are dedicated to Tantric deities—Bhairava/Bhairon, for instance—or to local aspects of the Goddess. All Hindu worship necessitates an image or icon as a substrate of worship, however modest it may be.

Not all Hindu temples[12] are Tantric. They are only Tantric when they house a Tantric deity. However, one may say that, generally speaking, with the exception of the most elementary structures, the foundation and construction of Hindu temples and the images of deities they contain are all made according to rules set down in Tantras, āgamas, and Tantric technical treatises. The basic texts being sacred, revealed scriptures, their precepts are deemed to be of divine origin. That such texts should issue from the deity may be considered normal, since the temple is not merely the deity's residence but an axial point of the godhead's presence in this world. It is a sacred place (*kṣetra*). It is also a ford (*tīrtha*), where one may cross over religiously from this world to the Supreme, since it is a place where devotees approach a deity to have its *darśan*.

The site where a temple is to be built is always to be carefully chosen. It must be auspicious, for which astrologers are to be consulted. It must also be correctly oriented (usually facing east) and metaphysically "stable," which does not exclude practical considerations, such as the preferences of those who have it built—the monarch, a social group (caste, guild, etc.), or some rich person. The structure is erected by qualified craftsmen (*śilpins*) headed by an architect, this always under strict control of expert Tāntrika Brahmins who see to it that all is done according to rule and who perform all prescribed rites during the building process. This is a long and complex process, which I shall not describe here. More interesting for us are the principles on which these rites, which sanctify the building, are based and that make them meaningful.

Being the abode of a deity, the temple is there either because the deity appeared there or because of some miraculous (as we would say[13]) sign that gave a reason for the temple to be built. Such events, which have evidently nothing to do with historical facts (known notably through inscriptions), are typically mentioned in the foundation myth of the temple (*sthalapurāṇa*)—the "history" (or rather the legend) of the place. As for the construction, the building site of the temple is to be square. This connects it with the earth (*Bhū* or *Pṛthivī*), whose outline is round but, as connected with the four cardinal points, is symbolically represented as square, or "four-cornered" (Ṛg Veda X.58). This is a first sign of the link between temple and cosmos. Once the area is found, delimited, ritually purified, and materially prepared, a diagram of the basic pattern of the building must be drawn upon it. This pattern is not seen as a mere geometrical architectural requirement but as a ritual diagram (*yantra*). It is called *vāstumaṇḍala*, or more precisely *vāstupuruṣamaṇḍala*, Puruṣa being the Cosmic Man, the origin and source of all that exists and therefore of the place (*vāstu*) where the temple is built. The *vāstumaṇḍala* is divided into sixty-four or eighty-one squares, filled up by the different parts and limbs of the *puruṣa*'s body. These divisions also correspond to cosmic divisions, heavenly bodies, or deities—a divine and cosmic totality. Then one digs the foundation.[14]

On this symbolic base, the temple, which is the residence of a god (or goddess), is built. The whole temple, which may include several architectural elements surrounding the center or leading to it, is not necessarily square in shape. But its inner sanctum, containing the central shrine (*garbhagṛha*)[15] that houses the icon of the main deity, is square. Above it is a pyramidal superstructure, usually called a *śikhara*. This is often pointed and curvilinear but can take on a great variety of forms and can be decorated in many different ways. The *śikhara* symbolically represents the axis of the world, the deity enclosed at its base in the darkness of the *garbhagṛha* being metaphysically in the center of the universe, of which the temple is a symbol.

The whole temple is charged with symbolism. It is, one may say, a symbolical construction. The sculptures that adorn it are not placed arbitrarily. They form a pantheon surrounding the main deity, its constitutive deities selected and placed according to the theological conceptions of the tradition proper to the temple. For instance, in a Śaiva temple, the images of the god present in the temple are those of the five "faces" of Sadāśiva, and they are placed in the directions prescribed in the āgamas: a fearsome form in the south, a peaceful one in the west, a feminine one facing north, and so on. There is an analogous placing of the god's aspects in Vaiṣṇava temples with the Vyūhas surrounding Viṣṇu. In the same way, carved figures showing constituent elements of the cosmos are tiered vertically from the base to the summit of the temple. Facing the entrance of Śaiva temples, there is a flagpole (*dhvaja*)—ritually chosen, erected, and decorated—placed on a platform on which the three *tattvas* that constitute the universe are ritually placed.[16] The first two, *Nara* and *Śakti* (the planes of humans and of energy), are on the pole, and the third, *Śiva*, is on the flag fastened to the top of the pole. Thus the whole universe is symbolically placed there, with the main deity, Śiva, on the top of the cosmic mountain that is the temple. The flagpole is usually considered as a variety of *liṅga*, the main and essentially important *liṅga* being, of course, the one in the *garbhagṛha*—immovable, approached only by priests. It goes without saying that this *liṅga* is ritually installed together with all the accessory elements that surround or support it, as are the other images of Śiva (notably portable ones, used in different rites) or the images of other deities present in the temple. The sanctum is also to be ritually consecrated.

Thus divinely "impregnated," the temple is not merely the residence of the main deity; it is a visible aspect of the deity's presence and power. It is entirely divine. The mantras, or the "vital breath" (*prāṇa*), the power of the deity, are infused in it as a whole and in its different parts by the *pratiṣṭhā* ritual. The temple itself is consecrated first, then the main icon present in the sanctum is permeated by the divine *śakti*, followed by the other temple images, especially the mobile images of the main deity, which remain unmovable in the sanctum. Thus the temple is fully permeated by the power of the deity.

Resting centrally on the *vāstupuruṣamaṇḍala*, the temple can be considered as Śiva's body (or that of any other deity, as the case may be). Thanks to the carved images of deities it houses and to the supernatural entities ritually installed there, the temple displays the mythology of the god's tradition on its walls and pillars for all who visit it.

According to the rules governing the construction of temples, its structure and proportion are, at least in theory, not left to the personal choice of an architect or of patrons, even if royal, but must follow textual prescriptions. However, there are different types of temples, large or small, of different architectural styles, that vary according to architectural or regional tastes—the peculiar Himalayan temples, for instance,[17] or the vast constructions in South India, the equivalent of which is never seen in the north. But even if different in style or size, all temples are held to have been built and structured according to strict and very precise traditional rules.

Temples are important centers of Hindu life. This is still the case today. With a few exceptions (archeological sites, ruined or abandoned sanctuaries), Hindu temples, Tantric or "mainstream," are not dead structures. As they were in the past, they are still today (sometimes intensely) active places, cared for by priests, their rituals attended by (sometimes crowds of) devotees. Like their building and architectural pattern, their activity is, in theory, all rule governed, codified in sacred texts, Tantras, and so on that are often ancient but still in use today. Temples are one more Indian place where past meets present. The main deity of the temple,[18] or the pair of deities—for, if Tantric, a deity very often has a consort (a fact to which an important exception is that of Sadāśiva, who is typically present in a *liṅga*, the main substrate of worship in surviving ancient Śaiva temples)—is to be treated as a person or persons to be honored and taken care of from their early awakening at dawn to their time for sleeping in the evening. These ceremonies, held at different fixed times of the day, are not mere social pretense but ritual acts of worship (*pūjās*) performed by a priest whose worship aims at identifying him with the deity. The public attending these actions attends a ceremony of worship (and, as it ends, partakes of the offerings to the deity, the holy *prasāda*, an important item of contemporary Hindu practice[19]).

These acts of veneration are said to be performed for the benefit of the world. In addition to the daily worship, cults are also performed at different dates of the lunisolar Hindu calendar. Some are modest events while others are more formal or festive, each carried out to pay homage to and glorify the deities of the temple. These may be "great festivals" (*mahotsavas*), where the deities are carried out in procession around the temple on ornamented chariots or palanquins, often drawn by devotees who attend these events in large numbers. Some well-known *mahotsavas* are those of Jagannāth at Puri or the feast of *Kārtikkai* in the great Śaiva temples of Tamil Nadu (a celebration associated with Annamalai [Tiruvaṇṇāmalai] in which devotees climb the sacred Arunāchala Mountain, carrying fuel for a fire to be lit on its summit commemorating the manifestation of Śiva as a column of fire). These feasts are conducted and ritually performed by temple priests (initiated Tantric Brahmins) helped by (sometimes numerous) ritual officiants, temple servants, chanters, musicians, and dancers (*devadāsīs*).[20]

The larger temples—notably those in South India—usually comprise different constructions, the temple complex including several sanctuaries, many halls, multiple kitchens, a bathing tank, numerous gateways, and so on. Temples were sometimes large land and property holders. Large tax-concessions were often conferred on them, as well as gold, jewelry, and so on—all this showing the power of those who founded, endowed, and patronized them. Thus temples had a social and political role,[21] a condition that, as we shall see, has not entirely disappeared today. If attending temple rites is not mandatory for Hindus, many do attend some ceremonies, daily worship, or festivals. They also have rituals performed by temple priests for their benefit, notably purification and expiatory or propitiatory rites. The temple (as we have said) is also the place where devotees feel near to the deity and receive (or rather exchange) its auspicious *darśan*.

Iconography

Like the temple, all the divine images it holds (as well as all images or icons for ritual use) are not supposed to be freely made by artists but made by craftsmen (*śilpins*) who carry out their creative activity according to precise iconographical rules expounded in āgamas and in their accompanying technical treatises. They often make beautiful images; however, their primary aim is not to create "things of beauty" but to create objects for spiritual or religious use that are to be ritually consecrated.

The rules concerning the making, consecration, use and upkeep, and disposal (when they are damaged or broken) of these images are numerous and are to be strictly respected. More creative freedom seems to be allowed for painted or drawn images, but these are not always for ritual uses. The patterns of *yantras* or *maṇḍalas*, which may include different kinds of images, are strictly rule governed—one cannot fashion them imaginatively. They must be drawn as prescribed by tradition. Carved images lining the outer walls of temples appear more freely composed, but this is possibly because they are also decorative. Notionally, they are of a canonical sort, since they transpose the visualizations of deities described in sacred texts in stone.

There are also erotic sculptures, the best known being those of Khajuraho and Konarak. Their nature and raison d'être is problematic. They may be patterned according to particular rules; some may figuratively transpose an esoteric erotic diagram (the *kāmakalā*, for instance). It has been suggested that their meaning could be deduced from their place in the temple. Do they figure real (if sometimes bizarre) sexual unions? Do they evoke fertility, cosmic or human vital effervescence? Or are they simply erotic scenes? This remains an open question.

In the end, one must not forget that everywhere in India and Nepal, there are not only small sanctuaries or shrines but also innumerable sacred images or symbols of all sorts, substances, and aspects—natural ("self-born" *svayambhū*) or due to human action—that are worshipped as religious icons and considered sacred by direct divine action without ever having been consecrated. They often, but not always, represent forms of popular religion ("self-born" *liṅgas*, for instance, are an officially recognized category of *liṅga*).

INSTALLATION

Before any image or object can be used for ritual, spiritual, or religious (or magical) ends, whether it is a temple image or an object for private worship or prayer (a rosary, for instance), it is first to be consecrated, united with the deity (or the absolute *brahman*), and infused by divine power. Because this power is sometimes conceived as a vital breath, this ritual action is often (probably sometime after the twelfth century) named "installation of breath" (*prāṇapratiṣṭhā*). In a temple, the main image is consecrated first, followed by its portable forms. The images of other deities abiding in the temple may also receive a *pratiṣṭhā*. There are Śaiva *pratiṣṭhātantras* describing the ritual process. These vary according to different traditions, but the general pattern as well as the spirit of the process is common to all systems.

The ritual is a complex one. For the main temple image, it may last two or three days. There are differences according to circumstances, but the general pattern is always the same, since one is always to infuse a power into an object. First, the image of a deity is to be ritually posited in its proper place, provided with all necessary symbolic elements, abundantly marked with mantras, infused with their power and, after other rites, ritually bathed. The eyes of the image (if anthropomorphic), which were deemed to be "closed" (though already engraved by the *śilpin*) until that time, are to be "opened" by the priest, who symbolically traces the contours of the pupils with a golden stylus. This is an important action, for the gaze of the deity is charged with power (hence the rite of *darśan*). This first gaze is considered especially powerful and dangerous—it must not fall on the officiating priest but on some peaceful, auspicious object. In practice, it is mostly after the opening of the eyes that power is effectively infused into the image by placing a series of mantras accompanied by other ritual actions on it (by *nyāsas*). Manipulation of power, use of mantras, abundant ritual action—the *pratiṣṭhā* process is typically Tantric.

ICONS, PANTHEONS

Tantric divine images come from different Tantric traditions. Though diverse, they share a number of common features. However, like in Hindu temples, deities, whether Tantric or not, are made and placed according to rules recorded in Tantric texts with few exceptions. As said in chapter 1, Tantra is, in many respects, nothing else than what became Hinduism from the fifth century AD onward.[22] From that time down to our days, all divine images are, if not Tantric, at least marked by Tantra—even in Jainism ("Tantric" Buddhism, as one knows, developed in the same period and sometimes together with Hindu Tantra).

These images are too numerous to be described here, this being all the less necessary because there are a number of well-illustrated books on Hindu iconography. Such images may have human features (they are "anthropomorphic") with sometimes several heads or animal heads (as the Yoginīs, for instance). Their bodily postures and gestures, clothing, ornaments, and attributes, or the objects they hold in their hands (the so-called weapons [*āyudhas*]), correspond and give expression to their nature and functions.[23] Thus Kālī, powerful and fearsome, is often shown garlanded by severed human limbs, standing on the lifeless (though sometimes ithyphallic) body of Śiva, or united with him when a deity is shown standing on top of this pair.[24] There are also cases where the Goddess is the main deity, dominating her male consort, and so is shown seated on his shoulders. Of Śiva, a fundamentally Tantric god, there are a large number of different forms corresponding to his different aspects, described notably in the Purāṇas (early Tantras typically include very few mythical elements). There are also Tantric forms of Viṣṇu, of his consort Lakṣmī, of his emanations (the Vyūhas), and of other Vaiṣṇava deities who are also described in the Purāṇas. A form of Viṣṇu from Kashmir called Vaikuṇṭha has three heads, one being that of a lion. The multiple arms and heads of a deity give an iconic expression to the infinite power and activity of the deity shown.

A characteristic trait of Tantric pantheons is their usual "maṇḍalic" disposition. The ancillary deities forming the retinue of a main god or goddess usually surround it in concentric circles (*āvaraṇas*) where the main deities are in the center with the others tiered around it in decreasing importance.

But the divine image is also sometimes "aniconic"—that is, without any human form. The most obvious case is that of the *liṅga*, whose forms are very varied. It can be more or less clearly phallic or not phallic at all, being a simple unadorned column. The *liṅga* may bear one to five "human" heads, those of Śiva (or Sadā Śiva). It is then a *mukhaliṅga* (*mukha* means "face"). It may be a stone polished by the flow of a sacred river, which is a variety of "spontaneous" (*svayambhu*) *liṅga*. An "aniconic" image may also be (as we have seen) an incised human skull (*tūra*) or any other object of human or of natural origin. Masks and painted cloths are also sometimes used, though they are more in popular cults (those of the Himalayas, for instance). The support of the ritual worship of any deity or of other divine elements of a ritual may also be a *kumbha*, a vase or pot filled with consecrated ("mantrified") water and other auspicious substances. In Tantra, there are a number of such symbols.

Among those, I should mention the ritual diagrams, named *cakra*, *yantra*, or *maṇḍala*. These three terms are used in different cases, applied to different geometrical patterns; however, they may be taken as roughly synonymous. Such geometrical patterns are not only Tantric; they are widely used in India (and in Asia) in Hinduism as well as in Buddhism. However, their role is particularly important in Tantric ritual and mental practices.

The *śrīcakra*

FIGURE 3

These ritual diagrams (sometimes called *cakra*, which means "wheel") have a central point that is surrounded by concentric triangles and/or petals, which are in turn enclosed in a square area with "doors." This is the case of the *śrīcakra*, the diagram of Tripurasundarī, and of those of a few other goddesses. Such diagrams are usually shown in books on "Tantric art," for they are often quite beautiful. They also allow, in the West, such philosophical speculations as those of Carl Gustav Jung and the use of these diagrams for mental concentration—which is not their role in Indian traditions. They may, however, be shaped quite differently. In the Trika of Kashmir, for instance, the two *maṇḍalas* of the tradition are square and enclose a trident, or three tridents with lotuses on their prongs. The *Śrīmaṇḍala* of the *Netratantra* is also square, and so on. For a number of ritual actions, *maṇḍalas* of different shapes and inside patterns suited to their functions are used. A case in point that we have seen is the *vāstupuruṣamaṇḍala*, drawn (or imagined) at the root of a temple. For a number of Tantric rituals, one draws *maṇḍalas* of different shapes and sizes according to need. These are not usually "centered" and are divided (as we saw for the temple) into smaller sections in accordance with the nature and aim of the action. On these, one often places vases (*kumbha*) provided with foliage and strings and filled with water consecrated by mantras, which represent the deities invoked for the ritual action. One may also draw letters of the alphabet or place mantras (therefore deities) on *cakras*, *yantras*, or *maṇḍalas*. Diagrams used in ritual (for *pūjā*, *dīkṣā*, etc.) are usually not small drawings but often large enough to allow the officiating adept to enter them when performing the ritual or an initiate to stand on them. These structures are often temporary, usually drawn with powders. (Many will have seen the vast and beautiful powder *maṇḍala* of Kālacakra Buddhism.)

Maṇḍalas can also be mentally imagined as present in the (yogic) body of an adept, where they are visualized and mentally worshipped. This happens, for instance, during the *pūjā* of Tripurasundarī, where the sections (*cakras*) of the *śrīcakra* are to be imagined as present in the bodily centers of the worshipper (see chapter 7). In chapter 14 of the *Kubjikāmatatantra*, the yogi is to imagine *maṇḍalas* of a cosmic dimension containing a host of deities on five of his bodily *cakras* so that he transcends entirely, mentally, his human body and fuses with the Absolute.[25]

Concluding on this subject, I will say that apart from some details, Tantric diagrams differ from non-Tantric ones more by the way they are used—by their aim and meaning—or by the spirit of the thing, rather than by their material form.

This brings us to another subject—namely, is it possible to distinguish clearly Tantric deities from those that are not Tantric? Answering this question is far from easy. Where does Tantra begin, and where does it end? I discussed this point in chapter 1. Concerning deities, an answer is all the more difficult to give because it would require taking into account both their particularities as described in texts and the sort of worship performed for them. One must also factor in how they are perceived or conceived by their worshippers, as practice and ideology go hand in hand. Kṛṣṇa, for instance, is not a Tantric deity except when worshipped as described in their tradition by the Vaiṣṇava sahajiyās. Viṣṇu is not basically a Tantric deity, but he is Tantric for the Pāñcarātra. Śiva, as described in the Purāṇas and worshipped by millions—or as worshipped by *smārta* Brahmins as one of the five divine entities of the *pañcāyatana*[26]—is not Tantric. Śaṅkarācārya never conceived of Śiva as a Tantric god. Nevertheless, one may say that in evolving from his Vedic form (Rudra), he became essentially Tantric in his main aspects, Bhairava and so forth (or as the bisexual Ardhanarīśvara). The *liṅga* on the *yoni*, a visibly sexual symbol, is iconographically Tantric even though it is not perceived and worshipped as such by devotees. The Goddess, in most of her aspects, is Tantric and worshipped as such. But not all goddesses are Tantric, whether in the "great tradition" or among local deities and in popular religion. (In this last category, there are interesting forms in the cults of local goddesses in the Himalayas.) Also in such cases, there are theologies, iconography, and ritual practices on the one hand and the perception and beliefs of the faithful on the other.

A basic Tantric notion is that the deity, when active, is polarized in masculine and feminine. In effect, almost all Tantric deities go by sexual pairs with a consort of the opposite sex—a Tantric Gaṇeśa (sometimes ithyphallic) has a *śakti*. But the role of the consort varies, being sometimes quite subdued. There are also Tantric "celibate" deities: Solitary Heroes or Heroines (*ekavīra*). And the principal deities of what were, for centuries, the dominant Tantric cults across much of the Indian world—namely, the Śaivasiddhānta and the Pāñcarātra—are also consortless. They are, respectively, the white five-faced and ten-armed Sadāśiva and Vaikuṇṭha (whom I mentioned above). Furthermore, non-Tantric deities are certainly not all celibate—Śiva abides with Pārvatī, Viṣṇu with Lakṣmī, Kriṣṇa with Rādhā, and so on.

Tantric deities also tend to multiply and form groups. For example, there are the eight Mothers (*mātṛ*), who are sometimes eight times eight; the nine Durgās, the ten Kālīs of the Krama; the ten Mahāvidyās; the sixteen Nityās; the fifty Rudras; the fifty-one Gaṇeśas; the sixty-four Yoginīs; and so on. One also says that there are 64,000, or even 640 million, Yoginīs. Tantric India is fond of large numbers, which may be an expression of power.

As mentioned above, such deities are often shown or conceived of as grouped in concentric circles (*āvaraṇa*). They are often fearsome. Their bodily parts or what they hold in their hands or bear on their bodies are sometimes seen as divine entities. This is the case of the "members" (*aṅgas*) of Śiva, which are not limbs but mantras; or of the eight supernatural powers (*siddhis*); or the ten mudrās of Śrīvidyā; and so forth. There are also, as (eminently) divine, the different forms of the Word (*vāc*)—phonemes of the Sanskrit alphabet, mantras, *vidyās*, and so on. There are many supernatural or divine entities one may call forth, worship, and manipulate for a variety of mundane or supramundane ends.

Finally, there are two often-mentioned points that I will underscore here. First, in practice, in spite of the visible and often impressive presence (and social role) of temples and the wealth of often beautiful divine images, the divine or supernatural entities to be worshipped or otherwise to be made use of are mainly to be mentally evoked and visualized. Their description as given in the *dhyānaślokas* of the compendiums of *mantraśāstra*, in hymns (*stotra*), or in other āgamic-Tantric texts are given, as the name implies, so as to visualize them mentally (*dhyāna*) not only during meditation but also (as we have seen above) during ritual. The word *ritual* implies actions sometimes applied to a surface or material image, but this action is effected with mantras. Thus the domain of ritual appears more as part of the domain of thought and word (sacred Word, mantra) than of concrete action. This is also why ritual is meaningful: it is not mere senseless gestures but is penetrated by thought—a conscious activity.

I will also underscore that mantras, the phonic form of deities, are their highest aspect, an aspect one may either enunciate or evoke mentally. Rites may well be performed using concrete images or symbols, but this mental work is done with mantras. Pantheons exist only insofar as they are evoked. They have no material consistency; they are made ritually present and are ritually worshipped using mantras. In conclusion, metaphysically (and even in ritual practice) Tantric pantheons are pantheons not of deities but of mantras.

PART III

Tantra Today

11

Tantra in India

Tantra, as we have seen, appeared in brahmanical circles and developed over the course of centuries within Hinduism, which it very largely pervaded. It became part of the Hindu socioreligious world and survived down to our days, many of its practices and notions being present in today's India as part of the Hindu world. We also saw that Tantra is inseparably made up of notions, ideology, and practices that are linked, the former giving their meaning and power to the latter. The Hindu world of yore, pervaded, in many respects, by Tantric elements, does not exist anymore, so that nowadays the two elements of practice and ideology are, in many cases, no longer together. Time inevitably alters the form, meaning, and uses of many elements. Also not to be forgotten is the fact that Tantra evolved over the course of centuries. A living tradition survives while evolving—"change and continuity."[1] Nowadays, one often finds Tantric elements, notions or practices, in a non-Tantric context. This is what I will discuss first. In the Indian subcontinent, there are also temples, ascetic groups or even social milieus, or regions where Tantric practices are (sometimes very intensely) recognized and "lived" as a part of everyday life. However, though part of everyday life somewhere, they may be judged negatively, and even condemned, elsewhere.

Let me add that I do not claim to be able to give a complete and precise image of Tantra in present-day India. I cannot do more than give some information and try to offer a general view of the subject. I hope that, though I am sometimes imprecise, I am never inaccurate.

Tantra: Pervasive but Not (or Hardly) Perceived as Such

An unprejudiced scholar of the Hindu world, when looking objectively at present-day India, cannot but note the pervasive presence of Tantric notions or practices in today's Hinduism. The scholar must also note that the Hindu users of such practices or notions often do not consider them as Tantric. In India (and in other—Buddhist—Asian countries[2]), there are what I might call "unconscious" uses and users of Tantra, mainly in the realms of ritual, religious/magical techniques, and iconography.

In ritual, the ritual worship of deities (*pūjā*) performed publicly in temples or in private for one's own benefit, remains today—in its pattern and its constitutive elements, and even, up to a point, in its spirit—the same as described in chapter 8: formally Tantric. This is evident in temples of Tantric deities and for avowed Tāntrikas, but such rites may be attended by large numbers of non-Tantric believers who are unaware of their real nature. This may also happen for other ritual practices, public or private.

In yoga, too, Indians (like Westerners) sometimes practice some form of *kuṇḍalinī* or haṭhayoga with its accompanying mental vision of *cakras* and *nāḍīs* without being in any way Tāntrikas.

Tantric mantras are sometimes used without their true nature being recognized—for instance, those of *kuṇḍalinī*-yoga, where deities are placed on *cakras* of the yogic body with mantras or recited in *japa*. The diagrams (*gahvaras*) used to select mantras belong to a Tantric practice sometimes also used outside Tantra. Tantric mantras are used in Āyurvedic medicine as well as in magic. Those in South India who resort to *mantirikars* or *mantiravātis*, who are Tāntrikas, do not necessarily know that they are.[3]

Temples, as we have seen, are built and structured according to Tantric rules, whatever their persuasion, and the Hindu pantheon of today includes many deities whose images were originally Tantric. Admittedly, Hindu myths are Purāṇic in origin, but many Purāṇas included Tantric elements. When a deity has Tantric and non-Tantric aspects, is the devotee aware of the difference? He may well be "unconsciously" Tantric. The same deity may also be worshipped in both a Tantric and a non-Tantric fashion.[4]

Except in large temples, traditional religious groups or organizations, and even among observant Brahmins, the role of ritual has decreased. In most places and circumstances, *pūjā* is very simplified, often consisting mainly of the waving of lights (*arati*; *ārātrika*, in Sanskrit) in front of the idol. This is due to the fact (an ancient phenomenon) that devotion (*bhakti*) tends to replace ritual—ritual minutiae are foreign to the spirit of our time. Modern life leaves little time for long and often complex rites. Because they do not know all the texts of their tradition, or because they are not fully initiated, temple priests at the time of this writing are often unable to perform some rituals, and sometimes devotees cannot afford them, for they are costly.

Tantra Variously Recognized as Such

Instruction given today for the performance of ritual in temples or in private consists mainly, in Śaiva cases, in teaching quotations from āgamas, Tantras, or ritual treatises such as the *Somaśambhupaddhati* and its twelfth-century commentary.[5] Also Tantric are, on the whole, rites of initiation (*dīkṣā*), funerary rites, and rituals for atonement and purification, as are those for the building and consecration of temples and the installation or disposal of cult images, rosaries, and so on. This is the case both in Śaiva and in Pāñcarātra milieus. Admittedly, these two traditions are only a part of Hinduism, but their rules are those followed in the main Hindu temples. They are also variously followed in smaller sanctuaries insofar as detailed rites are practiced. Today, the usual *pūjā* is limited to very few rites, more or less perfunctorily performed. (This, naturally, does not exclude the intense devotional participation of those who attend the worship.) Public or private, rites tend to be simpler than before. Priests, purohitas, and gurus are less ritually knowledgeable now than they were in ancient times[6] where, in fact, actual practice surely differed from the prescriptions of Tantras, āgamas, and other normative texts, but we do not know to what extent their rules were actually put into practice.

As we have observed, the growing place of devotion (*bhakti*)—perhaps, rather, of emotion—works against ritual precision and the belief in the efficacy of ritual, which is time-consuming and sometimes costly. Some traditional rites do not correspond to the spirit of our times. The profession of temple-dancer (*devadāsī*), long criticized by Hindu reformers but tolerated by the British, was forbidden by a wave of legislation culminating in the Madras Devadasi Act, passed in 1947, just after Indian independence. Nowadays, animal sacrifices (normally prescribed in Tantra) are outlawed (though still performed). Poor young Brahmins who formerly became priests or religious specialists now look for more financially and socially rewarding jobs. Usually only Brahmins remain entitled to be priests in the main temples. This ritual privilege was recently legally confirmed by an Indian court by reference to the āgamas. Today, ritual, with those who perform it—if somewhat "tuned down"—remains basically Tantric in Śaiva temples.[7] This is less so in

Vaiṣṇava temples, whose priests are sometimes Vaikhānasas, who claim not to be Tāntrikas. It goes without saying that many temples are not at all Tantric, even if their ritual does include elements from Tantra.

There are also cases where the acting person is fully conscious of the Tantric nature of the action they perform, participate in, or attend. We saw in chapter 2 that in some cases, Hindu princes, though today often in business or politics, have kept if not a real role in ritual ceremonies then at least their formal title as the main sacrificer (*yajamāna*) of their former realm. They therefore participate officially in the main festivals of the temple whose deity used to reinforce their power. This still happens, for instance, at Puri for the great festival of Jagannāth, a Vaiṣṇava deity with Tantric traits. Some mahārājas (in Gwalior, for instance) still have a Tantric *rājaguru*. One exercised real power for several years in the 1860s in Jaipur[8] (where there is still, in addition to the official, main, royal temple, a secret temple to the Goddess). A different sort of conflation between religious and politicosocial power is to be seen in the Kullu Valley of the Himalayas, where conflicts between royal and divine orders of precedence cause lawsuits between opposing villages, which are settled by officers of temples and individuals "possessed" by goddesses. Deities, most often goddesses, inhabiting these Himalayan valleys (Hidimbā at Manali, for instance) are still actively worshipped in their numerous sanctuaries, for they are fearsome. In the Kullu valley, their images are masks that, placed on palanquins, travel each year from temple to temple in festive ceremonies attended by the local population.

Tantra Recognized, Visibly Present

As an instance of the presence of openly acknowledged Tantric practices, there is—or rather, there was until 2008—the particular case of Nepal, which was the last surviving Hindu kingdom. In Nepal, Hindu as well Buddhist cults were fully Tantric. They were part of the social and political life of the kingdom, their main ritual events marking its yearly calendar. Some cults included large animal sacrifices, especially the royal Dasain Feast of Durgā. This Tantric world was present everywhere, deeply rooted in Nepalese (or, more precisely, Newar) society in the Kathmandu Valley. In Nepal, apart from the dominating Gorkhas, there are many other ethnic groups with a variety of more or less Hinduized local cults (and, as we shall see, Nāthas). Now that the country is a people's republic, conditions are very different. There are social changes and economic progress. But the numerous temples, sanctuaries, and monasteries, Hindu or Buddhist, some of which are in full activity, seem to survive—for the time being.[9]

Of this presence in the Indian subcontinent, there are evidently different modes and degrees.

Tantric Asceticism, Sadhus

Different groups of ascetics, called sadhus (*sādhu*) in common parlance, are overtly Tantric. Not all sadhus are Tantric. When Tantric, they are usually Śaivas—heirs, we could say, to the ancient kāpālika and Nātha traditions we saw in chapters 3 and 4. The most obvious and organized group of ascetics is, I believe, that of the Nāths (or Nāthyogis), also called Kānphaṭas ("Split-eared"), since the cartilage of their ears is split for the insertion of large earrings. They continue the Nātha tradition, whose importance, precepts, and practice we saw previously.[10] Their present role is not, by a long shot, what it was formerly, but they are very active, having adapted well to the world they live in. They patronize charitable organizations, their patrons include businessmen, and they have several centers, an important one is in Gorakhpur (in Uttar Pradesh), a city named after Gorakhnāth, their mythical founder, who has a shrine there. Other centers are at Haridvar, where the Ganges reaches the North Indian plains, Varanasī, Rajasthan, Karnataka, and so on. They have shrines in Pakistan, notably at Hinglaj (on the Makran coast of Baluchistan), which is one of the fifty *pīṭhas* of Satī, the shrine dedicated to a terrific goddess. They also have (or had) centers in Afghanistan.[11] They organize yearly festivals, traveling in groups to a main gathering point, always carrying with them their sacred fire, the *dhuni*. In Nepal, they have an important monastery at Caughera (in Dang province, near the Indian frontier), which is very prosperous and active. Surprisingly, even though the Nāthas are theoretically not Śākta, each year this monastery—dedicated to Gorakhnāth and to Bhairava—organizes a pilgrimage to a neighboring temple of the Goddess. Also unexpected is that the heads of the monastery are called *pīr*, a Muslim title. And there are roving Nātha yogis. But today, there are only a few thousand Nātha yogis. In Nepal, there is a particular Nātha group, the Kusle-Yogis, who are not renouncers but householders that form a caste (this also in Rajasthan). I alluded previously to the links between Nāths and Sufism. Of this, traces remain today among the Satpanthi Ismaelis of Gujerat, whose sacred hymns, called *ginān*, include many Hindu elements coming mainly from the Nāths.

There are sadhus of different kinds, roving or sedentary, often looked upon as magicians, with more or less transgressive ritual practices. Foremost are those called Aghoris, their bodies smeared with ash from funeral pyres. They stay in burning grounds where they practice their rituals at night, sometimes using corpses.[12] They are believed to eat flesh from corpses. They are worshippers of Bhairava. There are many Aghoris in Varanasi, the city of Śiva, where Bhairava has several shrines, but overall they are not very numerous. Sadhus such as the Aghoris usually smoke cannabis (*charas*), a practice that seems to go back to the eighteenth century.[13]

Goddesses and the Goddess

Goddess-cults are particularly important in some regions and deserve to be approached separately. Goddesses are not all Tantric, but the more fearsome ones often are, being usually associated with an aspect of Śiva/Bhairava. Kālī and Durgā, who have shrines all over India, are examples. In Nepal, Guhyeśvarī and the nine Durgās are especially worshipped, as is Tripurasundarī. The cult of Vaiṣṇo Devī, a form of Durgā, a fearsome killer of demons, worshipped in an underground sanctuary in the state of Jammu (near Kashmir), could be added to the Himalayan goddess cults I mentioned above. The boundary line here between what is popular and what might be considered properly Tantric is difficult to draw. Take, for instance, the cult of Yellama, a goddess whose temple—a very important pilgrimage place—is at Saundatti in Kerala, where possession by the Goddess plays an important role. Possession is often seen as a trait of popular Hinduism, but it is also a characteristic of several Hindu traditions. *Āveśa*, or *samāveśa*, which may denote penetration by, or fusion with, the Absolute, may also refer to possession and is often mentioned in Śaiva Tantric works—those of Abhinavagupta, notably (see chapter 9). Goddess sanctuaries, often of local deities, are innumerable, sometimes without any qualified priest in charge but well and devotedly attended by devotees. There are also temples of great goddesses whose cults are attended by huge crowds in large temples, as is the case of Mīnākṣī in Madurai.[14]

Tantra in Different Areas

In Kacch, a coastal region of Gujerat State, the Goddess is present everywhere in her fearsome aspects (Kālī, Durgā, Hinglaj, etc.). She is worshipped there as a goddess of the land (*deśdevī*), guardian deity of region and king, or as a lineage goddess (*kuldevī*)—guardian of the royal lineage and of local social groups. Goddesses also appear as living goddesses (*jīvan mātājī*), embodied in women of the Charan caste, a caste of bards and shepherds. This tradition's rites are still very much alive today; it is an essential social cohesive element.

But its more Tantric traits are fading because of the anti-Tantric "brahmanical" tendencies alive today in many parts of India.[15]

Bengal is the part of India where Tantra is most generally present and acknowledged, where goddess cults are the most widespread and widely practiced. Many Bengalis tend to consider the Goddess as their supreme deity above all other Hindu deities. The majority of Bengal's higher castes are Śākta, families guided in their ritual practices by a Tantric guru. The Goddess is worshipped mainly as Durgā, Killer of Demons. In addition to her common worship, she is feasted each year in October. This feast, the Durgāpūjā, is the main festival of Bengal, an essential part of Bengali religion. Durgā is worshipped together with three other goddesses: Jagaddhātrī ("She Who Supports the World"), associated with agriculture; the fearsome Kālī astride Śiva; and also Umā, Śiva's gentle wife, who is closer to the heart of many devotees and evokes longing. This is a complex theological ensemble.[16]

There are other goddesses prominent in Bengal, notably the fearsome ten Mahāvidyās, the first among whom is Kālī. But Kālī may also be felt as a peaceful auspicious Mother, as she was for Ramakrishna, who was a priest of her temple at Dakshineshwar. Her main temple in Calcutta, the Kālīghat, is crowded by devotees, and hundreds of young goats are sacrificed to pacify her. There are also local goddesses—Caṇḍī or Manasā, the goddess of snakes, and many others.[17] Male gods also have their roles, notably Śiva. Though usually subordinate to the Goddess, he is also the Great Yogi (*mahāyogin*), master of all (more or less transgressive) yogis.

In Bengal, there still are Vaiṣṇava Sahājiyās, heirs to those we saw in chapter 4, with the same transgressive beliefs and practices. A deviant category of ascetics proper to Bengal are the Bāuls—mystic bards extolling the glory of the "Man of the Heart" (*maner mānus*), the ideal form of the individual—a group whose sexo-yogic rites, and some notions, are more or less Tantric. Unexpected and interesting is the fact that there are also Muslim Bāuls, the so-called Fakirs (sometimes also called *āuls*), whose ideology fuses Sufi-Muslim and Hindu notions and terminology.[18]

The presence of such groups and practices is a reason—in spite of the pervasiveness of Śākta cults—why many Bengalis have an unfavorable idea of Tantra, which they believe to abound in illicit sex, secret magical practices, or sorcery. The presence of such secret sexual practices is also the reason another group, the Kartābhāja, which appeared in the eighteenth century in colonial Bengal, is disapproved of by the Bengali higher classes. This is also because the membership of the sect is definitely subaltern, asserting itself as the "Poor Company" and opposing the riches of the East India Company and its affluent Indian members or associates. The Kartābhajā conception of the body, as well as its sexual practices, is clearly Tantric. They use a secret language. Though they do not hold many festivals, the one they organize each year at Ghospara, near Calcutta, is attended by large numbers.[19]

Among Tantric groups in Bengal is also the Anand Marg, which we will consider further on. But I will touch upon this movement here because it is the present form of a development that, born in colonial Bengal, has survived until the present day, linking Tantra and revolutionary nationalism, the terrific goddess Kālī being used as an image of Indian political awakening. This interpretation of the figure of Kālī as a symbol of an oppressed motherland but also of a glorious liberated India first appeared in a novel by the Bengali author Bankim Chandra Chatterjee, *Ānandamaṭh* (Abbey of Bliss). It was taken over by young nationalists, among them Aurobindo Ghose, who was a convinced nationalist revolutionary advocating the use of violence, for which he was pursued by the British authorities and sought refuge in Pondicherry, where he remained in secrecy before becoming a world-renowned spiritual master.[20] In 1907, he published a pamphlet, "Bhawani Mandir" (The Temple of the Goddess), laying out his ideal of an order of young sannyasis fighting for the liberation of India. Indian nationalism was later to take on another, very different, form, but the idea of the Goddess as a symbol of India has (unfortunately) not disappeared.

Another region where Tantra is present is the state of Assam in the northeastern corner of India, this perhaps from early times. As mentioned in the introduction, the Himalayan region—and especially its eastern part—is believed to be one of the parts of India where Tantra first appeared. Indeed, three of the five main "seats" (*pīṭhas*) of the goddess of the Kula tradition are in that region, one of them being that of Kāmarūpa/Kāmākhya near Guhawati, the capital city of the state of Assam.[21] This *pīṭha* is particularly important for the cult of the Goddess, for it is the place where Satī's *yoni* fell from the shoulders of Śiva as he roamed, grief-stricken, all over India. In the temple, dedicated to the goddess Kāmākhyā, this *yoni* is a stone with a fissure, which is constantly watered. It "bleeds" every year in the month of *āṣāḍha* (June–July). These four days are deemed to be days of impurity for the earth, and no agricultural activity may take place. Her cult is extremely active. For devotees who wish to worship her, there are prepubescent girls (*kumārīs*) of different castes in the temple who can be used by devotees as icons symbolizing the goddess for a private worship of that deity.

In Assam, where 60 percent of the population is Hindu, there are many temples for the Goddess, usually Durgā. There is also a local Tantra, the

Kāmaratna tantra,[22] which is a collection of magical formulas dealing mostly with *kāma*.

Kerala, in southwest India, is another region where Tantric cults are very actively present. To quote Sarah Caldwell: "Tantrism . . . pervades Hindu practice at all levels of Kerala society."[23] These cults are mostly Śākta, most temples being dedicated to the Goddess and aspects of Kālī, Bhadrakālī usually, who may be peaceful and beneficent but also wrathful and fearsome. Though Tantric, these temples can only be entered by Brahmins. Officiating priests come from high-status Brahmin families and use ancient Tantric texts of pan-Indian reputation for their practice, such as the *Īśānaśivagurudevapaddhati* or, more locally extolled, the *Tantrasamuccaya*. Worship and other rituals are wholly Tantric but "of the right hand"—not transgressive. In the temple, there is usually a (non-Brahmin) oracle who is possessed by the goddess. There are also temples where priests and servants are of lower castes, their rites including sometimes "nonvegetarian" offerings or an animal sacrifice. Male gods are also worshipped, mainly aspects of Śiva associated with the Goddess, or Gaṇapati. A recent development is the popularity of the worship of Ayappan, a deity known in earlier times who could be considered a male counterpart to Durgā. Only men are permitted to take part in the yearly pilgrimage to his principle shrine at Shabarimala.

In Kerala as elsewhere, rites are performed using mantras, often put into practice using *yantras* or *maṇḍalas*, of which there is a large variety. Mantric practices are ubiquitous in Kerala. Their professional practitioners (*mantravādis*) are devotees of different deities, notably of a local god, Chattan, deemed to have magical powers. Traditional doctors also use mantras, *yantras*, or amulets. Kerala is known for its temple festivals, where episodes from myths of the Goddess are played by a particular caste of temple servants. They play before large audiences, for whom these are merely artistic performances. However, they are not mere theatre for the god's servants, who intensely "live" their parts, sometimes going as far as to feel that they are possessed by the deity they embody. To quote a performer: "When all these people are looking at us, that same divine power gets into us."[24]

Moving across to the southeast, we again encounter the Śrīvidyā, the "Vedantized" form of Tripurasundarī's cult, since the basic texts of this Śaiva tradition are (as we saw in chapter 4) Tantric. Today, its main center (*maṭh*) is in Shringeri, Karnataka. Another important center is in Kancipuram, not far from Madras/Chennai. The spiritual heads, the Shankaracaryas (*śaṅkarācārya*), of this tradition reside in these two places. There are also other Śrīvidyā temples. This very brahmanical tradition seems now only faintly Tantric, in spite of its use of the *śrīcakra* and *śrīvidyā*. The Shankaracharyas appear to have adopted the paraphernalia—deities, mantras, *maṇḍalas*—but none of the doctrines or other problematic features of the Tantric cult. (Similarly in the temples of Varanasi we find *daśanāmi*, sannyasis whom one cannot really consider as Tantric.) However, I mention this Southern tradition here because, in spite of its small number of adepts, it is socially very present in India: the Shankaracaryas are eminent Indian personalities who often enjoy political importance. I also mention it here because—in the states where it has adepts—it is described by some scholars as typically Tantric.[25]

It goes without saying that, today as before, there are many people in India who follow a Tantric *sādhana*, either individually or collectively, without being members of any recognized group, institution, or tradition. Several such groups or institutions surely exist, of which I am not aware. There are also Tantric gurus, or gurus whose teachings include Tantric notions or practices, and who have disciples. Going more than a century back—but important for the history of Indian spirituality—the Bengali "saint" Ramakrishna (1836–95) must be named, for he was, in many respects, an influential personality. A priest of Kālī, he was initiated by a female Tantric ascetic, a Bhairavī, and surely practiced some Tantric (not sexual) rites. His visions were often colored by his Tantric experience, but he never advocated Tantric practices, which he judged to be dangerous.[26]

To come back to our time, a few years ago in Allahabad (Prayag) there were disciples of a Tantric guru living in Jhansi who edited a journal, *Kalyan*, and books or booklets with the texts of unedited Tantras, or on the worship of Tantric deities, or on *mantraśāstra*. There are many such publications, often sold near temples, bought and read by many.

The abundance of such "popular" Tantric materials shows that in spite of what is said or believed about Tantra in India, it is not so generally condemned. For a more limited readership (though not only an academic one), there are also editions by universities or research centers of Śaiva or Vaiṣṇava Tantras or other such works in Sanskrit. Among these, one should mention the "Gaekwad Oriental Series," published under the auspices of the maharaja of Baroda since 1916. There is also the "Yoga-tantra-grantha-mālā" ("garland of books on yoga and Tantra") of the Sanskrit University of Banaras (Varanaseya Samskrit Vishvavidyalaya), notably with the collection of Tantras called *Tantrasaṃgraha*. Another example is the "Chowkhamba Sanskrit Series" of Varanasi, who edited (and go on editing) hundreds of Sanskrit texts and studies, including such important works as K. C. Pandey's *Abhinavagupta: An Historical and Philosophical Study*, issued in 1935, which was a pioneering enterprise and remains today a reference work on the subject. Among the internationally best-known series is that jointly published by the Institut Français de Pondichéry and the Pondicherry Centre of the École française d'Extrême-Orient,[27] which includes texts, translations, and studies. There are also translations in English as well as in other Indian languages. A well-known forerunner of this was Sir John Woodroffe, who used the pen name Arthur Avalon. He compiled the series called *Tantrik Texts* and a number of other works on Tantra.[28] Studies and editions of Tantric texts now regularly appear from academic presses around the world. Tantras are all the more easily available because many can now be found online. In India, there are surely a number of people who are interested in Tantra and sometimes follow its teachings, as there seems to be a renewed interest in the philosophical, spiritual, or religious content of Tantra—this being perhaps due in part to the present interest in the subject in the West.

The work and activity of some personalities is also proof of the living presence of Tantra. Gopinath Kaviraj (1887–1976), who was born in a Brahmin family of Bengal, was initiated by a Tantric yogi known for his supernatural powers. He lived thereafter as a scholar and teacher in Varanasi, where he was considered a master of Śaiva studies, as proven by his many publications in Bengali and Hindi.[29] He extolled Tantra, which he saw not as contradicting but as completing the ancient Vedic teaching because of its being more than a particular aspect of the quest for individual liberation, having "the potential to achieve a collective salvation . . . for mankind."[30]

I make special mention here of Swami Lakshman Joo (1907–91), an exceptional personality, whose ashram was in Nishat on Dal Lake, Kashmir. He was the last initiated guru of nondualistic (Trika) Śaivism, whose survival to this day in India and in the West owes much to him.[31] The 2007 foundation in Varanasi of a study center with a library, "Saṃvidālaya: Abhinavagupta Research Library"—aimed at helping research and encouraging publications on Kashmirian Śaivism—is one more token of the renewed interest in India for a philosophical and spiritual tradition that, in spite of its glorious past, remained until recently little known.

These are as drops in the ocean of the billion Hindus on the subcontinent. They are, however, worth mentioning because they show that, in spite of yesteryear's bigotry and today's development of fundamentalisms of various sorts, the intellectual value of Tantra (Hindu or Buddhist) is acknowledged by some. However, I will note that this is hardly the case among contemporary Indian professional philosophers who, when referring to the past, tend to remain prisoners of the mystical vision of Śaṅkara. Though surely an essential Indian philosopher—if very little known in his own time—he is, I believe, very much overestimated, in part because of the prevalence of Vedānta-biased doxographies.[32]

Tantra's presence in India today owes much to new religious sects differing from those we just saw because of their links with the Western world. Taking over only elements from Tantric traditions that suit their purposes, they produce new Tantric systems adapted to the world we live in now, systems whose novelty often comes from the West, where several developed, as we shall see. Of these, I will briefly touch on three.

First, I will discuss the Anand Marg/Ānanda Mārga. It was founded in Bengal in 1955 by Prabha Ranjan Sarkar (1919–2008), believed by his disciples to be an *avadhūta* ("one who has shaken off [worldliness]") and an incarnation of Śiva. This "Path of Bliss" aims, they say, at "spiritual development, social service and the spiritual transformation of society." Though without any ties to any earlier Tantric tradition, the Anand Marg insists on its continuity with traditional Tantric philosophy and on the practice by its members of a "*tāntrika sādhana*," which includes a particular form of dance associated with meditation and supposedly inspired by the "dance of Shiva." It has also a social philosophy, its goal being "self-realization and the welfare of all." But it insists on the role of violence it considers as "the very essence of life" and this sect has in fact been associated with terrorist activities. In 1971, its leader was arrested for abetting the murder of six former disciples. In 1982, seventeen of its members were murdered. In spite of all this, the Marg seems to prosper. It is said to have several thousand members all over the world, though most are located at its main center in Bengal.[33]

Another, very different, organization is the one founded in Pune (near Mumbai) in 1974 by a self-styled *ācārya*, henceforth known as Bhagwan Shri Rajneesh. He soon attracted many disciples, mostly young people, male and female, from Europe and the United States. They were drawn by a teaching consisting of indulging all their physical urges. "Humans," Rajneesh used to say, "are both body and soul: both must be indulged." Apart from (and as a consequence of) total freedom, he favored unfettered capitalism in a totally free, ideal society. He quickly amassed a great deal of money. However, he did this in such a way that he had to leave India in 1981, trailed by police and tax collectors. He came back to India in 1985 after being expelled from the United States and, under the name of Osho, founded a "multiversity" and a meditation center in Pune animated by the same hedonistic spirit as before. He went on garnering riches but avoided all that could again cause trouble. This organization survives his death and has members all over the world.

The last I will mention here is the Siddha Yoga Center at Ganeshpuri,

Maharashtra, where Nityānanda lived during his last years. He was an interesting personality, the guru of Muktananda,[34] the founder this organization. A mysterious man, usually silent, Nityananda claimed to have been born a *siddha* without any guru. It does not seem that he had any precise doctrinal position. The Siddha yoga's basic doctrine, however, is a modern, simplified, version of nondualistic Kashmirian Śaivism. It is therefore Tantric but it is from America. This is a case of the change a Tantric (or any) tradition incurs when it comes back into India after a stay in the West, where its doctrine and practices become modified in line with other Western values.[35]

12

Tantra in the West

Tantra being, in many respects, what is most profoundly Indian, one may well find it surprising that it should have spread out of the original Asian sphere of expansion of Indian civilization—unless this particular character should be the reason it draws attention, fascinates even. On the contrary, perhaps it is this very character that explains this attraction. Religious and spiritual quests are quests for the other—the divine Other—and for us, what is more "other" than Tantra? What could be more attractive in our present world than a message of power over oneself, over other humans, and over the world we live in—let alone sex and transgression? The presence of Tantra in the West is all the more interesting because it is one of the aspects of the relationship between the West and a largely imaginary, "fabricated" India, together with India's reaction to this vision (misinterpretations working both ways). It is also the insertion of Tantra in the globalized, merchandized, and hedonistic world we live in today.[1]

On this meeting of cultures (which is, at least in part, a "comedy of errors"), one must first mention again Sir John Woodroffe/Arthur Avalon (1865–1936), the pioneer of Tantric studies. It is true that his work represents, up to a point, a "deodorized Tantra" (to use Hugh Urban's words), published with the help of Bengali pandits eager to give a good impression of Tantra. Nevertheless, his work remains important. I will repeat that he was the first to say that Tantra was a basic aspect of Hinduism (see chapter 1). Sir John Woodroffe's case is also interesting because his was a dual personality: a British judge and member of Bengal's Supreme Court, he was also if not a Tantric initiate then "an Indian soul in a European body," as it was said. He was a passionate student of this domain, a friend of Bengali Tāntrikas, with whose help he pursued his work.[2] Some critics have reproached him for giving too favorable a view of Tantra.[3] The fact remains, nevertheless, that he was a transmitter (a "passeur," as we say in French) whose role in making Tantra known and showing its value to a larger public both in India and abroad is noteworthy. In this, he had all the more merit because in his time, the image of Tantra in India as well as in the West was an entirely negative one. The Indian elite and the Orientalists (not to mention the British colonizers) used to see nothing but immorality, superstition, and degeneracy in Tantra.

The legend of the Thugs, said to be present all over India, deceiving innocent travelers and strangling them as an offering to Kālī, is a remarkable instance of an image of India as a country of rampant violence and crime with Kālī, the Tantric goddess, as its patron.[4]

Conditions changed as India evolved from a semicolonial status to a modern state, open to the world, visited by many and, in particular, by Orientalists, who until then knew it solely through Sanskrit texts found in European or American libraries. Prejudices waned or tended to disappear. But India's fascination—the work of *māyā*?—went on working, so that even now the most absurd ideas—notably about Tantra—persist, as we shall see presently.

Serious approaches to Tantra are to be mentioned first. In the academic world, Tantra has ceased to be left aside. One has realized its importance in Indian/Hindu culture and history. In Europe, America, and Japan, important studies on the subject are now carried out in universities and research centers. This I cannot review here. I must, however, underscore the abundance and validity of the "scientific" work being done now, which enlarges the knowledge of a historically important socioreligious phenomenon. This is very useful. Less satisfactory is the fact that scholarly writings about Tantra have crossed over from academia into the lives of "ordinary" people and become responsible in part for some bizarre Western distortions of Tantra.

The psychoanalyst Carl Gustav Jung (1875–1961) deserves mention here because, though critical of yoga, he considered *maṇḍalas* as archetypal images and saw *kuṇḍalinī*-yoga as an inner energy that could help in the process of individuation. He wrote several books on the subject. However, his conceptions, if perhaps therapeutically useful, were "Indologically" mistaken and contributed noticeably to misconceptions.

To come nearer to Indian matters, I would mention Lilian Silburn (1908–93), in spite of the fact that she wrote in French,[5] for hers is a blameless case, and her work is especially interesting. She was the first in Europe to write on nondualist Kashmirian Śaivism. She also studied it in India with Swami Lakshman Joo. She published carefully introduced and annotated translations of important texts (*Śivasūtra, Vijnānabhairava, Spandakārikā*, Hymns by Abhinavagupta, etc.), underscoring their mystical import. Though "scientifically" valid, these translations were meant for a larger than purely academic readership, introducing readers to the notions and practices of such systems as Trika, Spanda, or Krama for their information, leading some, however, to a personal practice.

The work of many other academic scholars in Indology, sociology, and anthropology contributed usefully—and still contribute—to make known Tantric doctrines and practices. If these are perfectly blameless, the work of others were (are) more ambiguous or questionable.

Such was the oeuvre of Heinrich Zimmer (1890–1943), who taught Indology at Heidelberg University before emigrating to Great Britain and then to the United States. He is largely forgotten now, but he was, for a time, one of the most important and widely read Indologists of the twentieth century. He considered Tantra as the most authentically Indian form of religious thought and Tantric yoga—with the play of creative imagination—as the subtlest and most efficacious of all mental-spiritual techniques, this going together with a this-worldly, life-affirming attitude. Zimmer sharply contrasted this presence of the gods in the human body in a divinized world with the—for him—life-denying Judeo-Christian world we live in.

This was also, much more intensely, the viewpoint of the Italian Julius Evola (1898–1974). Born to a noble Sicilian family, his spiritual quest took a particular aristocratic heroic turn. For him, Tantra is not "eastern" but "in its spirit, more clearly *occidental* than the Christian soteriology." A convinced fascist, in 1943 he played a role in the organization of the last fascist government at Salo. He viewed Tantra as the sole aristocratic, heroic, virile way able to save the West from decadence—from its perverse, "womanly" preoccupations with sex. Nietzschean, antidemocratic, elitist, racist, he was one of the inspirers of European neofascist movements and of the so-called New Right (where one may still meet today a few Indologists). This conflation of Tantra and violence, though perhaps unexpected, is not entirely surprising. A *siddha* is a superman, above good and evil and, as we saw above, there can be links between Tantra and political violence. In his youth, Kālī was for Aurobindo an incarnation in this world of divine salvific power. (We also saw lately, in Japan, with the *Aum Shirinko* sect, a transition from Buddhist ideology to blind violence.)

Very different from the two preceding persons is the third I wish to mention: Mircea Eliade (1907–86). Born in Romania, he took part in the activities of the extreme right in his younger years. He was involved in the violence that swept across his country before and during the Great War. But he also went to India (1928–31) to study Indian philosophy and yoga. After the war, he came to France, where, not being able to get the university post he expected (and deserved)[6] for local political reasons, he went to the United States. There in Chicago he became an internationally known (and, for some, charismatic) personality. He was also prominent in European cultural life, being among those who actively participated in the well-known and well-attended yearly meetings of *Eranos* at Ascona, Switzerland. Unlike with Zimmer and Evola, the influence of Eliade's hermeneutical approach to history of religions is still perceptible today. Like them, however, he saw the paradox of a this-worldly transcendence of dualities in Tantra—the salvific identification of sacred and profane, the *coincidentia oppositorum*, the union of contrary principles. He once wrote that these would "fascinate [him] until the end of [his] life."[7] Some feel that there are "cryptofascist" elements in his work, which, I believe, is quite unfounded. He surely was profoundly antimodernist, but was he wrong in that?[8] Mircea Eliade was also a writer whose literary work is very much worth reading—in particular, the four volumes of his *Journals.*

The three Orientalist philosophers I have just mentioned saw Tantra as extolling and making accessible a larger vision of the world and of the place and role in it of humans, who would participate in the powers that animate it.

But the Western approach to Tantra was to take another turn, already discernible in the first years of the twentieth century. It was developed, intensified, and profoundly transformed after World War II, especially in the United States. In these cases, there is usually no attempt at understanding the nature of Tantra, but some Tantric elements (often misunderstood) are transposed and used to fabricate new systems suited to the Western modern socioeconomic context, "uniting spirituality and sexuality, sacred transcendence and material enjoyment."[9]

In a globalized Western world where the ancient beliefs and established religions have been loosening their hold, and where what is sometimes called "free-choice religion" tends to dominate, some try to cobble together a personal religion by selecting elements more or less haphazardly that seem to answer their spiritual needs. Hence the development in Europe and in America of "neo-Hindu" movements, either born in India or put together by some Western guru and linked only spiritually to India, some asserting themselves as Tantric.

They are of various values. When one logs onto Tantra websites that proliferate on the Internet, one soon realizes how worthless, misleading, and teeming with errors most of them are. Stress is usually laid on sex, a Tantric sex, "spiritual," "perfect," "transcended"—that is, "ecstasy online"—allowing intense and endless sexual enjoyment together with spiritual bliss. Thus Tantra is celebrated as "a cult of ecstasy," an aspect that is particularly developed in the United States. A link also appears between these new forms of Tantra and the socioeconomic situation of the contemporary capitalist, merchandized world. Tantric movements flourished in this world while also—from the 1960s—criticizing it.

Not by chance, I would say, the first Western Tantric organization was founded (in 1906) in the United States. There, too, later appeared—and continue to thrive today—the main (and various) forms of "pop," "neo," or "New Age" Tantra.

Though not our concern, we might note here that Tantric Buddhism went through the same transformations in America. For instance, there was the highly controversial Chogyam Trumpa (1939–90) who, after a traditional Buddhist upbringing—he was as a child abbot of the Surmang monasteries in northern Tibet—fled to India in 1959 and then came to the United States in 1970. In Boulder, Colorado, he founded the Naropa Institute, which attracted a number of people—dropouts and hippies but also students, artists, and writers—representative of American counterculture, all seduced by this bizarre, crazy-wisdom guru, whose organization continued to spread worldwide.

The first American neo-Tantric organization, the Tantric Order of America (with its *International Journal of the Tantric Order*), was founded in 1906–7 in New York City by the American Pierre Bernard (1875?–1955). He established an Oriental Sanctum in New York where he taught haṭhayoga (as the Omnipotent Oom) and bestowed a secret initiation upon rich followers who would thus come to have a new conception of love. All of this was a matter of scandal. In 1918, he bought a vast estate where he created the Utopian Tantric Community. Here he pursued his activities, attracting wealthy customers for secret physical treatments that always had a sexual side. His wife, Blanche de Vries, after having taught "oriental dancing," founded the Tantric Health System also meant for the wealthiest, and this became a very successful financial affair. Later, Pierre Bernard and his wife retired into a quieter but still very lavish lifestyle and finished their lives as millionaires. In all these respects, Pierre Bernard was a pioneering figure in the American reinterpretation of Tantra. By deliberately ignoring its real nature, he transformed it into a movement where sex and physical pleasure dominated.

Theos Bernard (1908–47), a nephew of Pierre Bernard, was also a pioneer of Tantra in the United States, but in the realm of Indo-Tibetan yoga. Having spent some time in Tibet, he was permitted to go to Lhasa, where he visited monasteries in which Tantric forms of Buddhism were transmitted. In 1937, he came back to the United States saying that he had been initiated, posing henceforth as the "White Lama." He settled in New York but traveled all over the United States lecturing. Practicing his narrative skills for a variety of audiences, he recounted his largely imaginary adventures in Tibet and India. Like his uncle in his last years, he associated with several of the major social, political, and cultural leaders of his time. He disappeared in Himalayan India during the troubles of Partition.[10]

New developments in American Tantra were to take place a few years later—from the 1960s and 1970s—associated with a vast movement of liberation from the shackles of tradition, and especially of "sexual repression," with counterculture and sexual liberation going hand in hand. In 1964, Omar Garrison's *The Yoga of Sex*, advocating Tantric techniques that prolonged sexual ecstasy and seeing in Tantra a cure from the ills of the Western world, was extremely successful. Sexual union, for him, could "open the way to a new dimension in life." (Mis)understood in this way, Tantra entered popular imagination as an element of American counterculture, a means for criticizing the prevailing sociopolitical order, which was seen as repressive and corrupt. The fearsome goddess Kālī became thus a symbolic figure of the fight against all these fetters, symbolizing both an immersion in obscure but renovating powers as well as the newly liberated feminine power. All this was celebrated by such figures as Alan Watts, the psychedelic guru of the Beat Generation—who saw in Tantra "a marvelous and welcome corrective to certain excesses of Western civilization"—and by poets of that group, such as Allen Ginsberg (all these being nearer, in fact, to Chogyam Trumpa than to Hindu Tantra).

Those American versions of Tantra were to become important elements in the development of what we today rather vaguely call "New Age," a term that lumps various alternative sociocultural, philosophical, and more or less religious movements that mix up "Euro-American" traditional elements and the counterculture of the 1960s together with Indian Tantric—or supposedly Tantric—elements. But in contrast to the antimaterialism of the sixties, and in total opposition to real Tantric teaching, New Age movements tended to sanctify material prosperity, uniting spirituality and financial success: "The more spiritual you are, the more you deserve prosperity." In this respect, Tantra was sometimes described in the United States as the tradition of modern times, "religion for the Age of Aquarius," the age of the commercialized world we live in. Typical of this New Age Tantra was Nick Douglas's New Tantric Order in America, a revival of Pierre Bernard's "Tantric Order of America" in harmony with our time, offering online "personalized" Tantric initiation with access to Tantra on its website. This has not caused any scandal—proof that this is adapted to today's Zeitgeist. On the contrary, to quote Hugh Urban: "Its brand of sacred sexuality seems to be remarkably at home in American consumer culture at the start of the millennium."[11]

A typical guru of this present age was Bhagwan Shri Rajneesh, whom we saw in the preceding chapter. Having to leave India, he came to the United States in 1981, which he considered as the country of freedom and of liberal capitalism. On his arrival, he announced himself as "the Messiah America has been waiting for." After a brief stay in New Jersey with numerous disciples, he bought a four-thousand-acre ranch in Antelope, Oregon, to create a new ideal society. "Rajneeshpuram," which quickly became a very profitable affair, amassed some twelve million dollars during its brief existence. The enterprise spread simultaneously in the United States and in Europe, an international ensemble uniting, it is said, more than twenty-five thousand members, promising them, as in Pune, both free love and liberation. But Rajneesh and his group, whose behavior and luxury (the famous twenty-five Rolls-Royces!) caused scandal, soon clashed with the residents of Antelope, whom they attempted to displace with violence. They thus came under investigation by the US government and were charged with criminal conspiracy, first degree assault, attempted murder, racketing, arson, and so on. Deported from the United States, Rajneesh returned to the Pune ashram in 1987, where, as Osho, he started a new sect that also has members in several countries, as we have seen above.

More important (and much less scandalous) and still active today is the Siddha Yoga Dham of America (SYDA) set up by Swami Muktananda (1908–82), who came to New York in 1971 with a mission: to create a "meditation revolution" based on a widespread realization of the universal Self, and who quickly became a key figure in the transmission of Tantra (also, some say, of sexual scandal) in America. The SYDA, whose center is now in South Fallsburg, New York, soon became extremely popular, attracting a number of personalities and becoming a vast and very rich international organization with more than five hundred meditation centers and ashrams the world over.

A disciple of the mysterious Nityananda of Ganeshpuri (see above), Muktananda's teaching is based mainly on nondualistic Kashmirian Shaivism and, in particular, on Abhinavagupta's Trika. It lays stress on the basic role of divine grace—or more exactly on the descent upon the disciple of divine power (*śaktipāta*)[12]—that will open for him the way to liberation. This divine power is that of the Goddess, Śakti Kuṇḍalinī, which is also present in the body of humans, whose progress toward salvation is to result from a transformation of sexual energy into spiritual energy. Muktananda seems to have gone through this process, though not without difficulty (and much sex). Through this process, it is said, he eventually became the ideal guru, whose sexual urge has been transformed into pure spiritual love. Muktananda's sexual behavior remains a more or less secret and embarrassing problem for the SYDA to this day. All this conforms to the spirit of a time where an obsession with sex prevails and a certain American perception of Tantra associates it with secret transgressive sexuality. The present guru of the SYDA is now a (very respectable) female disciple of Muktananda, Gurumayi Chidvilasananda. In its South Fallsburg main center, the organization gathers initiated members—swamis, male and female—who teach and guide spiritually, as well as many permanent members in charge of the day-to-day life of the center and of its business or social activities.

An unusual feature of the SYDA is its eagerness to maintain links with the academic world. A number of scholars and university professors of South Asian studies or of history of religions have become members of the Siddha Yoga or are invited by it to give talks or participate in meetings. Thus in 1999, the American Academy of Religions held a panel on the topic "Who speaks for Siddha Yoga," bringing together both critics and committed members of the movement. In 1997, the SYDA founded the Muktabodha Institute with a digital library whose goal was to digitalize and put manuscripts and rare editions of Tantric texts online, especially those of so-called Kashmir Shaivism. A number of such texts are now available, their collection and online edition progressing under the direction of Indian, European, and American scholars. Some activities of the institute or choice of editions by the library are criticized, but the work is generally extremely useful.[13]

A split in the movement after Muktananda's death resulted, among other things, in the foundation by one of his disciples—Rudrananda (an American)—of the Nityananda Institute, now located in Portland, Oregon. This movement considers itself as more faithful than the SYDA to Nityananda's teachings. It is a small movement, gathering a community whose members reside in the ashram while being active outside. It also keeps in touch with scholars, whom it invites for talks and teaching. It has neither the activity and presence nor the financial means of Siddha Yoga. It also seems less involved in our consumer world than SYDA; nevertheless, it is a typical case of the involvement of American Tantra in the American capitalist system.

Another aspect of Tantra in the United States that I will mention here is the academic one, this both for its own sake and because of its contacts with the movements we have just seen. In the United States, there was, and still is, an abundance of often high-quality academic studies on Tantra pursued in the South Asian studies departments and the departments of religion of many universities. Because the study of religions is not meant only for Indologists or Orientalists, these departments and studies effectively help develop an overt, liberal understanding of the Tantric phenomenon. This occurs much more in the United States than in Europe; however, an open approach to Tantra by the public has increased in recent years there, too. In the

United States, there is the Society for Tantric Studies, which every year hosts a well-attended Tantric conference in which foreign scholars also participate.[14]

On the subject of scholars and Tantra, one cannot avoid mentioning Agehananda Bharati (1923–91), a rather uncommon case. Born in Vienna, he came to the United States in 1958 and became a professor of anthropology at Syracuse University in New York. Interestingly, he believed that only the affluent Western world and especially the United States could become a new center for a revival of Tantra, which the traditional and morally repressive India could not be. He also warned against Western misinterpretations of Tantra, a subject he knew much about, for he was initiated in Tantra and put it in practice while in India. However, his views on these practices were far from those of all Indian Tantric traditions. For him, Tantra could only be a totally amoral hedonistic mysticism completely opposed to any rule or constraint. He stressed the enjoyment of all the pleasures of life, especially sex. This was the way to find *The Light at the Center*, to use the title of one of his main theoretical works. He did not approve of drugs and did not have any sympathy for extreme right-wing movements. He followed the "roads of excess" but was a humanist Tāntrika who practiced what he called "cultural criticism"—a questionable personality, but an interesting one.[15]

Tantra, or rather, neo-Tantra, is also present in other parts of the Western World, but nowhere as actively—or by the same numbers and with the same financial resources—as in the United States. Forms of Tantra adapted to the spirit of the modern world exist in many countries not merely as local sections of American movements, which, however, are often their most visible manifestation. This is true for Hindu Tantra but not for Buddhism, whose various "Tantric" forms have flourished in several countries, benefiting from the presence of Tibetan masters who left Tibet because of the destructive Chinese occupation of that country and brought with them the teachings of living traditions.

Some Hindu Tantric texts do appear in translations, even as paperbacks, but this does not mean that there are many committed adepts of their teachings. The translations, with some notable exceptions,[16] are often not good. In Europe as in the United States, the stress is usually on sex.[17] There is no point in dilating on the subject.

On the other hand, Western Tantric movements—European or American, large or small—usually only keep the traits from Indian Tantric traditions that correspond to their needs, oversimplifying their doctrinal teaching and generally ignoring what, in traditional India, were (and still are today) the basic Tantric elements. These are the "anthropocosmic" vision of the world and of humans—theology, pantheons, and rites. All that is existentially experienced, or "lived," by a true Tāntrika seems unnecessary to a Western adept who adopts the notions but not the culture where these notions were born and developed and is, naturally, not concerned by the all-important socio-religious side of the Tantric world. As I have already said, Tantra is deeply rooted in the Indian soil. It cannot be exported without these roots unless it is to be totally transformed in the process. I might perhaps say that what we see now in the West is a kind of new version of the approach to Tantra that was that of eighteenth-century Orientalists, but in a different spirit—not rejecting but adopting, while also misunderstanding it. It is a "comedy of errors," as I have said: the Western world goes on fabricating images of India.

To conclude this chapter and this book, I would first like to repeat that a Tantric phenomenon that is profoundly Indian does indeed exist. India acknowledged the existence of Tantric texts and traditions and of their notions and practices (both being necessarily conjoined). Western Orientalists discovered these piecemeal but, soon perceiving "family resemblances," hypostasized what they found in "an imaginative act of comparison and generalization," as Tantrism / Tantra. Decades later, they realized that there are actually different traditions that should not be put into the same bag. Today, Tantric studies is a vigorous and rapidly expanding field, for the quantity of available documents on the subject has infinitely increased. However, this is in academia. Outside the ivory tower, imagination is given free rein. Westerners, also hypostasizing the family resemblances within Tantra, misunderstanding and interpreting them according to their wishes and needs, have elaborated the forms of Tantra we have just seen, which have little to do with what Tantra really is. Admittedly, however "objective" outside observers wish to be, they cannot avoid being somehow affected by their own preconceptions or prejudices. Objectivity is something to which we can only aspire. But there is no need to reinvent Tantra to suit our own needs.

The reality, the real nature and life of Tantra, is not in the outside world. It is in India, in the past as well as today. It is a vast and fascinating universe of doctrinal constructions, of visions and ritual practices—a universe to be grasped and understood as a whole. Tantric traditions share the same vast pantheon in different ways. With different cosmogonies, they have a common view of the cosmos as a locus of powers both human and divine, these powers pervading and animating the universe while being grounded in a totally transcendent—but omnipresent—Absolute. This goes together with a conception of humans as being actively part of this universe of power, whose elements and traits they experience existentially as they live in it before eventually transcending it in unlimited fullness. All this, developed over centuries in Tantric texts, is still—if obscurely—perceptible in India today.

Tantra may, however, also be approached from outside, from where we are, not to adopt wholesale but to find elements that can lead to a fuller, more intense experience of life. I believe it is possible for us, without forsaking our own traditions, to find and to adopt from Tantra, without denaturing them, many concepts about the nature of the universe we live in and approaches to the Ultimate that would enrich our lives. Tantra underscores the essential point that our world is not made of an "inner" world that is different from the "outer world" that surrounds us, for it does not surround us—we are part of it and entirely pervaded by it. To live is to be open to the whole cosmos. Admittedly, all this is not explicitly stated in any Tantric text, but it is always implicitly there. For Tantra, to live is typically to transcend our daily human condition by an "élan," an intense lived thrust toward a divine, supreme One that is both in us and omnipresent (the "transpersonal" self [*ātmeśvara*] of the Pratyabhijñā tradition). There is also the notion that there is a basic, initial, originative level of speech that Tantra calls "supreme" (*parā*), therefore divine, but that some Western thinkers since Kant have also (as we noted) considered as the real foundation of speech. Thus Tantra may help us reach a deeper understanding of this fundamental notion. These are merely a few points among many others—and very clumsily expressed, I fear. Such borrowings (do we need to say so?) would evidently be entirely different from the Western deracinated transpositions we have seen in the last chapter of this book.

I have tried, more or less successfully, to give an overview of the extraordinarily rich diversity of Tantra. Surely this is a very limited and imperfect one. Much was also inevitably left aside. However, I will hope that I was able to offer a not untruthful general view of what Tantra, this truly essential aspect of India, really is. Admittedly, I described some elements that may appear strange or even bizarre. But even if this is so, I believe that Tantric India offers many interesting elements that may enrich our own view of human life—our destiny and place in this world. I hope that, however imperfect, this book will contribute somehow toward this end.

But I am very far from being sure of having succeeded in doing this. I will therefore conclude with the traditional Sanskrit final formula: *kṣamasva me tat* (forgive me this [imperfect work]).

Notes

Chapter One

1. On so-called Tantric Buddhism, Herbert Guenther once wrote, "The philosophical significance of the Mantrayāna has been much obscured by irresponsibly applying to it the name 'Tantrism,' probably one of the haziest notions and misconceptions the Western mind has evolved." *The Life and Teaching of Naropa* (Boston: Shambala, 1995), 112.

2. On this subject, see Gavin Flood, introduction to *The Blackwell Companion to Hinduism* (Oxford: Blackwell, 2003).

3. Hindu was furthermore originally an ethnic designator. It referred to the inhabitants of the region east of the Sindhu (the Indus) River, not to a religious ensemble.

4. They did not contrast Indian native traditions with those from outside, which were present in India but were treated as nonexistent by the Brahmin writers of Sanskrit.

Astika ("believer") is from the verbal form *asti*, which means "is, exists," and *nāstika* ("nonbeliever") is from "does not exist" (*na asti*), a group in which some authors included Śaṅkara's Vedānta, which they considered "crypto-Buddhist!"

5. Pursuing our deconstructive considerations, we could add that the notion of religion as we usually understand it is also foreign to India, as it is perhaps to all traditional cultures.

6. On John Woodroffe, see the study by Kathleen Taylor, *Sir John Woodroffe, Tantra and Bengal: "An Indian Soul in a European Body?"* (Richmond, UK: Curzon Press, 2001).

7. This is still the case nowadays, especially in Śaiva temples of Tamil Nadu and Kerala in South India, where officiants are sometimes not fully initiated because they cannot afford the expenses of a full initiation.

8. The *saṃskāras*, which mark the stages of life of caste Hindus from their conception to their funeral, include notably the *upanayana*, the initiation during which the sacred thread and a mantra are given to young boys, a rite that officially marks their entry in their caste. Girls are not entitled to this initiation. Therefore, Hindu women, whatever their caste, are ritually *śūdras*. This initiation is not to be identified with Tantric initiation into a sect, *dīkṣā*, which women can, at least theoretically, also receive.

9. "Āgamas." Though Pāñcarātra texts are usually called *saṃhitās*, *āgama* is a general term for Tantric scriptures. The Pāñcarātra scriptures are also sometimes called "Tantra."

10. On Abhinavagupta, see the section "Śaiva Postscriptural Works and Exegeses," chapter 4 of this volume.

11. This, we may note in passing, is typical Indian intellectual behavior: a different or new idea is not rejected as false but either considered virtually the same as the admitted one or as, though false, including elements that may lead indirectly to the discovery of truth. This behavior was famously called *Inklusivismus* by the Austrian indologist Paul Hacker.

12. Tantra is ritually transgressive but socially conservative. Some Tantras or exegetical works go as far as to limit the initiation of adepts to the three "twice-born" classes of Hindus, thus excluding *śūdras*. (Classes [*varṇa*] are divided in castes [*jāti*].)

13. The Mīmāṃsā (a word meaning "exegesis") is an interpretative exegesis of the Veda. At first a hermeneutic of Vedic ritual, it developed into a philosophical school, one of the six so-called views (*darśanas*) of Indian philosophy. It is the basic system of traditional Hindu orthodoxy.

14. Memory (*smṛti*) is the human tradition as opposed to what is heard (*śruti*), the divine revelation. These texts, though transmitted by humans, are deemed to have a divine origin. Among them are commentaries on the Veda, the Epics, the Purāṇas, and the works on the socioreligious Hindu rules (the *dharmaśāstra*).

15. The "classical" work of Rai Bahadur Srisa Chandra Vidyarnava, *The Daily Practice of the Hindus* (1949; repr., New Delhi: Sri Satguru Publications, 2008), describes first the Vaidikī then the Tāntrikī practice for each rite, treating them as equally valid.

16. See "The Textual Material," chapter 3 in this volume.

17. See "Tantric Places or Practices," chapter 10 in this volume.

18. *Techniques du Yoga* (Paris: Gallimard, 1948). The book, written in Paris, was based on lectures given in the University of Bucharest in 1934–35, when Eliade was back in Romania after a stay in India, where he studied yoga. A revised version was translated in English. I could not lay my hand on a copy of that translation. I therefore translated the sentences quoted here.

19. Louis Renou and Jean Filliozat, eds., *L'Inde Classique* (Paris: Payot, 1947).

20. This fascicule of Louis Renou's *Etudes védiques et pāninéennes* (Paris: Institut de civilisation indienne, 1955–1969) is on "Le destin du Veda en Inde." It is very much worth reading even for non-Indologists—if they know French.

21. Translated as *Hinduism, the Anthropology of a Civilisation* (New Delhi: OUP, 1989).

22. This, of course, insofar as the private life of a human being living in this world can be entirely separate from his or her social life. The whole life of a practicing Tāntrika cannot but be marked by his or her "Tantric," nondualistic way of thinking.

We could add here that the notion of the individual person as we generally conceive it is foreign to Indian traditional society—a point never to be lost sight of when considering India.

23. This has been shown by Michel Strickman in a fascinating study, *Mantras et mandarins: Le bouddhisme tantrique en Chine* (Paris: Gallimard, 1996).

24. It was, in fact, preceded in the same collection by Jan Gonda's *Medieval Religious Literature in Sanskrit* (Wiesbaden: Otto Harrassowitz, 1977), which reviewed the Pāñcarātra saṃhitās, the Śaiva āgamas, Pāśupata and Nātha works, and so on—all texts presented as so many aspects of Hindu literature.

25. In India, Tantric works went on, of course, being "published" (in manuscript form) from early times. Their modern, "scientific" approach is not recent. The Yogatantra Department of the Sanskrit (now Sampurnanand) University of Varanasi, for instance, was founded half a century ago; collections of philologically edited Tantric works by Indian learned institutions began much earlier. The Gaekwad Oriental Series of Baroda (where some Tantric works have also appeared in translation) began in 1924, while the first volume of Abhinavagupta's *Tantrāloka* in the Kashmir Series of Texts and Studies was issued in 1918.

26. See "Tantra in the West," chapter 12 in this volume.

27. David G. White, *Kiss of the Yoginī: "Tantric Sex" in Its South Asian Context* (Chicago: Chicago University Press, 2003).

28. Secrecy is an element of the "symbolic capital" and therefore of the power, of a group—hence its importance. On an aspect of this subject, see the study by Hugh B. Urban on the Kartābhajā sect, *Economics of Ecstasy: Tantra, Secrecy, and Power in Colonial Bengal* (Oxford: Oxford University Press, 2001).

Chapter Two

1. The Maitri Upaniṣad, for instance (seventh *prapāṭhaka*), where the ether (*nabhas*) pervading the inner void space of the heart (*kha*) is the supreme igneous energy (*paraṃ tejas*), which is associated with the ascending vital breath (*prāṇa*), and circulates in the body, then flows out of it as the mother (*mātr̥kā*; of the phonemes).

2. Notably in the Pāñcarātra, as we shall see.

3. Such is the case, even now, of the great Nepalese festival, the Dasain—the royal festival in honor of the goddess Durgā—as well as of many Śaiva feasts or pilgrimages.

4. The same "popular" influence perhaps explains the birth of so-called Tantric Buddhism.

5. The term *tapas*, which means "heat," or "warmth," is applied to religious austerity (asceticism) insofar as it "heats" the body. It is an ancient and important notion.

6. This is what I did in the original French version of this book. There are recent studies on the subject, especially one by Alexis Sanderson on "The Lākulas," *Indian Philosophical Annual* (2006), 143–217, whom he regards as "intermediate between the non-Tantric Pāśupatas and Āgamic Śaivism," to use the subtitle of his article.

7. In Alexis Sanderson, "The Śaiva Age: The Rise and Dominance of Śaivism during the Early Medieval Period," in *Genesis and Development of Tantrism*, ed. Shingo Einoo (Tokyo: Institute of Oriental Culture, University of Tokyo, 2009), 41–349.

8. On this Tantra and other ancient texts, see "The Textual Material," chapter 3 in this volume.

9. For the English translation, see Bhaṭṭa Jayanta, *Āgamaḍambara, Much Ado about Religion*, trans. and ed. Csaba Dezső (New York: New York University Press, 2005).

10. These Chinese translations can give credence to the idea that Tantra was Buddhist before being Hindu, which, though not impossible, does not seem likely for several reasons (the role of *śakti*, for instance).

11. I want to mention the important work of preserving, cataloging, and microfilming done over three decades by the Nepal-German Manuscript Preservation Project (NGMPP), now replaced by two other Nepalese and German programs run from Hamburg and Kathmandu.

12. See the well-illustrated book by Vidya Dehejia, *Yoginī Cult and Temple: A Tantric Tradition* (New Delhi: National Museum, 1986).

13. See "Tantric Traditions," chapter 4 in this volume.

14. A part of the Tibetan Buddhist canon, the Kanjur, consists of translations (or mistranslations) of Śaiva texts probably from Kashmir. They were done in part by Brahmins—another piece of evidence of the Hindu-Buddhist interaction, notably in Kashmir.

On Buddhism in Tibet, see, for instance, Goffrey Samuel, *Civilized Shamans: Buddhism and Tibetan Societies* (Washington, DC: Smithsonian Institution, 1993).

15. Marie-Louise Reiniche, preface to *Les dieux et les hommes: Etude des cultes d'un village du Tirunelveli* (Paris: Mouton, 1979).

16. This Śaiva predominance is remarkably described by Alexis Sanderson in the very erudite study, "Śaiva Age."

17. This existed until recently in Nepal, where the Kumarī is an incarnation of the secret royal goddess Taleju. Every year, the king reinforces his power through her.

18. Such rites were performed for the king of Nepal (See Gérard Toffin, *Le palais et le temple: La fonction royale dans la vallée du Népal* [Paris: CNRS, 1993]) until the end of the monarchy. They are still performed nowadays for the descendants of some formerly reigning Indian princes, whom one still sees present as such at some religious festivals—for instance, at Jagannath, Puri.

19. This lasted practically down to Indian independence.

20. See the remarkable book by M. S. Slusser, *Nepal Maṇḍala: A Cultural Study of the Kathmandu Valley* (Princeton: Princeton University Press, 1982).

21. This state of affairs is still very much present and visible in the Himalayan regions. See, for instance, Niels Gutschow et al., eds., *Sacred Landscape in the Himalayas* (Vienna: Austrian Academy of Sciences Press, 2003). It is an extremely interesting and beautifully illustrated work. See also Daniella Berti, *La parole des dieux: Rituels de possession dans l'Himalaya indien* (Paris: CNRS, 2001).

22. Those in Cambodia are particularly numerous and informative and are still being deciphered and studied.

23. In his book *Mantras et mandarins*, Michel Strickman noted that Tantra had transformed not only monks into Tantric kings but also kings into Tantric masters. *Mantras et mandarins: Le Bouddhisme tantrique en Chine* (Paris: Gallimard, 1996).

24. See Sanderson, "The Śaiva Age," *passim*. In this study, Sanderson underlines the fact that the Tantric age was essentially a Śaiva (and also Śākta) age. Vaiṣṇavism was of lesser importance.

Chapter Three

1. *Scripture* is not a good term for the Hindu revelations, for they are in essence oral—spoken, not written. In Sanskrit, Revelation is "what is heard" (*śruti*; see "The Tantric Word: Mantras," chapter 7 in this volume). Writing was known early in India but always considered as inferior to oral transmission and not to be used for sacred texts. The Veda, tenth century BC, was first committed to writing in the thirteenth century CE.

2. The term *mantraśāstra* is currently used to refer to the ensemble of works on mantras. It is, however, mainly a recent usage. In India, it tends to be applied especially to the magical use of mantras.

3. The different groups of texts considered here are exhaustively listed and described in Jan Gonda, *Medieval Religious Literature in Sanskrit*, A History of Indian Literature, vol. 2, no. 1 (Wiesbaden: Otto Harrassowitz, 1977); and Teun Goudriaan and Sanukta Gupta, *Hindu Tantric and Śaiva Literature*, A History of Indian Literature, vol. 2, no. 2 (Wiesbaden: Otto Harrassowitz, 1981).

4. Tantric deities tend to multiply—there are ten Śivas, fifty Rudras, fifty-one Gaṇeśas, etc. We shall see this in "Tantric Places or Practices," chapter 10 in this volume.

5. When it was founded in 1956, the Indological section of the Institut Français de Pondichéry undertook the collection of as many manuscripts as possible of the Śaiva āgamas and aimed to engage in their study and, in some cases, translation. In 2005, the manuscript holdings of the French research institutions in Pondicherry (namely the Institut Français de Pon-

dichéry and the Pondicherry Centre of the École française d'Extrême-Orient) were recognized by UNESCO as a "Memory of the World" collection entitled "The Śaiva Manuscripts of Pondicherry." The paper manuscripts of this collection are now accessible online.

6. As we shall see in "Tantric Traditions," chapter 4 in this volume, a *saṃhitā* dating probably from the fifth or sixth century, the *Niśvāsatattvasaṃhitā*, shows that the doctrines and practices of the earlier period of the Siddhānta did not differ very much from those of the Bhairava Tantras.

7. In fact, few āgamas include these four sections, whose normativeness (which has been questioned) is therefore theoretical. The *Mṛgendrāgama* has all four sections.

8. On the so-called classical Siddhānta, see "Tantric Traditions," chapter 4 in this volume.

9. Dominic Goodall, *The Parākhyatantra: A Scripture of the Śaiva Siddhānta*, Collection Indologie 98 (Pondichéry: Institut Français de Pondichéry, 2004).

10. Both have been translated into French and published in the series of the French Institute, Pondicherry.

11. The list, given in several texts (in the commentary of the *Tantrāloka*, for instance), appears as largely theoretical. It includes some Tantras that are unknown to us. The number eight is important in this group of texts—there are eight Bhairavas with eight goddesses, etc.

Concerning Tantras, we must note that the *Mahānirvāṇatantra*, often quoted because it was among the first published and the first translated (by Arthur Avalon in 1913, in the *Tantrik Texts* series *Tantra of the Great Liberation [Mahānirvāṇa Tantra]: A Translation of the Sanscrit with Introduction and Commentary* [London: Luzac, 1913]) is a nineteenth-century fabrication intended to give an accessible and respectable presentation of Tantrism. It is, however, interesting as an aspect of the modern survival of Tantra and a testimony to the ambiguous relationship between the Hindu tradition and the modern world.

12. Note that the Tantras are classified according to the sort of mantras they propound; mantras are deities (see "Tantric Word," chapter 7 in this volume).

13. In the Kashmir Series of Texts and Studies (KSTS).

14. There are several English translations of this text with Kṣemarāja's commentary. However, the best, most abundantly annotated translation to date is in Italian by Raffaele Torella, *Gli Aforismi di Śiva, con il Commento di Kṣemarāja* (Milano: Mimesis, 2013).

15. It was excellently edited, annotated, and translated (in French) by Hélène Brunner-Lachaux (1920–2005) and published in the series of the Institut Français de Pondichéry in four volumes (1963–98).

16. To date, the most (in fact, the only) complete survey of this exegetical literature is Alexis Sanderson's "The Śaiva Exegesis of Kashmir," in *Tantric Studies in Memory of Hélène Brunner*, ed. Dominic Goodall and André Padoux (Pondichéry: Institut Français de Pondichéry, 2007), 231–442.

17. John Nemec, *The Ubiquitous Śiva: Somānanda's Śivadṛṣṭi and his Tantric Interlocutors* (Oxford: Oxford University Press, 2011).

18. The only translation is in Italian by Raniero Gnoli. Abhinavagupta, *Tantrāloka*, trans. Raniero Gnoli (Milano: Adelphi, 1999).

19. The only substantial writing of Rāmakaṇṭha to have been completely translated is a commentarial work on liberation. Alex Watson, Dominic Goodall, and S. L. P. Anjaneya Sarma, *An Enquiry into the Nature of Liberation: Bhaṭṭa Rāmakaṇṭha's Paramokṣanirāsakārikāvṛtti, a Commentary on Sadyojyotiḥ's Refutation of Twenty Conceptions of the Liberated State (Mokṣa)* (Pondichéry: Institut Français de Pondichéry, 2013).

20. Many such temples follow the Vaikhanāsa tradition, which considers itself as Vedic in spite of the fact that its ritual practices include many Tantric traits.

21. This was done notably by Yāmunācārya, who was Rāmānuja's master—see "The Hindu Tantric Field," chapter 1 in this volume. Some Pañcarātrins go even as far as to assert that the Pāñcarātra is a Vedic school (*śākhā*).

22. Daniel H. Smith's *A Descriptive Bibliography of the Printed Texts of the Pañcārātrāgama*, vol. 1–2 (Baroda: Oriental Institute, 1975, 1980) gives a résumé of the contents of the main saṃhitās. See also Gonda, *Medieval Religious Literature*, 39–139. Many of these texts have been edited.

23. *Lakṣmītantra*, trans. Sanjukta Gupta (Leiden: Brill, 1972).

24. Already studied by Schrader during the First World War (1916).

25. The work has been translated into English: M. L. Gharote and G. K. Pai, *Siddhasiddhāntapaddhati: A Treatise on the Nātha Philosophy by Gorakṣanātha* (Lonavla: Lonavla Yoga Institute, 2005). On the Nāthas, the reader is referred to G. W. Briggs, *Gorakhnāth and the Kānphaṭa Yogis* (repr., Delhi: Motilal Banarsidass, 1982), dating from 1938 but still very much worth reading. The Nāthas and their role in the modern Indian scene are mentioned again in "Tantra in India," chapter 11 in this volume.

26. The names given to these two volumes are of the Theosophical Society's choice. They have no traditional or scientific import.

27. This seems to be the first Śaiva text to mention *haṭhayoga* (first mentioned in a Buddhist work, the *Guhyasamājatantra*). Its yogic teachings have been examined by Somdev Vasudeva in *The Yoga of the Mālinīvijayottaratantra*, Collection Indologie 97 (Pondichéry: Institut Français de Pondichéry, 2004), ch. 1–4, 7, 11–17.

28. The Theosophical Society is responsible for this selection and for its title, which have no traditional, scriptural base.

29. This was carefully studied by M.-T. de Mallmann in *Les enseignements iconographiques de l'Agnipurāṇa* (Paris: Presses Universitaires de France, 1963).

30. Somadeva's *Kathāsaritsāgara* was translated in ten volumes and given the title "Ocean of Stories," trans. C. H. Tawney, ed. N. M. Penzer (London: privately printed for subscribers only by Chas. J. Sawyer, 1924–1928).

31. It was translated into English under that title by Csaba Dezső (in the Clay Sanskrit Library). Many literary works quoted here are also available in translation.

32. A brief review of this literature was made by Sanjukta Gupta in Teun Goudriaan and Sanjukta Gupta, *Hindu Tantric and Śākta Literature*, A History of Indian Literature, vol. 2, no. 2 (Wiesbaden, Otto Harrassowitz, 1981). A not very recent but still valid study of the subject—on Bengali literature only—is Shashibhusan Dasgupta, *Obscure Religious Cults* (Calcutta: Firma K. L. Mukhopadhyaya, 1967).

33. In Indian studies, the term *medieval* refers conventionally to the period going roughly from the twelfth to the sixteenth centuries.

34. On this literature, see Rachel Fell McDermott, "Raising Snakes in Bengal: The Use of Tantric Imagery in Sakta Poetry Contexts," in *Tantra in Practice*, ed. David G. White (Princeton: Princeton University Press, 2000), 167–83; or Hugh B. Urban, *Songs of Ecstasy: Tantric Devotional Songs from Colonial Bengal* (Oxford: Oxford University Press, 2001). On ritual worship in Bengal, see also Akos Östör, *The Play of the Gods: Locality, Ideology, Structure, and Time in the Festivals of a Bengali Town* (New Delhi: Chronicle Books, 2004).

35. See "Tantric Places," chapter 10 in this volume.

36. On this, see Edward C. Dimock, *The Place of the Hidden Moon: Erotic Mysticism in the Vaishnava-Sahajiya Cult of Bengal* (Chicago: Chicago University Press, 1969).

37. On Tantric elements in Kabir's work, see Charlotte Vaudeville, *Kabir*, vol. 1 (Oxford: Clarendon Press, 1974).

38. On one of these poets, Nammāḻvār, see *Hymns for the Drowning: Poems for Viṣṇu by Nammāḻvār*, trans. A. K. Ramanujan (Princeton: Princeton Library of Asian Translations, 1981). All the work of A. K. Ramanujan, who was professor of South Asian languages, and a poet in his own right, is well worth reading.

39. I would be tempted to refer here to Vīraśaiva literature in medieval Kannaḍa, although it is not Tantric. This is because of the sheer beauty and emotional intensity of the *Vacanas* of Vīraśaiva mystical poets of the eleventh and twelfth centuries, and also because they are close in their form and feeling to Tamil Tantric works. They are immensely worth reading. They have also been beautifully translated by A. K. Ramanujan in *Speaking of Śiva* (Harmondsworth: Penguin Classics, 1979).

Chapter Four

1. Indian Veda-based philosophical systems have, since the twelfth century, been considered as being six in number, grouped in pairs. They are Mīmāṃsā and Vedānta (also called Uttaramīmāṃsā), the exegesis of the Veda and the metaphysical developments based on the ancient Upaniṣads: the Sāṃkhya, a classifying description of the universe and yoga, two closely interrelated systems—a philosophy and a practice—and the Nyāya, the "method" and Vaiśeṣika, which are also cosmic descriptions and logical systems. In the presentation of Indian traditions, other systems were added, including materialism, Buddhism, Jainism, and Śaiva or Vaiṣṇava traditions so as to have a total of sixteen systems. These were described and hierarchically classified in the thirteenth century in Mādhava's *Sarvadarśanasaṃgraha*, according to the author's Vedāntic prejudice—a work influential in the reconstruction (Western and Indian) of Indian philosophy.

2. The number of *tattvas* vary. Śaiva traditions have usually thirty-six *tattvas*. The Pāñcarātra has less.

3. *Puruṣa*, as the first of the principles (*tattva*), is not a divinity. Hence the notion that the Sāṃkhya was originally an atheistic system.

4. Tantric traditions attribute to the godhead the simultaneous powers of occlusion or concealing (*tirodhāna*), which puts obstacles to liberation, and of bestowing grace (*anugraha*), which opens the ways (*adhvan*) to liberation.

5. See "The Textual Material," chapter 3 in this volume.

6. There are varying lists of Mothers. A commonly occurring one is Brāhmī, Māheśvarī, Kaumārī, Vaiṣṇavī, Indrāṇī, Vārāhī, Cāmuṇḍī, and Mahālakṣmī.

7. Sometimes shown in nondualist Śaivism as a thirty-seventh *tattva*.

8. They are shown in this way in the circular Yoginī temples of central India, the Yoginīs being in a circle with Bhairava in the center. The same pattern is found in Buddhist pantheons. It is considered as the usual pattern of pantheons in South Asia. Sometimes sanctuaries of deities are spread over a territory so as to form a *maṇḍala*—see "Tantric Places or Practices," chapter 10 in this volume.

9. Not the Śaivasiddhānta.

10. This appears notably in the *Niśvāsatattvasaṃhitā*, a work of the fifth to sixth century of

which a ninth-century Nepalese manuscript was recently discovered. It is now being studied, edited, and translated by Dominic Goodall and a first volume appeared after this book was first submitted for publication. Dominic Goodall, Alexis Sanderson, and Harunaga Isaacson, eds., *The Niśvāsatattvasaṃhitā: The Earliest Surviving Śaiva Tantra*, vol 1 (Pondichéry: Institut Français de Pondichéry, 2015).

11. Thus, if I may attempt to translate the French of Pierre Hadot in his *Eloge de la philosophie antique* (Paris: Allia, 2001), 66, "Attitude existentielle qui fonde l'édifice dogmatique."

12. To this day (2016), the best brief overview of the different Śaiva Tantric traditions is Alexis Sanderson, "Śaivism and the Tantric Traditions," in *The World's Religions*, ed. S. Sullivan et al. (London: Croom Helm, 1988), 660–703. It is a scholarly study but easily readable by the uninitiated. The different schools of Kashmirian Śaivism are the subject of a very erudite study by Alexis Sanderson, "The Śaiva Exegesis of Kashmir," in *Tantric Studies in Memory of Hélène Brunner*, ed. Dominic Goodall and André Padoux (Pondichéry: Institut Français de Pondichéry, 2007), 231–442.

13. This is one of the senses of the Sanskrit *pūrva*. The East—the orient, where the sun rises—is the primal point, always mentioned first in ritual.

14. See John R. Dupuche, *Abhinavagupta: The Kula Ritual as Elaborated in Chapter 29 of the Tantraloka* (New Delhi: Motilal Banarsidass, 2003).

15. On the Devī cult in Bhaktapur, I refer the reader to the very interesting study of Robert I. Levy, *Mesocosm: Hinduism and the Organization of a Traditional Newar City in Nepal* (Berkeley: University of California Press, 1984).

16. Hindu deities, and especially Tantric ones, are figured holding symbolic objects, called "weapons" (*āyudha*) in their hands, but these are not necessarily instruments of violence. Tripurasundarī, for instance, carries an elephant-goad, a noose-like fetter, and a bow and arrows.

17. On this text and on the problem of "the Goddess," see Thomas B. Coburn, *Devī Māhātmya: The Crystallization of the Goddess Tradition* (Delhi: Motilal Banarsidass, 1984).

18. In North Indian sculpture, they are often shown with infants. In South Indian sculpture, however, they never hold infants and are referred to as *kanyakā* (girls).

19. The most complete study of this exegetical literature is Alexis Sanderson, "The Śaiva Exegesis of Kashmir," in *Tantric Studies in Memory of Hélène Brunner*, ed. Dominic Goodall and André Padoux (Pondichéry: Institut Français de Pondichéry, 2007), 231–442, but it is not meant for the lay reader. Usefully readable, however, is Sanderson's earlier overview, "Śaivism and the Tantric Traditions."

20. It has been excellently edited, commented on, and translated in French by Hélène Brunner-Lachaux. *Somaśambhupaddhati*, trans. Hélène Brunner-Lachaux (Pondichéry: Institut français d'indologie, 1963–98).

21. The best annotated translation to date of the *Śivasūtra* is in Italian by Raffaele Torella, *Gli Aforismi di Śiva* (Milano: Mimesis, 2013).

22. The *Stanzas on Vibration* with their four commentaries have been translated and commented on by Mark Dyczkowski (Albany, NY: SUNY Press, 1992).

23. In the British sense of this word, a person versed in aesthetics, not a beautician.

24. On the subject of remembrance (*smṛti*, *smaraṇa*), which is considered a means to conquer time, Abhinavagupta once wrote, "In truth, only Śiva remembers."

25. *Samāveśa* is difficult to translate. The notion, too, is not easy to define. It is somehow different from "possession" (*āveśa*)—"(mystical) absorption," perhaps.

26. The system of the twelve Kālīs is described and explained by Lilian Silburn with her

French translation of the *Kramastotra*. I am not aware of an English translation of this text, but the Krama exegesis is carefully studied in Sanderson's "Śaiva Exegesis of Kashmir," 200–350.

27. See Friedhelm Hardy, *Viraha-Bhakti: The Early History of Kṛṣṇa Devotion in South India* (Oxford: Oxford University Press, 1983).

28. On this subject, see the studies of Glen A. Hayes, who has edited a curious Sahajiyā text, *The Necklace of Immortality*. I borrow here some of his terms.

On the Vaiṣṇava Sahajiyās, see Edward C. Dimock, *The Place of the Hidden Moon: Erotic Mysticism in the Vaishnava-Sahajiya Cult of Bengal* (Chicago: Chicago University Press, 1969); Shashibhusan Dasgupta's *Obscure Religious Cults* (Calcutta: Firma K. L. Mukhopadhyaya, 1967) is extremely informative and still very much worth reading.

29. I refer here to Leo Frobenius's classification of "primitive" society into "magical" and "mystical."

30. Several Tantric texts use the trilogy *śānti*, *puṣṭi*, and *abhicāra* for the peaceful, nourishing, and hostile effects of mantras.

On magic in India, see the study by Teun Goudriaan, *Māyā Human and Divine: A Study of Magic and Its Religious Foundations in Sanskrit Texts* (Delhi: Motilal Banarsidass, 1978), a very informative work. On magic in contemporary India, I refer the reader to Lee Siegel, *Net of Magic: Wonders and Deceptions in India* (Chicago: Chicago University Press, 1991). The book is enjoyable, amusing, and informative.

31. In his study of yoga, *Sinister Yogis* (Chicago: Chicago University Press, 2009), 165–66, David G. White quotes the Tantric scholar Gopinath Kaviraj (1887–1976), describing his own knowledge and practice of this power.

32. This more in Buddhism (in Southeast Asia, the Himalayas, and Tibet or Japan) than in Hindu India.

Chapter Five

1. This was done by Gavin Flood in *The Tantric Body: The Secret Tradition of Hindu India* (London: I. B. Tauris, 2005), the original text of which was unfortunately partly suppressed by the publishers.

2. Notably in Jain cosmographies.

3. One of the best-known descriptions of the system of *cakras* is the *Ṣaṭcakranirūpaṇa*, edited and translated by Arthur Avalon in *The Serpent Power: The Secrets of Tantric and Shaktic Yoga*, 5th ed. (Madras: Ganesh, 1953), first published 1919 by Luzac. It is still available in countless reprints and worth reading.

4. On the role and "functioning" of *kuṇḍalinī* according to Tantric texts, I would refer the reader to Lilian Silburn, *Kuṇḍalinī: Energy of the Depths* (Albany, NY: SUNY Press, 1988).

5. "Conscious Is Up," p. 15 of George Lakoff and Mark Johnson, *The Metaphors We Live By* (Chicago: University of Chicago Press, 1980).

6. On this subject, see David Gordon White, *The Yoga Sutra of Patanjali: A Biography* (Princeton: Princeton University Press, 2014).

7. *Tarka* is one of the elements of the six-limbed yoga of the *Maitri* (or *Maitrāyaṇīya*) Upaniṣad, which may date from before our era. It mentions also *suṣumnā* (6.21), saying that an ascending *prāṇa* flows in it together with *OṂ*, which unites the adept with the Absolute.

8. Some traditions—the Trika, for instance—say there are two *dvādaśāntas*, an upper one above the head and a lower one "at the end of the outgoing breath." On the *uccāra* of mantras, see "The Tantric Word," chapter 7 in this volume.

9. On the history and the present practice of yoga, I would refer the reader to an interesting study by J. S. Alter, *Yoga in Modern India: The Body between Science and Philosophy* (Princeton: Princeton University Press, 2004).

10. On the Tantric initiations, see "Tantric Ritual," chapter 8 of this volume. When describing this ritual (and other ones), I use the masculine, since normally only male disciples are initiated and temple priests and officiating Brahmins are normally male.

11. On the *kalās* of *OṂ*, see "Tantric World," chapter 7 in this volume.

12. For a more precise description of this *japa*, see my translation of the *Yoginīhṛdaya: The Heart of the Yoginī*, trans. André Padoux with Roger-Orphé Jeanty (New York: Oxford University Press, 2013), 145–60.

13. On this, see James Mallinson's article on haṭhayoga in Jessica Frazier, ed., *The Continuum Companion to Hindu Studies* (Leiden: Brill, 2011). On haṭhayoga, see Jason Birch's paper, "The Meaning of *Haṭha* in Early Haṭhayoga," *Journal of the American Oriental Society* 131, no. 4 (2011), 527–54.

14. For more details on the subject, see the chapter on *nyāsa* in André Padoux, *Tantric Mantras: Studies on Mantraśāstra* (London: Routledge, 2010), 54–80.

15. As the saying goes: "Without becoming Śiva, one cannot worship Śiva" (*nāśivaḥ śivam arcayet*).

16. To quote Jacques Lacan on Bernini's statue of St. Theresa in ecstasis: "Obviously she is having an orgasm."

17. Alchemy is, however, one of the sixteen *darśanas* of Mādhava's *Sarvadarśanasaṃgraha*. It is placed ninth in this ("vedantically" biased) hierarchical overview of Hindu traditional systems, among those deemed to be able (though not aptly) to lead to liberation.

18. The most complete and well-informed study of Indian alchemy and of its relationship with Tantra is, to date, David G. White, *The Alchemical Body: Siddha Traditions in Medieval India* (Chicago: Chicago University Press, 1984).

19. A number of studies (in English, French, and Italian) on Indian medicine are grouped in Eugen Ciurtin and Oscar Botto, eds., *The Human Body, at the Crossroads of Multiple Indian Ways of Knowing: Papers Presented to Arion Roşu by his Colleagues and Friends on the Occasion of his Eightieth Birthday* (Paris: De Boccard, 2004). See also Axel Michaels and Christoph Wulf, eds., *The Body in India: Ritual, Transgression, Performativity* (Berlin: Akademie Verlag, 2009).

20. A. K. Ramanujan, "A Hindu to His Body," in *The Collected Poems of A.K. Ramanujan* (Delhi: Oxford University Press, 1995). This poem ends with the wish of the poet—when he dies, he wants to rise with the sap of trees and plants.

On the image of the body, the classical work remains Paul Schilder, *The Image and Appearance of the Human Body: Studies in the Constructive Energies of the Psyche* (New York: International Universities Press, 1950).

The most comprehensive approach to the Indian aspect of the subject that I know of is V. Bouillier and G. Tarabout, eds., *Images du corps dans le monde hindou* (Paris: CNRS, 2002).

Chapter Six

1. In this, I disagree with David G. White who, for instance, wrote in *Kiss of the Yoginī: "Tantric Sex" in Its South-Asian Context* (Chicago: Chicago University Press, 2003) that "sexualized ritual practice is the sole truly distinctive feature of South Asian Tantric traditions" (13). This is because he does not consider, as I do, the field of Tantra as having permeated the whole Hindu world, where the sexual aspect, though central, is of a comparatively limited importance. If one

looks at Tantra as an aspect of the whole Hindu domain (and of a part of Mahāyāna Buddhism), the common basic trait would not be sex but ritual—as shown, for instance, by the structure of *pūjā*, both Hindu and Buddhist.

2. The French anthropologist Hélène Trottier, who had a personal experience of such sexual practices, used to say that the Indian woman is "both goddess and slave." We must not forget that the Indian discourse on women is a "male construction of femaleness."

On the male Indian's attitude toward or emotional reaction to women, see, for instance, G. Morris Carstairs, *The Twice-Born: A Study of a Community of High-Caste Hindus* (London: Hogarth Press, 1957), 157–59, 167–68. Another psychoanalytic approach of the subject is in Sudhir Kakar, *Shamans, Mystics and Doctors: A Psychological Inquiry into India and Its Healing Traditions* (New Delhi: Oxford University Press, 1982), chapter 6, "Tantra and Tantric Healing."

3. In the pantheon of the Śrīvidyā, for instance. See André Padoux with Roger-Orphé Jeanty, trans., *Yoginīhṛdaya: The Heart of the Yoginī* (New York: Oxford University Press, 2013), chapter 3.

4. See "The Tantric Word," chapter 7 in this volume.

5. See ibid., where this passage of the *Tantrasadbhāva* is referred to.

6. The totality of the Word (*vāc*) and therefore of the cosmos is thus present there.

7. The *adhovaktra* is also called "Mouth of the Yoginī" (*yoginīvaktra*). It is the source, commentators say, of the secret teachings of nondualistic Śaivism.

On *kāmakalā*, see the study by David G. White, "Transformations in the Art of Love: Kāmakalā Practices in Hindu Tantric and Kaula Traditions," *History of Religions* 38, no. 2 (1998): 172–98, which stresses the sexual side of the subject.

On the philosophical and theological aspects of *kāmakalā*, the main Sanskrit work is Puṇyānandanātha, *Kāmakalāvilāsa*, trans. Arthur Avalon (Madras: Ganesh, 1953). The commentary by Naṭanānandanātha and notes by Arthur Avalon (originally produced in 1922), while useful, leave carefully aside anything sexual.

8. Nor, I may note, do we find there the sacred character of the cow. Vedic Indians were not vegetarian.

9. J. Schotermann, ed., *Yonitantra* (New Delhi: Manohar, 1980). No complete scholarly translation has been published.

10. Texts often say that the woman is to be of low caste, or a prostitute, which increases the transgressive aspect of the ritual. Note that in the Hindu traditional conception, a prostitute, the "never married" (therefore "never widow") is a woman out of norms. On this, one may read the novel by U. R. Ananthamurthy, *Samskara: A Rite for a Dead Man*, trans. A. K. Ramanujan (Oxford: Oxford University Press, 1979). The place and role of the courtesan in classical Indian society is well known.

11. According to Vidya Dehejia, *Yoginī Cults and Practices: A Tantric Tradition* (New Delhi: National Museum, 1986), such rites are still practiced today.

12. This chapter was read by Lilian Silburn with pandit Lakshman Joo of Kashmir, who had her promise not to reveal its secret teachings. Dr. Silburn, therefore, referred only to the mystical aspects of this practice in her *Kuṇḍalinī: Energy of the Depths* (Albany, NY: SUNY Press, 1988). The whole chapter—text and commentary—has since been translated, with notes and the transliterated Sanskrit text by John R. Dupuche, *Abhinavagupta: The Kula Ritual as Elaborated in Chapter 29 of the Tantrāloka* (New Delhi: Motilal Banarsidass, 2003).

13. The "caste" must be "any of the outcaste ones" and the choice to be done "without regard to age, beauty, etc.," says Jayaratha.

14. This, I may note in passing, is a general fact. Marcel Mauss developed this theme. Even

Augustine—if I may quote him in this context!—noted it, referring to the truths he experienced *per sensus corporis mei* (*Confessions*, X.6).

15. In India, aesthetic experience at its acme is akin to mystic experience. It raises the subject above time, space, and the flow of ordinary life, opening the heart to the Absolute. *Camatkāra*, the ecstatic wonder of the highest aesthetic experience, is also a state of pure and total intense consciousness. That great mystic Abhinavagupta was not the main Indian master of aesthetics by accident.

16. The best of which is made with grapes. "Wine [*surā*]," says Abhinavagupta, quoting a Tantra, "is pure by nature, it is light, bliss, and consciousness, forever cherished by the gods; therefore, [the adept] should always drink it" (TĀ. 29, 13).

17. This ritual is described from the male practitioner's viewpoint. Though the supreme knowledge comes from the "mouth" of the *dūtī*, she nevertheless remains an instrument for the spiritual quest of the yogi, who is both the main performer and the beneficiary of the ritual process.

18. This is the case with the Bāuls. See "Tantric Places or Practices," chapter 10 in this volume.

19. Man's anatomy does not allow this. A tube must therefore be inserted in the urethra.

20. When vajroli is used to mix semen and menstrual blood, it symbolically combines the energies, male and female, of both partners, thus intensely enhancing the power of the yogi. In such cases, to quote Martha Ann Selby, "the 'poetics'of gender and sexuality . . . is largely based . . . on two colors . . . red and white. Women and the 'feminine' are red, men and the 'masculine' are white." Professor Selby's (of Austin, Texas) study of the subject is very interesting: "Narratives of Conception, Gestation, and Labour in Sanskrit Āyurvedic Texts," *Asian Medicine* 1, no. 2 (2005), 254–75. On the Nāthas, see "Tantric Traditions," chapter 4 in this volume.

21. Some such descriptions are abundantly quoted and commented by White in *Kiss of the Yoginī.*

22. For instance, many rites prescribed in the *Vāmakeśvarīmata*, a basic Śrīvidyā text, aim mainly at conquering women.

23. Some of these rites are also fully described in White, *Kiss of the Yoginī*. According to the French anthropologist Dominique Sila Khan, analogous practices seem to exist today among Ismaelis of Rajasthan.

24. Or even to behave like a woman. A well-known case is that of the Bengali Saint Ramakrishna (1836–86), a devotee of Kālī.

25. A recovery of time past (*le temps retrouvé*) for Marcel Proust, who did not go as far as our Śaivas.

Chapter Seven

1. I refer the reader to two "classical" books on the subject. See J. L. Austin, *How to Do Things with Words* (Oxford: Oxford University Press, 1975); and John R. Searle, *Speech Acts: An Essay in the Philosophy of Language* (1969; repr., Cambridge: Cambridge University Press,1980).

2. "The Veda is understood to be a manifestation of the ultimate Word (*śabda*) that underlies phenomenal existence . . . [and] is more important for what it *is* and what it *does* than what it means." See David Carpenter, "Bhartr̥hari and the Veda," in *Texts in Context: Traditional Hermeneutics in South Asia*, ed. Jeffrey R. Timm (Albany, NY: SUNY, 1992), 17–32.

3. I gave an overview of these ancient notions in the first chapter of my book *Vāc: The Concept of the Word in Selected Hindu Tantras* (1990; repr., Delhi: Shri Satguru, 1992).

4. In spite of the fact that the Vedic seers (*r̥s*) are deemed to have "seen" the Vedic hymns.

5. The great Indian poet Kālidāsa, in the first line of his poem *Raghuvaṃśa: Vāgarthāv iva saṃpṛktau.*

The grammatical way of reasoning played, in many respects, the same role in the development of Indian theoretical thought as mathematical reasoning has done in the development of Western thought since the Renaissance. Louis Renou, one of the greatest French Indologists, famously wrote, "Adhérer à la pensée indienne, c'est raisonner en grammairien," a formula we might transpose into English as, "To reason as an Indian is to reason as a grammarian."

6. This passage is published only in the form of a quotation in Kṣemarāja's commentary on *Śivasūtra* 2.3, and in Naṭanānandanātha's commentary on stanzas 26–27 of the *Kāmakalāvilāsa*, where it is quoted with some variants. The full Tantra, a voluminous work, survives transmitted in Nepalese manuscripts, but it has not been edited and printed.

7. The heart is the resting place of the Lord, Śiva, both cosmically and mystically.

8. These worlds (*bhuvana*) are infernal, terrestrial, and celestial—the whole cosmos.

9. *Paranināda* is the first infinitely subtle stirring of sound, the initial movement of phonic energy.

10. The term *mathitā* (from the verbal root *MATH, MANTH*), translated as "churned," evokes the movements of sexual union—of Śiva and Śakti uniting sexually.

11. Limiting forces allow the empirical, limited world to appear.

12. Śiva and Śakti, that is.

13. The shape assumed by *kuṇḍalinī* evokes the written form of the letter *A*, the first letter of the alphabet deemed to be the essence of all the phonemes and therefore of the whole cosmos.

14. She becomes fivefold because there are five *brahmamantras*, the first of which is Sadyojāta.

15. See "The Textual Material," chapter 3 of this volume.

16. I have described "the manifestation of sound" of *Vāc* in chapter 3 of this volume.

17. See figure 1 in "The Tantric Body," chapter 5 of this volume.

18. See "Tantric Traditions," chapter 4 of this volume.

19. We may note here that today in Europe (and, I presume, in the United States), there are thinkers (linguists and philosophers) who—building on the theory of the great German anthropologist and linguist of the nineteenth century, Wilhelm von Humboldt, rather than merely following Guillaume de Saussure's structural view of speech as made of an opposition of arbitrary signs—have propounded a genetical view of speech seen as evolving by stages from a basic intentionality in consciousness. There are notions of the same kind in Japan.

20. Louis Renou defined it as "the vital aspect of the *ātman*," which underscores its ambiguous nature.

21. For an overview of mantras in Hinduism, see chapter twenty-two in G. Flood, ed., *The Blackwell Companion to Hinduism* (Oxford: Blackwell Publishing, 2001). On mantras generally, the only attempt at a comprehensive study remains to this day H. Alper, ed., *Understanding Mantras* (Albany NY: SUNY, 1989; repr., Delhi: Motilal Banarsidass, 2012). It includes a bibliography that has, unfortunately, not been updated. On Tantric mantra, see A. Padoux, *Tantric Mantras: Studies on Mantraśāstra* (Abingdon: Routledge, 2011).

22. Western Tāntrikas who believe they can compose mantras are completely mistaken.

23. The six *jātis* are *namaḥ*, *svāhā*, *vaṣaṭ* (or *vauṣaṭ*), *hūṃ*, and *phaṭ*, each used according to the mantra's purpose.

24. Somdev Vasudeva has shown convincingly that this order can be explained by placing the phonemes in such a way as to form the body of the goddess from head to foot. See "Synæsthetic Iconography: 1. The *Nādiphāntakrama*," in *Tantric Studies in Memory of Hélène Brunner*,

ed. Dominic Goodall and André Padoux (Pondichéry: Institut Français de Pondichéry, 2007), 517–50.

25. See "Tantric Body," chapter 5 in this volume.

26. A work of this sort was published with a few other such texts in 1913 as the first volume of the *Tantrik Texts* series edited by Arthur Avalon. See the bibliography.

27. A Tantric treatise, the *Spandasandoha* by Kṣemarāja (eleventh century), has interestingly underlined the fact that mantras work "together with their user's mind"—mental concentration is fundamental in mantric practice.

28. This goes back to ancient Vedic times since, according to the Mīmāṃsā exegesis, there are in truth no deities but only mantras, the notion being taken over in Tantra in a somewhat different way. The essential nature of deities is mantra.

29. These diagrams, used especially in Śaiva systems, have various shapes. They are called displays (*prastāra*) or caverns (*gahvara*)—a place where the mantra is hidden.

30. The number of respiratory breaths in twenty-four hours is in effect normally twenty-one thousand. Ancient Indians knew this. *Haṃsa*, the swan, is traditionally a symbol of the Supreme or of the soul as identical with the Supreme.

31. I have described these rites in a paper, "A Hindu Rosary Ritual (*Jayākhyasaṃhitā*, chapter 14)," published with other papers, notably one on *japa*, in a volume of collected essays of mine in English called *Tantric Mantras: Studies in Mantraśāstra* (Abingdon: Routledge, 2011), 81–88.

Chapter Eight

1. The activity of a South Indian temple of the Goddess is described in C. J. Fuller, *Servants of the Goddess: The Priests of a South Indian Temple* (Cambridge: Cambridge University Press, 1964). On the organization and performance of a "great festival" (*mahotsava*), see Richard H. Davis, *A Priest's Guide for the Great Festival* (New York: Oxford University Press, 2010), which gives the text along with a well-annotated translation of a ritual manual of the twelfth century that is still in use today. The most complete study of āgamic temple ritual is, however, Françoise L'Hernault and Marie-Louise Reiniche, eds., *Tiruvannamalai, un haut lieu saint śivaïte du sud de l'Inde*, vol. 3, *Rites et Fêtes* (Pondichéry: École française d'Extrême Orient, 1999).

I will also note here that in addition to festive religious processions, there were also royal processions, which were a form of political action showing the power of the monarch.

2. On possession by ghouls or vampires, see *Vetālapañcaviṃśatikā* [Twenty-Five Tales of the Vampire], a section of Somadeva's vast twelfth-century collection of stories the *Kathāsaritsāgara* [Ocean of Stories], which was translated by C. H. Tawney in 1884 then reedited and revised by Penzer in 1924. A more recent translation is that of J. A. B. van Buitenen, "The King and the Corpse," in *Tales of Ancient India* (Chicago: Chicago University Press, 1959).

3. A Sanskrit saying on the ways to liberation says, "Knowledge is to be gained by serving a master or by giving over riches. It can also be gained starting with another knowledge. There is no fourth way."

4. As said before, the *pūjā* I describe here is the private, domestic one, performed "for oneself."

5. *nādevo devam arcayet*, in Sanskrit. This principle goes back to Vedic times.

6. This is underlined in Richard H. Davis, *Ritual in an Oscillating Universe: Worshipping Śiva in Medieval India* (Princeton: Princeton University Press, 1991).

7. This is a general Tantric rule: one invokes and worships the aspect of the deity corre-

sponding to the goal aimed at through the ritual worship, be it devotion, liberation, or some mundane or magical result.

8. See the table entitled "The Thirty-Six Tattvas of Tantric Traditions" in chapter 4 of this volume.

9. The showing of lights (together with the recitation of mantras) to the deity is called *ārātrika*, a rite whose simplified modern form is the *ārati.*

10. On this, see André Padoux with Roger-Orphé Jeanty, trans., *Yoginīhṛdaya: The Heart of the Yoginī* (New York: Oxford University Press, 2013).

11. The question is examined in an excellent study of *pūjā* according to the Śaivasiddhānta by Davis, *Ritual in an Oscillating Universe.*

12. The term *liṅga* may be used for all types of icons of Śiva, of which there is a great variety. The icon may be a sculpture, a painting, or different shapes and substances (a cloth, earth, a reflection in a mirror, etc.). If it is cylindrical icon that bears a face (or faces) of Śiva, it is called a *mukhaliṅga.*

13. Those to Sadāśiva, the principal deity of the Śaivasiddhānta, and to the Vaiṣṇava god Vaikuṇṭha, are "lactovegetarian."

14. The translation and the meaning of *mudrā* in Tantra are problematic. In the present case, one hardly sees the reason grains should be included in this list. In Tantric Buddhism, *mudrā* is the female partner of a sexual ritual.

15. A practice still found today among the Bāuls and Fakirs of Bengal (see "Tantra in India," chapter 11 in this volume). Note that the use of psychotropic products, bhang, etc., being a comparatively recent practice, is not prescribed in Tantric texts—it is mainly a popular practice.

16. Literally, "rule [-based] initiation." The "rules" in question are the rules of post-initiatory conduct.

17. On this important ritual manual, see "The Textual Material," chapter 3 in this volume.

18. Stanzas 186–292 of that chapter are on the initiations to be practiced after the sexual *kulayāga*, some of which are rather unexpected. Stanzas 236–270 are on the *vedhadīkṣā*—they are partly translated in Lilian Silburn's *Kuṇḍalinī: Energy of the Depths* (Albany, NY: SUNY Press, 1988).

19. This ambiguity was underlined in Teun Goudriaan's remarkable book, *Māyā Human and Divine: A Study of Magic and Its Religious Foundations in Sanskrit Texts* (Delhi: Motilal Banarsidass, 1978).

20. A seeker may be only a seeker of liberation, not a *bubhukṣu* looking for rewards. Interestingly, in regard to the hierarchy of situations, women as well as children are usually classified by the Tantras among the seekers of liberation (*mumukṣu*) only.

21. The eight *siddhis* (after *aṇimā*) are, in this order, lightness (*laghimā*), greatness (*mahimā*), obtaining all one wishes (*prāpti*), to be irresistible (*prakāmya*), to dominate (*īśitva*), to impose one's will (*vaśitva*), and to be able to be wherever one wishes (*yatrakāmāvasāyitā*).

22. Our distinction between nature and culture is unknown in traditional Indian thought.

Chapter Nine

1. Gnosticism accompanied by the downplaying of ritual is represented, for instance, in a Śaiva Tantra called the *Devīkālottara.* Nirañjanasiddha, ed., *Devīkālottarāgamaḥ*, trans. Pt. Vrajavallabha Dwivedi (Varanasi: Shaiva Bharati Shodha Pratishthanam, 2000).

2. This is the claim of the celebrated work of Frits Staal, *Ritual and Mantras, Rules without Meaning*, 1st ed. (New Delhi: Motilal Banarsidass, 1996). For Śaivism, a ringing rejoinder has

been given by Alexis Sanderson in his substantial article "Meaning in Tantric Ritual," in *Essais sur le rituel III. Colloque du Centenaire de la section des sciences religieuses de l'École pratique des hautes études*, ed. Anne-Marie Blondeau and Kristofer Schipper (Paris: Peeters, 1995), 15–95.

3. On the subject of possession, I refer the reader to Frederick M. Smith, *The Self Possessed: Deity and Spirit Possession in South Asian Literature and Civilization* (New York: Columbia University Press, 2006).

4. The place of images in human consciousness is fundamental. This is universally true. Images are on a deeper level of consciousness than language, not to speak of notions/ideas. Tantric prayer is mainly a play of images, as shown by Dominic Goodall in the preface to his edition of the *Pañcāvaraṇastava*. Dominic Goodall, Nibedita Rout, R. Sathyanarayanan, S. A. S. Sarma, T. Ganesan, and S. Sambandhaśivācārya, eds., *The Pañcāvaraṇastava of Aghoraśivācārya: A Twelfth-Century South Indian Prescription for the Visualisation of Sadāśiva and His Retinue* (Pondichéry: Institut Français de Pondichéry, 2005).

5. The two terms, *āveśa* and *samāveśa*, appear sometimes as synonymous and sometimes as referring to different experiences. *Āveśa* would thus be possession by a deity, demon or spirit; whereas *samāveśa* would be union (rather, "conpenetration") with the Absolute, absorption in the Absolute, fusion of the soul with the godhead—the realization of the identity of *ātman* and *Brahman*, "the perfect entry into one's own true nature," to speak like Abhinavagupta. Entering into, not being entered. On this, see Smith, *Self Possessed*, part IV, 10, "Possession in Tantra."

6. Śiva is considered as having five cosmic activities (*pañcakṛtya*): creation/emission (*sṛṣṭi*); maintenance of the universe (*sthiti*); its resorption (*saṃhāra*); veiling (*tirodhāna*), through which he veils himself and keeps bound souls; and bestowing of grace (*anugraha*), which saves them. There is a similar conception in the Pāñcarātra, the five activities being assigned to five hypostases (*vyūha*) of Viṣṇu.

7. *Śāṃbhava* is the adjective derived from Śaṃbhu. The final *a* of this term fuses with the initial vowel of *upāya*, hence *śāmbhavopāya*. *Śāktopāya* is in the same way composed from *śākta*, the adjective derived from *śakti*, and similarly *āṇavopāya*, from *āṇava*, itself from *aṇu*.

8. We have seen (in "Sex," chapter 6 of this volume, on *japa*) the practice of *SAUḤ*.

9. Or seventy, according to the edition referred to.

10. In French: "Un néant environné de Dieu, et rempli de Dieu, s'il veut." Cardinal de Bérulle (1575–1629) was the founder of the Oratory in France.

11. In Utpaladeva, *Shaiva Devotional Songs of Kashmir: A Translation and Study of Utpaladeva's Shivastotrāvali* (Albany, NY: SUNY Press, 1987). See also Ashok Kaul, ed. and trans., *Śivastotrāvalī of Utpaladeva: A Mystical Hymn of Kashmir* (New Delhi: D. K. Printworld, 2008). Swami Lakshman Joo's exposition in this work is very much worth reading.

12. They were edited and translated into French with an insightful commentary by Lilian Silburn in her *Hymnes de Abhinavagupta, traduits et commentés* (Paris: Publications de l'Institut de Civilisation indienne, 1970).

13. On these cults, see Alf Hiltebeitel, ed., *Criminal Gods and Demon Devotees: Essays on the Guardians of Popular Hinduism* (Albany, NY: SUNY Press, 1989).

14. Sir George Grierson and Lionel D. Barnett, ed. and trans., *Lallā-Vākyāni, or the Wise Sayings of Lal Dĕd, a Mystic Poetess of Ancient Kashmīr* (London: Royal Asiatic Society, 1920).

Chapter Ten

1. Described for goddesses in the state of Andhra by David Shulman, *Spring, Heat, Rains: A South Indian Diary* (Chicago: University of Chicago Press, 2008). See also Rachel Fell Mc-

Dermott, *Revelry, Rivalry, and Longing for the Goddess in Bengal* (New York: Columbia University Press, 2011), where the fate of Durgā's daughter, Umā, evokes a feeling of nostalgia among devotees.

2. This mystical geography and its internalization is described by Mark Dyczkowski in "The Inner Pilgrimage of the Tantras: The Sacred Geography of the Kubjikā Tantras with reference to the Bhairava and Kaula Tantras," in *A Journey in the World of the Tantras*, ed. Mark Dyczkowski (Varanasi: Indica Books, 2004).

3. On Banaras/Varanasi, the best study and guidebook is, I believe, Diana L. Eck, *Banaras: City of Light* (London: Routledge, 1983).

4. In India, one finds guidebooks for all pilgrimage places describing the deities and quoting local myths and legends.

5. On this subject, see Diana L. Eck, *Darśan: Seeing the Divine Image in India* (Chambersburg: Anima Books, 1981), an excellent study of the subject. There is more than a matter of gaze in the presence in a temple for a Hindu devotee. To quote a passage from David Shulman's profoundly perceptive book, *Spring, Heat, Rains*: "Here is a moving insistence on touching and being touched: what is god is 'only' an intensified mode of this sensate givenness, God is physical, not metaphysical" (30).

6. This pilgrimage is described together with a few others in John S. Hawley and Donna Marie Wulff, eds., *Devī: Goddesses of India* (Berkeley: University of California Press, 1996). The priests in charge of the main temple try today to tone down the Tantric character of this pilgrimage, which is linked to the soil, so as to attract a larger number of pilgrims.

7. On this, see Eck, *Banaras*.

8. See the study by Robert L. Levy, *Mesocosm: Hinduism and the Organization of a Traditional Newar City of Nepal* (Berkeley: University of California Press, 1984).

9. On this subject, see Niels Gutschow et al., eds., *Sacred Landscape in the Himalayas* (Vienna: Austrian Academy of Sciences Press, 2003).

10. In Puri, for instance, until recently, the local rājā was an official participant (together with two *rājagurus*) of the vast Jagannātha annual festival. (The temple was built by the command of one of his ancestors in the thirteenth century.)

The link between royalty and temple also appears in the fact that the temple dancers, "servants of the god" (*devadāsīs*), could also be "servants of the king" (*rājadāsīs*). The two categories are sometimes distinguished in the *Uttarakāmika āgama*, for instance, whose seventy-third chapter describes several sorts of temple servants—among them dancers—all "untouchables" but all said to go to heaven after their death.

This went on in South India until the profession of temple dancer, considered "immoral," was abolished in 1947 by the Tamil Nadu government, reducing all temple dancers to utter poverty. On *devadāsis* (and on the role of the king in religious ceremonies), the only comparatively reliable study available to day is by Frédérique Apffel-Marglin, *Wives of the God-King: The Rituals of the Devadasis of Puri* (Oxford: Oxford University Press, 1985). On the presentation of temple dancers in *Uttarakāmika* 73, see Dominic Goodall, introduction to *Śaiva Rites of Expiation: A First Edition and Translation of Trilocanaśiva's Twelfth-Century Prāyaścittasamuccaya* (Pondichéry: Institut Français de Pondichéry, 2015), 41ff.

11. To distinguish between popular and "mainstream" Hinduism is not always easy—this all the more so because it sometimes happens that, due to social circumstances or developments, a minor, local, or "popular" deity evolves and comes to be worshipped as a widely recognized Hindu deity.

12. On the Hindu temple, the reference work remains the second of the four-volume study

by Stella Kramrisch, *The Hindu Temple* (Delhi: Motilal Banarsidass, 1976), where the symbolic and metaphysical aspects of the Hindu temple are carefully studied. The two volumes reprinted in India are illustrated with photographs by Raymond Burnier.

13. There are no so-called miracles in India, merely supernatural events—the supernatural being an extension of the natural world. Deities are always present or near (and not "difficult to reach") in a world that is not "disenchanted."

14. On the symbolism of the *vāstupuruṣamaṇḍala*, see the chapters on the subject in Kramrisch, *Hindu Temple.*

15. For instance, this central position of the main deity is to be seen at Elephanta, where the impressive image of Śiva is that of the five-faced Sadāśiva (it is not a "*trimūrti*"). On this, see the study by Stella Kramrisch, "The Great Cave Temple of Śiva in Elephanta: Levels of Meaning and Their Form," in *Discourses on Śiva: Proceedings of a Symposium on the Nature of Religious Imagery*, ed. Michael W. Meister (Pennsylvania: University of Pennsylvania Press, 1984), 156–69.

16. This refers to a division of the cosmos into three planes, or levels: those of man (*nara*), of energy (*śakti*), and of the deity Śiva. There are several such divisions, which are valid on different planes. The three "worlds" (*loka*), the twenty-five or thirty *tattvas*, the five *kalās*, the six *adhvans*, etc., for example.

17. On this, see a not very recent but still interesting book by M. S. Randhava, *Travels in the Western Himalayas In Search of Paintings* (Delhi: Thomson Press, 1974).

18. In traditional Indian law (*dharmaśāstra*), the deity is the legal owner of the temple. This rule is still valid today.

19. This is something that vacillates from generation to generation. For some centuries, eating the deity's food (*nirmālya*) was unthinkable, hence the creation of *nirmālya-devatas* such as Caṇḍeśa to deal with it. See Dominic Goodall, "Who is Caṇḍeśa?," in *Genesis and Development of Tantrism*, ed. Shingo Einoo (Tokyo: Institute of Oriental Culture, University of Tokyo, 2009), 351–423.

20. On these people, and, more generally on the life of a temple, see C. J. Fuller, *Servants of the Goddess: The Priests of a South Indian Temple* (Cambridge: Cambridge University Press, 1984).

21. This has already been discussed. See "Origins, History, Expansion," chapter 2 in this volume, "A Tantric World?"

22. There were images of Hindu/brahmanical deities in India from the first centuries of our era—perhaps earlier.

23. A deity's *āyudhas* are sometimes shown as little human figures holding the "weapons" that they represent on their heads—these anthropomorphised weapons are called *āyudhapuruṣas.*

24. The Mahāvidyā Chinnamastā, for instance, holding in her hand her severed head while her blood flows into the mouths of other deities.

25. On these ritual diagrams, I refer the reader to Gudrun Bühnemann et al., *Maṇḍalas and Yantras in the Hindu Traditions* (Leiden: Brill, 2003). The work is illustrated and very informative.

26. "The fivefold support" is a group of five deities, Viṣṇu, Śiva, Durgā, Sūrya, and Gaṇeśa, worshipped together by Brahmins referred to as *smārta* because they adhere to the authority of the scriptural corpus *smṛti.*

Chapter Eleven

1. On today's presence and practice of Tantric rites, see the papers collected in David G. White, ed., *Tantra in Practice* (Princeton: Princeton University Press, 2000).

2. As is the case (which we have noted previously) of haṭhayoga in the West.

3. Mantirikars were described by Carl Gustav Diehl in *Instrument and Purpose: Studies on the Rites and Ritual of South India* (Lund: C. W. K. Gleerup, 1956). Things seem not to have changed very much since that time. Diehl noted that some mantirikars are Muslims. Popular Hindu books on mantras sometimes include drawings or amulets including Arab letters.

4. Rai Bahadur Srisa Chandra Vidyarnava, *The Daily Practice of the Hindus* (1949; repr., New Delhi: Sri Satguru Publications, 2008). This modern ritual handbook gives the Tantric and the non-Tantric ritual for each deity or ritual function.

5. In Madras/Chennai, an association of South Indian temple priests (*arcakas*) edits "A Collection of Essential Quotations from All Śaiva Agamas for Temple Worship," a *Sakalāgama-sāra-saṃgraha* for temple priests.

6. But was it not already a topos in earlier Sanskrit literature to lament the loss of knowledge of Brahmins in *kaliyuga*?

7. In the great Śaiva temple of Chidambaram, the Brahmin priests claim to be *vaidika* but their ritual manuals reveal a pervasive Tantric influence.

8. He was called by the Mahārāja to get rid of the overwhelming power (and financial cost) of gurus of another persuasion.

9. The case of Nepal as it was before 2008 was studied (in French) in an exemplary fashion by Gérard Toffin in *Le Palais et le temple: La fonction royale dans la Vallée du Népal* (Paris: CNRS, 1993). On Nepal more generally, see Robert I. Levy, *Mesocosm: Hinduism and the Organization of a Traditional Newar City in Nepal* (Berkeley: University of California Press, 1990). On the goddess Taleju, see Bronwen Bledsoe, "An Advertised Secret: The Goddess Taleju and the King of Kathmandu," in *Tantra in Practice*, ed. David G. White, 195–205.

10. On the Nāths, the basic study remains, I believe, that of George Weston Briggs, *Goraknāth and the Kānpaṭha Yogis* (1938; repr., Delhi: Motilal Banarsidass, 1982). More recent and more up-to-date are the studies of James Mallinson. There are two good studies by Véronique Bouillier in French—see the bibliography.

11. These holy places are described by Briggs, *Goraknāth*, 74–124.

12. This ritual is an essential element in the *Kathāsaritsāgara*, an eleventh-century collection of tales. In *Yoginī Cults and Practices: A Tantric Tradition* (New Delhi: National Museum, 1986), Vidya Dehejia writes, "The practice is not uncommon today: when there is a death in a poor home, the family is approached with an offer of money for the use of the corpse for one night. Indeed, in the town of Kāmākhya, people rarely leave a corpse uncremated overnight for fear of losing it to Tantric practitioners" (60; also on this page is a photograph of a sculpture showing a Yoginī consuming human flesh).

13. The consumption of cannabis (*bhang*) seems to have come to India in the sixteenth century from the Near East.

14. On this temple, see J. C. Fuller, *Servants of the Goddess: The Priests of a South Indian Temple* (Cambridge: Cambridge University Press, 1984).

On Indian Goddesses, see John S. Hawley and Donna Marie Wulff, eds., *Devī: Goddesses of India* (Berkeley: University of California Press, 1996).

15. The Charan and the worship of these goddesses are fully described (in German) by Helene Basu, *Von Barden und Königen: Ethnologische Studien zur Göttin und zum Gedächtnis* (Frankfurt: Peter Lang, 2004).

16. On this, I refer the reader to the perceptive study of Rachel Fell McDermott, *Revelry, Rivalry, and Longing for the Goddesses of Bengal* (New York: Columbia University Press, 2011), who describes minutely the festival with the numerous temporary worshipping places (*pandals*) erected all over Calcutta, showing also its emotive atmosphere.

17. On these deities, Tantric or popular, see Akos Östör, *The Play of the Gods: Locality, Ideology, Structure, and Time in the Festivals of a Bengali Town* (New Delhi: Chronicle Books, 2004).

18. On Bāuls (both Hindu and Muslim), see June McDaniel, *The Madness of the Saints: Ecstatic Religion in Bengal* (Chicago: Chicago University Press, 1989). The "classic" book on the Bāuls remains Edward C. Dimock, *The Place of the Hidden Moon: Erotic Mysticism in the Vaiṣṇava Sahajiyā Cult of Bengal* (Chicago: Chicago University Press, 1966).

There is, for those who read French, a very interesting book by Hélène Trottier, who lived for several years with a Muslim Bâul as her companion (and sexual partner), *Fakir: La quête d'un Bâul musulman* (Paris: L'Harmattan, 2000).

19. On the Kārtabhajās, see the two volumes by Hugh B. Urban, *The Economics of Ecstasy: Tantra, Secrecy, and Power in Colonial Bengal* (Oxford: Oxford University Press, 2001); and *Songs of Ecstasy: Tantric and Devotional Songs from Colonial Bengal* (Oxford: Oxford University Press, 2001). This, in many respects, is a very interesting study.

20. When in Pondicherry, Aurobindo's view of the Goddess evolved considerably. Thereafter, for him, the Great Goddess was not the fearsome Kālī but the divine Mother, whom he eventually identified with a French woman born in Paris, Mira Alfassa (later Mira Richard), who came to his ashram in 1914. He eventually came to see her as his counterpart and complement. She led the ashram until her death in 1973.

21. See the section on *pīṭhas* in "The Spiritual Aspect," chapter 9 of this volume.

22. This Tantra was printed and translated and is available online.

23. Sarah Caldwell, *Oh Terrific Mother: Sexuality, Violence and Worship of the Goddess Kālī* (Oxford: Oxford University Press, 1999).

24. Ibid., 258.

25. This is how Śrīvidyā was described by Douglas R. Brooks in *The Secret of the Three Cities: An Introduction to Hindu Śākta Tantrism* (Chicago: Chicago University Press, 1990).

26. On Ramakrishna, one may usefully read Jeffrey J. Kripal, *Kālī's Child: The Mystical and the Erotic in the Life and Teachings of Rāmakrishna* (Chicago: Chicago University Press, 1995), which underlines the homoerotic side of Rāmakrishna's personality. This interesting but somewhat controversial book provoked intense criticism among the saint's admirers and devotees.

27. This Pondicherry series maintained by French institutions of research in India has changed names more than once. It was the "Publications de l'Institut Français d'Indologie," then the "Publications du département d'indologie," and is currently, since 2004, the "Collection Indologie."

28. See "The Hindu Tantric Field," chapter 1 in this volume.

29. Gopinath Kaviraj (1896–1987) was a devotee of Mā Ānanda Mayī (or Moyi), who was believed to be an incarnation of Durgā. He was also near to another spiritual personality of Varanasi—Shri Shobha Ma (born in 1921) who, rather surprisingly, was considered an incarnation of both Krishna and the Goddess, two deities she incarnated at different times.

30. To quote part of a sentence in Urban, *Tantra*, 189.

31. Lilian Silburn and Alexis Sanderson studied with him for years, notably reading the whole *Tantrāloka* with him. I did, too, for a much shorter time, which was still very useful to me. A fine, illustrated book edited by Bettina Bäumer and Sarla Kumar, *Saṃvidullāsaḥ: Manifestation of Divine Consciousness; Swami Lakshman Joo, Saint-Scholar of Kashmir Śaivism,* A Centenary Tribute (New Delhi: D. K. Printworld, 2007), was dedicated to him. Illustrated with many photographs, it brings together several studies, among which a remarkable one by Alexis Sanderson ("Swami Lakshman Joo and His Place in the Kashmirian Tradition"). Also worth quoting is Sadananda Das and Ernst Fuerlinger, *Sāmarasya: Studies in Indian Arts, Philosophy*

and Interreligious Dialogue; In Honour of Bettina Bäumer (New Delhi: D. K. Printworld, 2005), including studies concerning Tantra. Western publications on or attributed to Lakshman Joo are generally not reliable.

32. See Andrew J. Nicholson, *Unifying Hinduism: Philosophy and Identity in Indian Intellectual History* (New York: Columbia University Press, 2011).

33. The activities of Anand Marg were abundantly reported in Indian press. On this movement, see Raphael Voix, "Denied Violence, Glorified Fighting," *Nova Religio* 12, no. 1 (August 2008), 3–25; and Helen Crovetto, "Ananda Marga and the Use of Force," *Nova Religio* 12, no. 1 (August 2008), 26–56.

34. Swami Muktananda wrote an autobiography that is interesting as a description of a Tantric *sādhana.* See *Play of Consciousness* (South Fallsburg: SYDA Foundation, 1978). Also worth reading is the well-known autobiographical work of pandit Gopi Krishna, *Living with Kundalini: The Autobiography of Gopi Krishna* (Boston: Kundalini Research Foundation, 1993 [repr.]).

35. The process of intercultural mimesis by which Europeans reformulate Hindu philosophy and then export it back to India has been called "the pizza effect" by Agehananda Bharati. Pizza, a local Neapolitan dish, was exported to the United States, where it was transformed, and came back to Italy to become a signature Italian dish, a status it had never enjoyed before.

Chapter Twelve

1. On the subject, and more generally on Tantra and the West, I cannot do better than refer the reader to Hugh B. Urban, *Tantra: Sex, Secrecy, Politics, and Power in the Study of Religion* (Berkeley: University of California Press, 2003), an excellent and most perceptive study to which this chapter is largely indebted.

2. On Sir John Woodroffe, see Kathleen Taylor, *Sir John Woodroffe, Tantra and Bengal: "An Indian Soul in a European Body?"* (Richmond, UK: Curzon Press, 2001).

3. This notably in 1913, with the edition of the *Mahānirvāṇa tantra,* which, as I have remarked above in a note to chapter 3, appears to be a nineteenth-century work composed in order to give Tantric thought and practices a better name than they enjoyed at the time.

4. This legend took place in the period between 1830 and 1860. It is marked by Major W. H. Sleeman's works, the best known being *The Thugs or Phansikars of India* (1839; repr., Oxford: Oxford University Press, 1973) which, together with his *Rambles and Recollections of an Indian Official,* was reprinted by Oxford in 1973.

5. Except for Lilian Silburn, *Kuṇḍalinī: Energy of the Depths* (Albany, NY: SUNY Press, 1988).

6. His two first books (and the only strictly Indological ones) were *Techniques du Yoga* (Paris: Payot, 1948) and *Yoga, Immortalité et liberté* (Paris: Payot, 1954).

7. Mircea Eliade, *Journal IV, 1979–1985,* trans. Mac Linscott Ricketts (Chicago: Chicago University Press, 1990).

8. An antimodernist upholder of "la Tradition éternelle" who was a figure of French intellectual life between the two wars was René Guénon (1886–1951). He was not without some influence among those interested by Indian thought at the time, though he was rejected by scholars. Among his works are *Introduction générale à l'étude des doctrines hindoues* (Paris: M. Rivière, 1921) and *L'homme et son devenir selon le Vedanta* (Paris: Les éditions traditionnelles, 1925), which were influential because there were practically no valid works on the subject in French at the time. He was one of the most outspoken enemies of the modern world. One important work of his is *Le règne de la quantité et les signes des temps* (Paris: Gallimard, 1945), whose criticism of our present merchandised world agrees paradoxically in some respect with that of the

situationistes—Guy Debord, for instance. Well known and translated in Europe, René Guénon is, I believe, little known in the United States.

9. Urban, *Tantra*, 207.

10. See Paul G. Hackett, *Theos Bernard, the White Lama: Tibet, Yoga, and American Religious Life* (New York: Columbia University Press, 2012). This detailed biography is interesting as a study of early American approaches to Indian and Buddhist spirituality.

11. Ibid., 228.

12. See "The Spiritual Aspect," chapter 9 in this volume.

13. Rather paradoxically, the Muktabodha Foundation subsidizes a *Vedashala* at Satara, Maharashtra, whose aim is to perpetuate Vedic rituals. Such contradictory positions are not unusual, even in a traditional context. For a modern instance, I remember a Vedic funeral ceremony for Rudrananda a few years ago in the (Tantric) Nityananda Institute at Portland, Oregon.

14. I have been one of them and keep pleasant memories of meetings in Menlo Park, California, Charlottesville, Virginia, and Flagstaff, Arizona.

15. Born as Leopold Fischer, he learned Sanskrit early and was accepted as a Hindu at the age of sixteen. Drafted in the German army, he joined the Indian legion of Subhas Chandra Bose as an interpreter in occupied France. He came to India in 1949, first becoming a monk of the Ramakrishna Math and Mission (an order he left), then being initiated as Agehananda Bharati in the Daśanāmi order, and eventually joining Benares Hindu University, from which he was expelled in 1954 for his "Tantric activities." He came to the United States in 1958 and became a professor of anthropology at Syracuse University, where he remained until his death in 1991. His autobiography, *The Ochre Robe*, 2nd ed. (Santa Barbara, CA: Ross-Erikson, 1980), is worth reading. His book, *The Tantric Tradition* (1970; repr., London: Rider, 1986), was the first overview of the subject. An interesting in-depth study of his case is to be found in a chapter of Jeffrey J. Kripal's *Roads of Excess, Palaces of Wisdom: Eroticism and Reflexivity in the Study of Mysticism* (Chicago: University of Chicago Press, 1964), 208–49.

16. In Italy, excellent scholarly translations are published by literary firms (Raniero Gnoli's translation of the *Tantrāloka* published by Adelphi being a remarkable instance); some are edited in paperback.

17. Note that in Europe as in the United States, there are "gay" Tantric groups. This would be understandable if Tantra could be seen to mean sexual freedom. But this is basically wholly mistaken and contradictory, since the Tantric conception of the deity—and therefore of the cosmic play of power and of the functioning of the world—is that of a male/female polarity.

Glossary

Sanskrit terms whose meanings are customarily well known (*brahman*, *liṅga*, *māyā*, *mudrā*, *śakti*, and *cakra*, for instance) are not included here, nor are the names of deities. (Nearly) all terms are listed in the index. Within the entries below, terms that are followed by an asterisk have themselves separate entries in the glossary.

ābhāsa: projection or apparition (notably of the cosmos).
abhicāra: black magic.
abhiṣeka: ritual sprinkling or shower; consecration; the ritual initiation of a *sādhaka** and of an *ācārya**.
ācārya: initiated spiritual master; initiated head of a monastery or of a sect or religious group.
ādhāra: in ritual, it is the concrete support of a deity; it is also a center or nodal point of the yogic body.
adhvan: path or way of cosmic manifestation to be followed to reach liberation.
advaita: nondualistic (*advaitatācāra*); the nondualistic behavior of a *kaula**.
āgama: "tradition"; the term used to designate scriptures of all Tantric traditions, also named *tantra* and *saṃhitā**.

The system of asterisks follows that of the multilingual five-volume dictionary of Tantric terminology, of which three volumes have so far been published from the Austrian Academy of Sciences in Vienna. The most recent volume is: Dominic Goodall and Marion Rastelli, eds., *Tāntrikābhidhānakośa III: Dictionnaire des termes techniques de la littérature hindoue tantrique* [A Dictionary of Technical Terms from Hindu Tantric Literature], Beiträge zur Kultur- und Geistesgeschichte Asiens 76 (Vienna: Verlag der Österreichischen Akademie der Wissenschaften, 2013).

ājñācakra: command; the *cakra* between the eyebrows where the adept is deemed to receive the command of his guru.

ākāśa: ether, one of the five lowest *tattvas**.

akṣamālā akṣasūtra: rosary. Rosaries are ritually made, consecrated, used (in *japa**), and disposed of.

akula: a name of the Absolute in the Kula system.

āmnāya: scriptural transmission, of which there are four in the Kula tradition.

amṛta: ambrosia, nectar of immortality. It can be ritually produced; it may ooze from the body in yogic states.

ānanda: "bliss"; *brahman* is bliss. *Ānanda* is not to be confused with pleasure (*sukha*). There are, in Śaivism, several levels of *ānanda*, as the polymath Abhinavagupta explains in his magisterial work on Tantra, the *Tantrāloka* (5, 44–454).

aṇu: "atom"; the limited being, individual soul.

anugraha: divine grace bestowed upon all beings (syn. *śaktipāta**) and to the whole cosmos; one of the five cosmic activities (*karmapañcaka**) of Śiva.

ārātrika (or ārati): waving of lights before the image of a deity. The common simplified form *ārati* is widely used today.

ardhacandra: crescent moon; one of the divisions (*kalā**) of the utterance (*uccāra**) of a *bījamantra**, such as *OṂ*.

arghya: water or other fluid specially prepared for ritual offering.

Atimārga: the Outer Path accessible only to ascetics. It is composed primarily of two divisions, the Pāśupata* and the Lākula*.

ātman: the Self.

āvaraṇa: circle of ancillary deities or powers surrounding a main deity, forming its retinue.

āveśa: possession by a deity or a supernatural power; spiritual fusion or absorption (see *samāveśa**).

avidyā: ignorance, especially metaphysical ignorance, which is the cause of human bondage (syn. *ajñāna*).

āyudha: "weapon"; the name for the instruments or objects a deity holds in his or her hands.

bhakti: devotion.

bhāvanā: intense creative and identifying meditation.

bhukti: mundane or supramundane rewards or joys, as opposed to *mukti**/*mokṣa**, liberation. Many Tantras say their teaching gives both *bhukti* and *mukti*.

bhūta: gross elements, the five lowest *tattvas*: ether, air, fire, water, and earth.

bhūtatantras: Tantras on the cult of spirits or demons.

bīja, bījamantra: "seed"; seed-mantra (always monosyllabic).

bindu: dot, drop (of power); the *cakra* also named *ājñācakra**.

brahmarandhra: the opening of Brahmā, the thousand-petaled lotus on the top of the head.

cakrapūjā: the name of the worship of Tripurasundarī performed using a diagram, the *śrīcakra** (see chapter 9, "Mysticism in Ritual"); a Tantric worship done by adepts grouped in circle (*cakra*) around their guru.
cit: "consciousness"; divine unlimited consciousness (syn. *saṃvit*).
citta: human (limited) consciousness, reason.

dakṣiṇa: right; the right side of a figure. When applied to Tantras, they are a category of Tantras as opposed to those of the left (*vāma**), for they are supposedly more staid than the *vāma* ones.
Dakṣiṇāmnāya: The Southern Transmission of the Kula, that of the cult of Tripurasundarī (with Bhairava), also called Kāmeśvarī (with Kāmeśvara).
*darśana**: "viewpoint"; the main philosophical systems of Hinduism. They are described and classified from the point of view of Śaṅkara's Vedānta in Mādhava's doxographical work, the *Sarvadarśanasaṃgraha*.
dhāraṇā: meditative fixation on a place of the body or on an element.
dharma: the eternal law of the Hindus, governing their status and rules of behavior.
dhātu: constituent elements of the body, traditionally five or six in number.
dhyāna: meditation, visualization.
dhyānaślokas: verses stating the aspect of deities to be visualized.
dīkṣā: initiation in a particular Tantric tradition.
dūtī: "messenger"; the female partner of a Tantric ritual.
dvādaśānta: the *cakra* twelve finger-breadths above the head, the highest point reached by the ascending *kuṇḍalinī**.

granthi: "knot"; a name for the *cakras* of the yogic body, also called *padma* (lotus).
guṇa: quality, property, notably the three qualities that pervade all the *tattvas*: *sattva*, *rajas*, and *tamas*.

homa: ritual offering in the fire, done notably at the end of the *pūjā*.
hṛd, hṛdaya: the heart as a *cakra* and as a mystical center.
hṛdayabīja: the seed-syllable mantra that is a deity's heart.

icchā: will.
icchāśakti: the power of will of the deity. It is the highest of the five cosmic powers of Śiva.

japa: ritual recitation of a mantra, usually done using a rosary (*akṣasūtra**)
jīvanmukta: liberated in this life.
jīvanmukti: liberation in this life.
jñāna: knowledge, gnosis.
jñānaśakti: the divine power of knowledge.

Kālīs: goddesses who animate the body and the cosmos in a sequential process called Kālīkrama.

kāma: Eros or passion, though not necessarily sexual. All that attracts the senses.

kāmakalā: a ritual diagram symbolizing the sexual union of Śiva and Śakti.

kāmya: rites undertaken to attain desired aims.

kapāla: skull worn by a yogi.

kapālavrata: the observance of the skull; a religious observance characterized by wearing ashes from the cremation ground and accoutrements garnered from corpses.

kāpālika: a skull-bearing ascetic who has therefore taken the *kapālavrata**, the observance of the skull.

karmapañcaka: the fivefold cosmic activity of Śiva: manifestation (*sṛṣṭi*), maintenance (*sthiti*), resorption (*saṃhāra*), concealment (*tirodhāna*), and grace (*anugraha*).

kaula: an adjective meaning "of the Kula."

khaṭvāṅga: skull-topped staff; one of the attributes of Śiva, worn by some Śaiva ascetics, notably those following the *kapālavrata**.

Krama: sequence, phase. The name of one of the nondualist Kaśmirian Śaiva traditions.

Kubjikāmata: the doctrine of Kubjikā, the hunch-backed goddess. It is the doctrine of the Paścimāmnāya* of the Kula*.

Kula: clan, family, originally that of the Yoginīs. Each *kula* is headed by a Mother (*mātṛ*/*mātrikā**). The Kula is represented by one of the largest surviving bodies of Tantric scripture, which is divided into five *āmnāyas**. In these traditions, the term *kula* is used for the highest (but not transcendent) divine plane, and it is also used for the human body seen as a microcosm.

kuṇḍagola(ka): a pellet (*gola*) made of various substances, notably of sexual origin, which is offered to the deity in Kaula cults.

Lākula: a division of the Atimārga*.

madhyamā: the Intermediate, the level of *vāc** between the Visionary (*paśyantī**) and the lower level of *vaikharī**.

Mantramārga: the path of mantras open both to ascetics and to married householders, leading both to liberation and to supernatural powers.

mantrapīṭha: the "seat of mantras" grouping the Tantras dedicated to Bhairava.

mantraśāstra: "the teaching of mantras"; a general term for all the works and notions concerning mantras.

mantrasādhana: the ritual to be followed to master a mantra.

mātṛ, mātṛkā: "mother"; these goddesses are Yoginīs, and they number either seven or eight. In Śaiva systems, a usual list is Mahālakṣmī, Brahmī, Kuleśvarī, Kaumārī, Vaiṣṇavī, Vārāhī, Indrāṇī, and Cāmuṇḍā. *Mātṛkā* ("little Mother") is used for the phonemes of the Sanskrit alphabet, each being considered as a (*bīja*) *mantra**.

mokṣa, mukti: liberation from the fetters of this world.
mūlādhāra: the "root-support"; the bodily *cakra* on the level of the perineum, where the *kuṇḍalinī* lies coiled.
mūlamantra, mūlavidyā: root-mantra or *vidyā**.

nāda: subtle phonic vibration.
nāḍī: channel of the yogic body.
nyāsa: ritual placing of mantras on the body or on some support.

parā: the Supreme, the highest transcendent omnipresent level of *vāc**.
Paścimāmnāya: the Western Transmission of the Kula, that of the Goddess or goddesses.
paśu: "beast"; a bound soul.
Pāśupata: a follower of the Śaiva system of Atimārga*.
paśyantī: the Visionary; the stage of the Word (*vāc**) where a vision of speech or of the cosmos appears in the deity and in the human mind.
pīṭha: "seat"; spiritual centers of a tradition; seats of the Goddess.
prakāśa: light, characteristic of the supreme Consciousness.
prakṛti: the primal matter; source of the cosmos.
prāṇa: vital and respiratory breath.
prāṇapratiṣṭhā: installation of vital breath in an icon.
pratyabhijñā: "recognition"; The philosophical doctrine of Pratyabhijñā was expounded first by Somānanda and then developed by Utpaladeva, Abhinavagupta, and Kṣemarāja.
pūjā: ritual worship of a deity.
Pūrvāmnāya: the Eastern, or the first, Transmission of the Kaula tradition.

rasāyana: alchemy.

śabda: sound.
sādhaka: an initiated adept looking to possess supernatural powers (*siddhi**).
Sahajiyā: a Vaiṣṇava Tantric tradition of Bengal.
Śaivasiddhānta: dualist Śaivism whose texts are often called *āgama* in secondary literature, centered on the cult of Sadāśiva.
śaktipāta: the descent of Śakti (see *anugraha**).
samāveśa: complete absorption in the divine.
saṃhāra: cosmic resorption; one of the five cosmic actions of Śiva (e.g., *sṛṣṭi**, etc.).
ṣaṭkarman, ṣaṭkarmāṇi: the six (magical) actions of Tantric traditions.
siddhi: supernatural power.
spanda: "vibration"; the subtle vibration of the divinity that pervades and animates the universe.
śrīcakra: the ritual diagram of the Śrīvidyā tradition embodying symbolically the cosmic activity of the goddess Tripurasundarī.

Śrīvidyā: the Southern Transmission (*dakṣināmnāya**) of the Kula.
sṛṣṭi, sthiti, saṃhāra: the cosmic cycle of emanations (*sṛṣṭi*), preservation (*sthiti*), and resorption (*saṃhāra*) of the universe going on eternally from age (*yuga*) to age.
śruti: "what has been heard"; all the "revealed" sacred texts of the Hindu tradition.
śūnya: void; a name for auxiliary centers of the yogic body.
suṣumnā: the main vertical channel of the yogic body along which *kuṇḍalinī* moves or travels.
svātantrya: absolute autonomy.

tantraśāstra: a term for the ensemble of Tantric texts and notions.
tantrāvatāra: the descent of the Tantra; its coming down from the deity who enunciates and thus reveals it to the level of humans.
tarka: reasoning, one of the six members (*aṅga*) of the *ṣaḍaṇgayoga* of Tantra.
tattva: the fundamental realities or principles that constitute the universe, from the deity down to the earth.
Trika: "triad"; a Tantric system that teaches the doctrine of three supreme divine powers: Parā, Parāparā, and Aparā.
trikoṇa: triangle, a symbol of the female sexual organ.

uccāra: utterance of a mantra; upward movement of *prāṇa**.
upāya: means or way toward liberation.
Uttarāmnāya: the Northern Transmission of the Kula.

vāc, vāk: the Word.
vaidika: Vedic, as opposed to *tāntrika*.
vaikharī: the Corporeal; the lowest level of *vāc**, that of human speech.
vajrolimudrā: a yogic technique for extracting the secretions of a ritual sexual intercourse.
vāma: left, as opposed to *dakṣiṇa**.
vidyā: a feminine mantra, that of a goddess.
vidyāpīṭha: "the seat of Vidyās"; a division of the Tantras of the Goddess, which is itself divided into Union Tantras (*yāmalatantra*) and Power Tantras (*śaktitantras*).

yoginīvaktra: "the face of the Yoginī"; the sexual organ of the female partner in a sexual ritual.
yoni: the sexual feminine organ.
yonipūjā: the ritual worship of the *yoni**.

Bibliographical References

The bibliography of Tantra is huge and of a varying quality. I list here, in addition to most of those alluded to in the notes, only certain books that may help the reader gather more information on the subject of Tantra without burdening him or her with erudite or arcane details—general works on Hinduism, a few translations of Tantric texts, and some studies on particular points, sometimes scholarly but within the reach of a non-Indological reader. With very few exceptions, only works in English are quoted. A few books mentioned in the notes, especially when not in English, are not included here.

General Studies, Overviews

Doniger, Wendy. *The Hindus: An Alternative History.* New York: Penguin Books, 2009. An idiosyncratic but interesting study. The book has been banned in India since 2014.

Flood, Gavin. *An Introduction to Hinduism.* Cambridge: Cambridge University Press, 1996.

———, ed. *The Blackwell Companion to Hinduism.* Oxford: Blackwell, 2003.

Frazier, Jessica, ed. *The Continuum Companion to Hindu Studies.* Leiden: Brill, 2011.

Gonda, Jan. *Medieval Religious Literature in Sanskrit.* A History of Indian Literature, vol. 2, no. 1. Wiesbaden: Otto Harrassowitz, 1977.

Goudriaan, Teun, and Sanjukta Gupta. *Hindu Tantric and Śākta Literature.* A History of Indian Literature, vol. 2, no. 2. Wiesbaden: Otto Harrassowitz, 1981.

Goudriaan, Teun, Sanjukta Gupta, and Dirk Jan Hoens. *Hindu Tantrism.* Handbuch der Orientalistik, 2 Abt., 4. Bd., 2. Abscht. Leiden: E. J. Brill, 1979.

White, David G., ed. *Tantra in Practice.* Princeton: Princeton University Press, 2000.

Texts

Abhinavagupta. *Tantrāloka.* Translated by Raniero Gnoli. Milano: Adelphi, 1999.

Avalon, Arthur, trans. *Tantra of the Great Liberation (Mahānirvāṇa Tantra): A Translation of the Sanscrit with Introduction and Commentary.* London: Luzac, 1913.

———, trans. *The Serpent Power: The Secrets of Tantric and Shaktic Yoga.* 5th ed. Madras: Ganesh, 1953. First published 1919 by Luzac.

———. *Kulārṇava Tantra/Introduction Arthur Avalon (Sir John Woodroffe)/Readings M.P. Pandit/Sanskrit Text Tārānātha Vidyāratna.* Madras: Ganesh, 1965.

Bailly, Constantina Rhodes. *Shaiva Devotional Songs of Kashmir: A Translation and Study of Utpaladeva's Shivastotravali.* Albany, NY: SUNY Press, 1987.

Brunner-Lachaux, Hélène, trans. *Somaśambhupaddhati.* 4 vols. Pondichéry: Institut français d'indologie, 1963–98. This work is in French, but it is such a basic work on Tantric Śaiva ritual practices that it must be mentioned here.

Coburn, Thomas B. *Encountering the Goddess: A Translation of the Devī Māhātmya and a Study of Its Interpretation.* Albany, NY: SUNY Press, 1991.

Dupuche, John R. *Abhinavagupta: The Kula Ritual as Elaborated in Chapter 29 of the Tantrāloka.* New Delhi: Motilal Banarsidass, 2003.

Gharote, M. L., and G. K. Pai. *Siddhasiddhāntapaddhati: A Treatise on the Nātha Philosophy by Gorakṣanātha.* Lonavla: Lonavla Yoga Institute, 2005.

Goodall, Dominic. *The Parākhyatantra: A Scripture of the Śaiva Siddhānta.* Collection Indologie 98. Pondichéry: Institut Français de Pondichéry / École française d'Extrême-Orient, 2004.

Goodall, Dominic, Alexis Sanderson, and Harunaga Isaacson, eds. *The Niśvāsatattvasaṃhitā: The Earliest Surviving Śaiva Tantra.* Vol 1. Pondichéry: Institut Français de Pondichéry / École française d'Extrême-Orient, 2015.

Gupta, Sanjukta, trans. *Lakṣmītantra.* Leiden: Brill, 1972. Reprint Delhi: Motilal Banarsidass, 2000.

Jayantabhaṭṭa. *Āgamaḍambara: Much Ado about Religion.* Edited and translated by Csaba Dezső. New York: New York University Press, 2005.

Kaul, Ashok, ed. and trans. *Śivastotrāvalī of Utpaladeva: A Mystical Hymn of Kashmir.* New Delhi: D. K. Printworld, 2008.

Nammāḻvar. *Poems for the Drowning, Poems for Viṣṇu.* Translated by A. K. Ramanujan. Princeton: Princeton Library of Asian Translations, 1981.

Padoux, André, with Roger-Orphé Jeanty, trans. *Yoginīhṛdaya: The Heart of the Yoginī.* New York: Oxford University Press, 2013.

Puṇyānandanātha. *Kāmakalāvilāsa.* Translated by Arthur Avalon. Madras: Ganesh and Company, 1953.

Śivasūtra. *Śiva Sūtras: The Yoga of Supreme Identity.* Translated by Jaideva Singh. Delhi: Motilal Banarsidass, 1979. The best translation is in Italian by Raffaele Torella. *Gli Aforismi di Śiva, con il Commento di Kṣemarāja.* Milano: Mimesis, 2013.

Somadeva. *Kathāsaritsāgara* [Ocean of Stories]. Translated by C. H. Tawney, edited by N. M. Penzer. London, 1924. Available online.

Spandakārika. *The Stanzas on Vibration: The Spandakārikā with Four Commentaries.* Translated by Mark Dyczkowski. Albany, NY: SUNY Press, 1992.

Vasudeva, Somdev. *The Yoga of the Mālinīvijayottaratantra.* Pondichéry: Institut Français de Pondichéry / École française d'Extrême-Orient, 2004.

Watson, Alex, Dominic Goodall, and S. L. P. Anjaneya Sarma. *An Enquiry into the Nature of Liberation: Bhaṭṭa Rāmakaṇṭha's Paramokṣanirāsakārikāvṛtti, a Commentary on Sadyojyotiḥ's Refutation of Twenty Conceptions of the Liberated State (Mokṣa).* Pondichéry: Institut Français de Pondichéry / École française d'Extrême-Orient, 2013.

Secondary Sources

Alper, Harvey P., ed. *Understanding Mantras.* Delhi: Motilal Banarsidass, 2012. First published 1989 by State University of New York Press.

Alter, J. S. *Yoga in Modern India: The Body between Science and Philosophy.* Princeton: Princeton University Press, 2004.

Ananthamurthy, U. R. *Samskara: A Rite for a Dead Man.* Translated by A. K. Ramanujan. Oxford: Oxford University Press, 1978.

Apffel-Marglin, Frédérique. *Wives of the God-King: The Rituals of the Devadasis of Puri.* New York: Oxford University Press, 1985.

Bansat-Boudon, Lyne. *An Introduction to Tantric Philosophy: The Paramārthasāra of Abhinavagupta with the Commentary of Yogarāja.* London: Routledge, 2010.

Basu, Helene. *Von Barden und Königen: Ethnologische Studien zur Göttin und zum Gedächtnis in Kacch (Indien).* Frankfurt: Peter Lang, 2004.

Bäumer, Bettina, and Sarla Kumar, eds. *Saṃvidullāsaḥ: Manifestation of Divine Consciousness; Swami Laksman Joo Saint-Scholar of Kashmir Śaivism.* A Centenary Tribute. New Delhi: D. K. Printworld, 2007.

Bharati, Agehananda. *The Tantric Tradition.* London: Rider, 1965.

———. *The Ochre Robe: An Autobiography.* 2nd ed. Santa Barbara, CA: Ross-Erikson, 1980.

Biardeau, Madeleine. *Hinduism: The Anthropology of a Civilization.* Oxford: Oxford University Press, 1989.

Bouillier V., and G. Tarabout, eds. *Images du corps dans le monde hindou.* Paris: CNRS, 2002.

Briggs, George Weston. *Gorakhnāth and the Kānphaṭa Yogīs.* 1st ed. 1938. Delhi: Motilal Banarsidass, 1982.

Brooks, Douglas R. *The Secret of the Three Cities: An Introduction to Hindu Śākta Tantrism.* Chicago: University of Chicago Press, 1990.

Bühnemann, Gudrun. *The Iconography of Hindu Tantric Deities.* 2 vols. Groningen: Egbert Forsten, 2001.

——— et al. *Maṇḍalas and Yantras in the Hindu Traditions.* Leiden: Brill, 2003.

Caldwell, Sarah. *Oh Terrific Mother: Sexuality, Violence and Worship of the Goddess Kālī.* Oxford: Oxford University Press, 1999.

Carstairs, G. Morris. *The Twice-Born: A Study of a Community of High-Caste Hindus.* London: Hogarth Press, 1957.

Coburn, Thomas B. *Encountering the Goddess*: see above "Texts."

Dasgupta, Shashibhusan. *Obscure Religious Cults.* Calcutta: Firma K. L. Mukhopadhyaya, 1969.

Davis, Richard H. *Ritual in an Oscillating Universe: Worshiping Śiva in Medieval India.* Princeton: Princeton University Press, 1991.

Dehejia, Vidya. *Yoginī Cults and Practices: A Tantric Tradition.* New Delhi: National Museum, 1986.

Diehl, Carl Gustav. *Instrument and Purpose: Studies on the Rites and Ritual of South India.* Lund: C. W. K. Gleerup, 1956.

Dimock, Edward C. *The Place of the Hidden Moon: Erotic Mysticism in the Vaiṣṇava Sahajiyā Cult of Bengal.* Chicago: University of Chicago Press, 1966.

Dyczkowski, Mark. *A Journey in the World of the Tantras.* Varanasi: Indica Books, 2004.

Eck, Diana L. *Darśan: Seeing the Divine Image in India.* Chambersburg: Anima Books, 1981.

———. *Banaras: City of Light.* London: Routledge, 1983.

Einoo, Shingo, ed. *Genesis and Development of Tantrism.* Tokyo: Institute of Oriental Culture, University of Tokyo, 2009.

Eliade, Mircea. *Techniques du Yoga.* Paris: Gallimard, 1948.

Flood, Gavin. *Body and Cosmomogy in Kashmir Śaivism.* San Francisco: Mellen Research University Press, 1993.

Fuller, C. J. *Servants of the Goddess: The Priests of a South Indian Temple.* Cambridge: Cambridge University Press, 1984.

———. *The Camphor Flame: Popular Hinduism and Society in India.* Princeton: Princeton University Press, 1992.

Goodall, Dominic, and Harunaga Isaacson. "Tantric Hinduism." In *The Continuum Companion to Hindu Studies,* edited by Jessica Frazier. Leiden: Brill, 2011.

Goodall, Dominic, and André Padoux, eds. *Mélanges tantriques à la mémoire d'Hélène Brunner* [Tantric Studies in Memory of Hélène Brunner]. Pondichéry: Institut Français de Pondichéry / École française d'Extrême-Orient, 2007.

Goudriaan, Teun. *Māyā Divine and Human: A Study of Magic and Its Religious Foundations in Sanskrit Texts, with Particular Attention to a Fragment on Viṣṇu's Māyā Preserved in Bali.* Delhi: Motilal Banarsidass, 1978.

———, ed. *Ritual and Speculation in Early Tantrism.* Albany, NY: SUNY Press, 1992.

Guenther, Herbert V., trans. *The Life and Teaching of Naropa.* Boston: Shambala, 1995.

Gutschow, Niels, Axel Michaels, Charles Ramble, and Ernst Steinkellner, eds. *Sacred Landscape in the Himalayas.* Vienna: Austrian Academy of Sciences Press, 2003.

Hardy, Friedhelm. *Viraha-Bhakti: The Early History of Kṛṣṇa Devotion in South India.* Oxford: Oxford University Press, 1983.

Hawley, John S., and Donna Marie Wulff, eds. *Devī: Goddesses of India.* Berkeley: University of California Press, 1996.

Hiltebeitel, Alf, ed. *Criminal Gods and Demon Devotees: Essays on the Guardians of Popular Hinduism.* Albany, NY: SUNY Press, 1989.

Kakar, Sudhir. *Shamans, Mystics and Doctors: A Psychological Inquiry into India and Its Healing Traditions.* Oxford: Oxford University Press, 1952.

Kramrisch, Stella. *The Hindu Temple.* Delhi: Motilal Banarsidass, 1976.

Kripal, Jeffrey. *Kālī's Child: The Mystical and the Erotic in the Life and Teaching of Ramakrishna.* Chicago: University of Chicago Press, 1995.

Lakoff, George, and Mark Johnson. *The Metaphors We Live By.* Chicago: University of Chicago Press, 1980.

Levy, Robert I. *Mesocosm: Hinduism and the Organization of a Traditional Newar City in Nepal.* Berkeley: University of California Press, 1990.

MacDermott, Rachel Fell. *Revelry, Rivalry, and Longing for the Goddesses of Bengal.* New York: Columbia University Press, 2011.

McDaniel, June. *The Madness of the Saints: Ecstatic Religion in Bengal.* Chicago: University of Chicago Press, 1989.

Michaels, Axel, and Christoph Wulf, eds. *The Body in India: Ritual, Transgression, Performativity.* "Paragrama." Berlin: Akademie Verlag, 2009.

Nemec, John. *The Ubiquitous Śiva: Somānanda's Śivadṛṣṭi and His Tantric Interlocutors.* Oxford: Oxford University Press, 2011.

Östör, Akos. *The Play of the Gods: Locality, Ideology, Structure, and Time in the Festivals of a Bengali Town.* New Delhi: Chronicle Books, 2004.

Padoux, André. *Vāc: The Concept of the Word in Selected Hindu Tantras.* Delhi: Shri Satguru, 1992. First published 1990 by SUNY Press.

———. *Tantric Mantras: Studies on Mantraśāstra*. London: Routledge, 2011.

Rai Bahadur Srisa Chandra Vidyarnava. *The Daily Practice of the Hindus*. 1949. New Delhi: Sri Satguru Publications, 2008.

Ramanujan, A. K. *Speaking of Siva*. Harmondsworth: Penguin Classics, 1979.

Renou, Louis. *Etudes védiques et pāninéennes*. Paris: Institut de Civilisation Indienne, 1955–69.

Samuel, Geoffrey. *Civilized Shamans: Buddhism and Tibetan Societies*. Washington, DC: Smithsonian Institution, 1993.

Sanderson, Alexis. "Śaivism and the Tantric Traditions." In *The World's Religions*, edited by S. Sunderland et al. London: Croom Helm, 1988.

———. "Meaning in Tantric Ritual." In *Essais sur le rituel III: Colloque du Centenaire de la section des sciences religieuses de l'École pratique des hautes études*, edited by Anne-Marie Blondeau and Kristofer Schipper, 15–95. Louvain: Peeters, 1995.

———. "The Lākulas: New Evidence of a System Intermediate between Pāñcārthika Pāśupatism and Āgamic Śaivism." *Indian Philosophical Annual* 24 (2003–2005; appeared 2006), 143–217.

———. "The Śaiva Age: The Rise and Dominance of Śaivism during the Early Medieval Period." In *Genesis and Development of Tantrism*, edited by Shingo Einoo, 41–349. Tokyo: Institute of Oriental Culture, University of Tokyo, 2009.

Schilder, Paul. *The Image and Appearance of the Human Body: Studies in the Constructive Energies of the Psyche*. New York: International Universities Press, 1950.

Siegel, Lee. *Net of Magic: Wonders and Deceptions in India*. Chicago: University of Chicago Press, 1991.

Silburn, Lilian. *Kuṇḍalinī: Energy of the Depths*. Albany, NY: SUNY Press, 1988.

Sleeman, W. H. *Rambles and Recollections of an Indian Official*. London: Hatchard, 1844.

Slusser, M. S. *Nepal Maṇḍala: A Cultural Study of the Kathmandu Valley*. Princeton: Princeton University Press, 1982.

Smith, Daniel H. *A Descriptive Bibliography of the Printed Texts of the Pañcārātrāgama*. 2 vols. Baroda: Oriental Institute, 1975–80.

Smith, Frederick M. *The Self Possessed: Deity and Spirit Possession in South Asian Literature and Civilization*. New York: Columbia University Press, 2006.

Strickman, Michel. *Mantras et mandarins: Le Bouddhisme tantrique en Chine*. Paris: Gallimard, 1996.

Taylor, Kathleen. *Sir John Woodroffe, Tantra and Bengal: "An Indian Soul in a European Body?"* Richmond, UK: Curzon Press, 2001.

Toffin, Gérard. *Le palais et le temple: La fonction royale dans la vallée du Népal*. Paris: CNRS, 1993.

Urban, Hugh B. *Songs of Ecstasy: Tantric and Devotional Songs from Colonial Bengal*. Oxford: Oxford University Press, 2001.

———. *The Economics of Ecstasy: Tantra, Secrecy, and Power in Colonial Bengal*. Oxford: Oxford University Press, 2001.

———. *Tantra: Sex, Secrecy, Politics, and Power in the Study of Religion*. Berkeley: University of California Press, 2003.

White, David, G. *The Alchemical Body: Siddha Traditions in Medieval India*. Chicago: Chicago University Press, 1984.

White, David, G. *Kiss of the Yoginī: "Tantric Sex" in Its South Asian Context*. Chicago: University of Chicago Press, 2003.

———. *Yoga in Practice*. Princeton: Princeton University Press, 2012.

Index

West, Tantra in the, 166–76
women, role of, 87–88, 187n2. *See also* female/male polarity; *specific topics*
Woodroffe, John (aka Arthur Avalon), 6, 39, 163, 166
worship. See *pūjā*; *specific topics*

yāmala (Union Tantras), 53
yāmalatantras (Union Tantras), 33
yantras, 68, 84, 139, 141, 144, 146, 148, 161
yoga, 47; "Tantric," 74–76. *See also specific topics*
Yogasūtra (Patañjali), 47, 67, 74–76
yogic aspects of mystical states, 128–29. *See also* mystical states
yogic body, 42, 73, 77, 81, 82, 89, 94, 105, 135; of the adept, 109; *cakras* of, 65, 74, 76, 95, 127, 148, 154; internalized image of, 75; *kuṇḍalinī* and, 74, 75, 89, 109, 128; *maṇḍalas* and, 148; mantras in, 109, 110, 154; *nāḍīs* of, 65, 74, 79; Nāṭha conception of, 65; ritual and, 113, 122, 128; Tantric yoga and, 74–76; worship and, 127
yogic practices, 76–80
Yoginī cults, 34, 49, 53–54, 114, 137, 187n11, 195n12
Yoginīhṛdaya: The Heart of the Yoginī, 34, 35, 49, 50, 82, 111, 128; on the adept, 135; *japa* and, 111, 186n12; *mudrās* of, 50, 81; *nyāsas* and, 82; Tripurasundarī in, 78, 128
yoginī-melana and *yoginī-melaka*, 95
Yoginīs, 50, 55; Bhairava and, 65, 94, 137, 183n8; *cakras* of, 95; Krama and, 56; mouth of, 91, 93, 94, 187n7 (see also *adhovaktra*); Nāṭha and, 65; number of, 49, 149; sexual rites/ritual sex and, 90, 114; temples dedicated to, 23; worship of, 65, 90
Yoginī temples, 21, 23, 58, 183n8
yoginīvaktra, 91, 93, 187n7. See also *adhovaktra*; Yoginīs: mouth of
yoni, 90f; *liṅga* and, 89, 148–49; ritual and, 34, 89, 91; Satī and, 89, 137, 160; Śiva and, 89, 91, 138, 160; worship of, 34, 138
Yonitantra, 34, 91
yonitattva, 91

Zimmer, Heinrich, 168